THUNDERBIRD RISING

THUNDERBIRD RISING

by

Stephanie Big Eagle

© Copyright 2021 by Stephanie Big Eagle – All rights reserved.

ISBN 978-1-7375122-0-2, Big Eagle Publishing.

It is not legal to reproduce, duplicate, or transmit any part of this document in either electronic means or printed format. Recording of this publication is strictly prohibited.

The story you are about to read is true. Only the names have been changed to protect the innocent.

This book contains terminology and formatting that respects and recognizes the cultural integrity of Indigenous Peoples and is intended to legitimize Indigenous identities, institutions, and collective rights that have been historically oppressed.

Front Cover Photograph by Stephanie Big Eagle (2022) at Thunderbird Rising Studios, Indianapolis, Indiana. Back Cover Photograph by Jason Sinn (2017) at D-Q University, Davis, California.

Cover design by Stephanie Big Eagle (© 2023).

Printed in Great Turtle Island, aka the United States of America.

This book is dedicated to:

Rah (Raniera) Tamati, my spiritual brother who took his life two days before I was inspired to write this book. To my children, especially during the times they have suffered from depression and suicidal thoughts. To Pouoterangi Ngaropo-Tawio, an extended family member who took his life due to childhood trauma. To Jonathan Quick Bear, a victim of bullying who took his own life, and to all those who have also given up because this world is filled with the dis-ease of separation. You will never be forgotten!

This book is especially dedicated to those who persist despite facing incredible odds. I honor and acknowledge these resilient survivors transformed into warriors, those who dedicate themselves to transforming the darkness that has enslaved this planet for far too long.

I acknowledge and thank our ancestors, who guide us out of chaos and into beauty, and who remind us that no matter how alone we may feel, we are always surrounded by a powerful team of helpers. We only need to recognize them and call upon them for help.

To those who bring darkness and dis-ease upon others, this book is also dedicated. May this story inspire you to go within, find healing, and rise with us to break the cycle of abuse, separation, and darkness. We are all in this together!

CONTENTS

Introduction ix
Chapter 1: Return Home 15
Chapter 2: It Began in Hawaii 38
Chapter 3: "Adulting" 70
Chapter 4: Creating the Next Generation 85
Chapter 5: Remembering 108
Chapter 6: Cuauhtémoc 125
Chapter 7: Texas Honey 183
Chapter 8: Flying Dreams 195
Chapter 9: Round Two 200
Chapter 10: Moonlight Bay 214
Chapter 11: The Standing Rock Tattoo 237
Chapter 12: We Are Still Here 259
Chapter 13: Artistic Freedom 274
Chapter 14: We Are Forever 312
Bibliography 342
Acknowledgments 345
About the Author 349

INTRODUCTION

"Sometimes I think this whole world is one big prison yard. Some of us are prisoners, some of us are guards." ~ Bob Dylan

In 2010 and 2012, I was imprisoned in Rapid City, South Dakota's Pennington County Jail (PCJ). This city and its jail are built over the heart of my people's ancestral homelands – Paha Sapa, or the Black Hills, a Sacred Site to our Nation. My people, the Oceti Sakowin, or the Seven Council Fires of the Great Sioux Nation, are comprised of the Lakota, Dakota, and Nakota bands. In 1868, our ancestral leaders placed their signatures on the Fort Laramie Treaty, ensuring that our Nation would have the "absolute and undisturbed use and occupation of" unceded lands, including the sacred Black Hills. In exchange, huge portions of our homelands were ceded to the U.S. government to create peace between our Nations. However, when gold was discovered in the Black Hills in 1874, the U.S. violated the Treaty – despite its Constitutional status as the "Supreme Law of the Land" – and invaded the Black Hills.

War between our Nations ensued, and eventually, our warriors who fought to protect our Treaty Rights were overwhelmed by the intense swell of gold miners, soldiers, and settlers. Our camps were raided, and men, women, and children alike were imprisoned on reservations and starved. Our main source of sustenance, the Plains buffalo, were targeted and slaughtered to the brink of extinction to further weaken our ancestors and to force their reliance upon food commodities provided by the U.S. government. The children of our ancestors were "legally" kidnapped and placed in extremely abusive boarding schools run by priests and nuns, resulting in the deaths of thousands of our young relatives. Most who survived were held captive in these schools until they were adults. At that point, they were mostly assimilated into Euro-American society via the "kill the Indian and save the man" indoctrination system that was insidiously enacted through strict authoritarian rule and forced Christian and European ideals.

Utilizing these war crime tactics, the U.S. government gained illegal possession of the Black Hills. Rapid City was then established in 1876 as a goldmining city and was soon occupied by tidal waves of Euro-American settlers. As prophecy foretold, in the five generations that followed, almost everything was taken from our people as we struggled to survive an invasion fueled by the dis-ease of separation that was forecast to spread across the entire Earth.

Fast forward to the year 2010, just 130 years later, as I, an Oceti Sakowin descendant, am barred in grey and white stripes, the mark of a prisoner of the Pennington County Jail. Since its inception in 1875 by the U.S. government, PCJ was contrived to detain our people who got in its way as it ruthlessly and criminally claimed our ancestral homelands. My incarcerations during 2010 and 2012 reflect the historical truth of this takeover, as I discovered that 98% of the inmates were Lakota or Dakota, even though we formed only 10% of Rapid City's population. Furthermore, over half of the children in the foster care system also belonged to the Oceti Sakowin! My child and I were forced to contribute to these statistics.

According to the official website of Pennington County, in 1878, PCJ's "presence... was a sure sign of civilization.... [By 1921] there was a 16-person cell block on each floor for a total capacity of 32. Males stayed in one cell and females and children in the other.... The space was so tight only one person could stand at a time.... In 1971, a jail addition was added to the 1921 facility along with a remodel.... A new $10.2 million jail opened in 1989, more than doubling previous available jail space.... By 2014 the jail daily inmate count surpassed 400.... In 2017, $1.75

million was awarded [to] the Pennington County Jail [because it] continues to embrace progress [and] adapts to meet the ever changing needs of the citizens of Pennington County." This self-told, fictional fable deceptively hides a grim truth – that the jail's so-called "honorable and justified" inception and generational expansion mask its true origin as a genocidal, prisoner of war detention center that has targeted Oceti Sakowin men, women, and children since 1875, and because of it, has also made an enormous illegal profit.

I was initially held in PCJ in 2010 for twenty-seven days due to an excessively high bond. This was just long enough for Child Protective Services (CPS) to file an abuse and neglect petition against me during a secret court hearing. The petition claimed I "neglected" my son because I couldn't afford to bond out. Thus, my rights to my child were "legally" removed and he was admitted into the foster care system. One day later, my bond was finally reduced, and I bailed out.

Over the next two years, I battled with Pennington County CPS and its court system, however, my parental rights to my son were quickly terminated, a year and a half *before* I pled guilty, while in a state of duress, to the criminal charges upon which the removal of my son were based. After blatantly ignoring my sovereignty claim, and with no due process of law, my son and I were permanently separated, and he was given to strangers, all of whom were of Euro-American descent. To this day, we remain separated. Intentionally, he's been kept from attending our Traditional Ceremonies and being taught our way of life. He carries a name that doesn't belong to him, has no idea who he truly is or where he comes from, and furthermore, *was* placed in numerous foster care placements where he was abused and neglected.

Our story is just one of many examples of cultural genocide – an invisible genocide enacted under the color of law and via the Doctrine of Discovery – that Indigenous People on an international level face every single day. My son and I are one of thousands of cases in Pennington County alone in which "Indian" parents and their children were arbitrarily separated. Life for most Indigenous Peoples has been extremely difficult for generations. I'm sharing my story to help reveal the truth of what many of us have, and continue to survive, and what many have not.

I've lived through what some call "hell," and what others think is normal. I endured despite extreme violence, sexual assault, betrayal, political imprisonment, isolation, neglect, cruel and unusual punishment, and physical and spiritual theft, including the separation from almost all my children. I've survived suicidal tendencies and murder attempts. Both of my parents have dealt with substance addictions for as long as I can remember, and at some point, so have I. I've not been given any privilege in life, and everything I have gained has been earned through overcoming the toughest of challenges. If I know anything well, it's surviving and persisting against all odds.

Yet, I cease to complain, because it was through this darkness that I grew close to the power and healing that is found in Nature and I began to understand that Wakan Tanka – Dakota for the "Common Creator of all Life," or the "Great Mystery," has an extraordinary plan for me. I discovered that our natural parents are Mother Earth and Father Sun, and that our spirits are always protected and guided by these influences, along with a powerful team of helpers from the animal, plant, elemental, and Spirit Worlds. Thus, a beautiful way of life etched within my own DNA was unearthed that is healing what I survived. Now, the suffering I endured is transmuted into natural power, resilience, and fortitude that creates an impenetrable shield of spiritual wisdom, wealth, and guidance, not only for me, but for others. I know that all of us are capable of this, and that our choices, perceptions, and willingness to work on ourselves are the keys to unlocking our greatest potential.

Thunderbird Rising retraces the underdog journey of the first half of my life, and my later rise from the ashes into an empowered and connected Indigenous woman. I am not defined by the abuse and oppression I survived that was inflicted by certain members of my family, along with governmental institutions and organizations such as the Catholic Church, CPS, the Bureau of Indian Affairs (BIA), the law enforcement system, the court system, the health care system... *the system* itself. An interwoven, international system that is an invisible form of slavery and genocide that inflicts abuse that seems to have no end. Currency is its slave master, and the main victims are the culture, lands, resources, identity, and unity of the people, in particular, Indigenous People. This era, however, must come to its end.

I know I'm not the only one that's survived against all odds and who now stands in their power in this time of chaos, confusion, and prophetic transition. I'm not the only one that's graduated from the most challenging of warrior training grounds! I'm not the only one who was brainwashed but can now see through the insanity, and I'm not the only one preparing for the battle that's been building for generations! I know that I'm just one of countless resilient others.

We are still here, which is a testament to ancient prophecies that have been passed down for generations from our Elders and the Star Nation! Even though it may appear that we have lost everything, we have only just begun. This book intends to help us remember who we truly are as humanity, and to remind those who read it, to find and create the beauty in the chaos that provides the strength and clarity to carry on, despite the odds that are stacked against us. It's a reminder that things are not what they seem, and that a miraculous transformation awaits us at the end of any dark tunnel if we're willing to walk through the shadows of uncertainty with Wakan Tanka, or Creator, as our guide.

Thunderbird Rising

I have a recurring dream. In it, I have massive wings that stretch to five times my height. A supernatural sense allows me to feel the approach of demons. When I detect them, I call out to the people. They huddle under my magnificent wings as I stretch them around us into a halo. The demons swirl around us, but we don't look at them; we don't acknowledge them at all. We only close our eyes and remain nestled together, allowing the power of the wings to shield us. When the demons realize they can't penetrate the shield, they leave, and the people finally return to living!

Look at us. We are older than America.
Surviving genocide because we have to,
We are strong enough to endure.
We are energy. We are Power.
Our resistance, our struggle,
Is not sacrifice lost.
It is natural energy properly used.
We must remember Earth.
We must remember what life is all about!
It is all up to us.
Look at us. We are of Earth and Water.
Look at them. It is the same.
– John Trudell
February 15, 1946 – December 8, 2015

CHAPTER ONE

RETURN HOME

I sit on the raised patio of my desert home, nestled in the luscious vegetation of a red rock cove. The peaceful flow of Oak Creek serenades me as I begin to share my story under the swaying branches of Sycamore, Cottonwood, and Oak trees. A bamboo chime knocks and clanks, playing a grounding melody as the wind rocks it gently back and forth. Hummingbirds dive-bomb their tiny bodies at each other, gracefully battling for positions before the feeder whose nectar easily earns their company. Suddenly, one of these tiny warriors levitates before me, flashing its iridescent hues. It's either a challenge, or a curious inspection. Either way, I'm enchanted by its unexpected attention! Like a mysterious light bullet, it hums away as quickly as it appeared.

Summer tanagers, thunder hawks, red-breasted mergansers, purple finches, yellow warblers, and over forty distinct species of birds also call this cove home. Their presence brings me close to heaven! Spiny lizards run up and down the trees hunting innumerable insects. Occasionally, I spot a tarantula and one of its only predators, the tarantula hawk, a wasp notorious for having the most painful sting of any venomous creature. Both remind me that I'm in the desert. My direct environment often causes me to forget this with its lush greenery, diverse species count, and constant water flow; all features of this unique desert-riparian ecosystem. Grandfather rocks – the type we use in our Inipi, or Traditional Sweatlodge – sit majestically along the creek's edge. Some are so enormous and haunting that I suspect they might be dinosaur eggs. Triggered, my mind wanders back into last night's riveting dream.

I felt like half of me was still there, in that place where grotesque beings attacked me with everything they had, after *she* – a witch disguised as my friend – told them they needed to "activate my powers." I fought with them, defending, blocking, and flying in fantastic swirls. Horizontally and vertically, my body zipped around, dodging their every move! A looming, swirling eye opened in the sky above me – a programming machine. I hovered beneath it, my belly facing the sky. It surged with full force, assaulting me with a barrage of negative thoughts that tried to overtake and control my perceptive energy, but my mind proved impenetrable. As I deflected every attack, my energy and power increased exponentially!

Suddenly, a tall and powerful shapeshifter lunged at my throat and clenched it before I could escape. His tightening hands fired electricity throughout my entire body, tasering me, but I concentrated the energy and shot it into the sky above us as lightning. Thunder exploded all around us! He surged into my vessel a second time. I isolated his energy again, transformed it into lightning, and deflected it from my body into the earth. Thunder boomed, pulsating the earth in waves!

A loud bang suddenly awakened me, leaving the unfinished fight replaying through my groggy mind. I sat up lazily, switched on the lamp and sloppily recorded my dream with one eye open – the only one awake – and added it to the pages of the filling book of my visions, each displaying the journey of my progress through the worlds I visited while my body fitfully slept.

Dreams like this dominated my psyche when I began this book. I lived in Sedona, Arizona, which is known for being one of the largest New Age spiritual communities in the world. Spiritual practitioners of all modalities live and gather there. I didn't know Sedona existed until two months before I visited but did travel close when I spoke at the 2009 "Return of the Ancestors Gathering" that was held a half hour away in Cottonwood. During this gathering, the Eagle and Condor prophecy given to the Sayaka Inka village in Peru 500 years ago, was fulfilled through the Condor Dance. After this dance, a condor feather was gifted to the Eagle People. The prophecy foretold that the time would come when the Eagle (the Indigenous People of North and Central America) and the Condor (the Indigenous People of South America) would unite and fly together in the same skies, ushering in an era of higher consciousness for all of humanity.

After witnessing this powerful fulfillment of prophecy and then sharing my message from the Star Nation to the people, I drove through miles of the desert surrounding Sedona, eventually stopping to explore an intriguing path. I climbed out of my car, stepped a few yards down the trail, and approached a tree standing proudly before me with a perfect circular hole in its trunk. This portal-like opening held an extraordinary, red clay Pipe with a spiral inscribed onto it, much like the spiral that is now tattooed on my forehead. I traded evenly for that special Pipe and still carry it with me to this day. Other than this remarkable visit years ago, Arizona and I had nothing in common. Yet, in November of 2018, I felt a strong urge to go to Sedona and answered that call a few months later.

Before my arrival, I toured for four months in a zig-zagging loop from Standing Rock, North Dakota to the Southwest, and finally through the entire state of California, to anchor Traditionally Handpoked Tattoos. In that four-month period, I tattooed over one hundred clients — a huge task considering that my method, like all machine-free artistries, requires at least twice the work output and time to complete! It was an empowering journey, but also extremely demanding. I put my self-care to the side to just barely meet the needs of my son, my clients, and myself during the tour. I realized the hard way that I couldn't maintain life on the road as a single mom while taking on such intense energy work, especially if I didn't give myself the time I needed to recharge.

Exhausted from this nomadic lifestyle, I decided to settle into a home where my clients instead came to me. My biggest consideration was where? Living in *any* city felt like being trapped in the matrix, and my usual go-to, Northern California, was scarred by devastating wildfires that destroyed entire cities and forests, affecting air quality, travel, and resources. Coupled with erratic periods of droughts and floods, my preferred home base was transformed into a ticking time bomb. Furthermore, recurring dreams of coastal tsunamis burned in the back of my mind. The threats far outweighed the familiarity. California was no longer an option. I began to look carefully into the places we visited during the tour to see if they were good options for a new home.

The first time I drove into Sedona on a drizzling, January day, I was blown away by the intense beauty of its red striated mountains and cliffs that stood in stark contrast to the barren and endless desert that surrounded it! Resembling an exotic temple of the gods taken from a far-away land and dropped into this high desert, this obviously holy land whispered hints of a once-hidden rejuvenation oasis whose secret had long since been discovered.

I pulled the car over immediately, grabbed my tobacco, and knelt upon the red rock temple. My body shook and vibrated for over twenty minutes while the energy of the land coursed through my veins like lightning! I introduced myself, my son, and our lineage, and laid my tobacco down as an offering upon this sacred earth, in respect and gratitude to the caretakers that inhabited this holy place long before it carried the "Sedona" name.

During my first week there, I split my time between handpoking tattoos on my clients and climbing up vortexes with my son. A vortex is a concentrated energy center, like a tornado, but instead of energy visualizing in tornadic form, it's invisible, and flows up and down from both the ground and sky. Although I loved the energy of the land, I loathed the slow-moving swarms of come-and-go tourists that clogged all travel, even on the trails, during their season. I was especially perturbed by the "Native American" art and spirituality that were sold mostly by non-Indigenous people and shops as part of the New Age tourist trap that Sedona had become.

As Nature is rapidly converted to concrete, and thus, a spiritual connection to the land is difficult to maintain, it is reasonable that tourists would flock to a place like Sedona to enjoy its incredibly rare beauty coupled with the opportunity for a guided spiritual experience. The problem is, how does one know *who* is genuine in a place filled with self-proclaimed healers, shamans, and gurus? And how does one know *what* is real in a place where white-owned stores sell supposedly "authentic" Native American art and spiritual items for a hefty price without the presence of the Native American people themselves?

I told one of my local clients that I was thinking about moving to Sedona, but she discouraged me because "only white people live there." Yet, in this place that "only white people lived," an inexcusable amount of Native American Ceremonies, art, ideas, and teachings were sold, by people who had no Traditional or genetic connection to them. Known as cultural appropriation, this is defined by Oxford dictionary as the "unacknowledged or inappropriate adoption of the customs, practices, and ideas, of one people or society by members of another and typically more dominant people or society." Those who are subjected to it, know it's a much nicer way of describing and concealing cultural genocide – the invisible continuation of the physical genocide of the entire Native American population that began in 1492, and continues to this day in the form of the theft of, misrepresentation of, and removal of their customs, cultures, and Traditions!

Sedona has a notorious history of "Native American" Ceremonies being held for profit by people who lack the proper training and ancestral connection to do so. As a result, those who don't know any better can pay a hefty and unexpected price. In 2009, New Age "guru" James Arthur Ray ran an imitation Sweatlodge at his New Age "warrior retreat" in Sedona. Purporting himself as a "shaman," and the experience as an authentic "Native American Purification Ceremony," he swindled $10,000 from each participant. However, the lodge was completely lined with plastic, which produced a deadly amount of heat and steam once the "Purification" began. His self-proclaimed "shamanic knowledge" cooked two of the participants to death inside the misconstructed lodge, and sickened nineteen others, one of whom later died after a ten-day coma! None of the participants, "Lodge" leaders, nor the mock "Sweatlodge" itself were Native American!

This example of cultural appropriation proves how dangerous it can be for someone who isn't taught the proper protocol to conduct Ceremonies that do not belong to them. It is also offensively marginalizing to the Indigenous Keepers of the Ceremony, for a self-proclaimed shaman to place themselves into the Ceremonial leader position, and furthermore, to collect an exuberant fee from participants! This type of "shaman" or "guru" is no more than a thief and a liar who preys on both the Native American people and culture, *and* those to whom they sell the "Ceremony."

In spiritual matters like these, the truth will always surface, as seen in the case of those who died in James Arthur Ray's fake Sweatlodge. One must learn to exercise caution when entering any Ceremony or buying any item that is labeled as "authentic," especially when it is labeled in a "Native American" package. Often, you aren't getting what it claims, especially in a place like Sedona where almost all its Indigenous people were forcefully removed, while their sacred way of life is exploited for profit. It can be quite easy to get taken advantage of and unintentionally contribute to cultural appropriation, or in more truthful terms, cultural genocide.

Meanwhile, the final night of my first visit to Sedona ended with a bang! My youngest son Zeke and I stayed atop the Airport Mesa, in the swirl of its vortex. Beneath a crisp, star-filled sky, I watched the "blood wolf moon" eclipse, the intriguing effect created when our planet passes in between the moon and the sun and blocks the light of the sun from reaching the moon. This impact turns the moon coppery red as it is slowly swallowed by the earth's shadow. I slept peacefully after watching the entire eclipse.

That night, I dreamt that I purged and spilled out my guts while everyone around me laughed. Yet, I didn't feel embarrassed. Someone whispered to me, "You're like Lucille Ball now!" and then I woke up. I processed this puzzling dream, and soon realized that Lucille Ball was a revolutionary woman in her field. The comedic star of "I Love Lucy," she brought the gift of laughter to a wide audience. People loved her because she gave them joy in challenging times. She was beautiful, but it wasn't her beauty that made her. It was her ability to make everyone laugh, and to raise their frequency by lightening their hearts, a significant form of healing.

Her fearlessness paved the way for future women in both comedy and in Hollywood. Her on-screen marriage with real-life husband Desi Arnaz, who played Rick, became the first multiethnic relationship to air on television. Lucille refused to do the show if her husband wasn't given the lead role as her on-screen husband. Thus, the first public multiracial relationship was normalized in the 1950s, in a time when discrimination and separation based on skin color were still considered publicly acceptable.

Thankful for the insights, I transferred the dream into my journal, foreshadowing my stay in Sedona, where I'd have the peaceful space I needed to finally tell my story through this book – or to purge my past, like my dream, in a healthy manner that would hopefully lighten other's hearts in a Lucille Ball sort of way. After all, dreams give us good paths to follow!

As we left town the next day, I stopped on an intuitive hunch at a local arts center. The ladies behind the counter looked up as my son and I entered, but neither acknowledged us. It didn't really matter to me, at first. I asked one of the ladies if I could take pictures. She looked up, briskly said "yes," and then looked away with a scowl. As we walked away, I heard the women eagerly thank someone for coming in, as they wished him "a lovely day!" I was surprised by their joy towards him because I was given the impression that they were quite grumpy. I laughed a bit to myself but didn't focus on it. I scanned the gallery for inspirational beauty but soon found cultural appropriation instead. At least half of their pieces were high-priced portraits or sculptures of Native American people.

A new couple walked in. They were happily greeted: "Welcome to the Arts Center!" Now, the hair on the back of my neck stood up, so I noted the differences between us: color, features, tattoos, and perception. Instantly, I understood why I was inspired to go there! My son and I – living representations of Native People – were snubbed and judged by outsiders that got paid to sell our people and culture. Instantly infuriated, I wanted to confront them both! Instead, I gave them another chance.

I stood in the middle of the gallery, and obviously stared at them. I wondered if we really were that worthless to them. Did the old-time portraits and sculptures of our ancestors, and the jewelry made by invisible Native modern-day artists only get respect because of the dollar sign that they attached to it? Did we only matter when we could be "authentically" sold for thousands of dollars?

I stared at them as they hustled cheerily about with their European clients, answering questions with certainty, and joyously sharing smiles. I stared while they refused to look back. I watched as one of the women walked right past us, looked at my beautiful boy, and checked his hands to see if he was holding any merchandise! She saw nothing, so looked up with her nose in the air and scuffled away, once again refusing to look me in the eye.

I seized that opportunity to explain to my son in a calm but fierce tone, "My son, this is what some of this world has come to. They glorify our ancestors to sell their image, while we, the ones that are still here, the ones that survived what they did to our ancestors, stand right before them, and are ignored as if we are worthless! We aren't even greeted with a basic "Hello!" They want our culture and image to line their pockets, but they don't want us! I'm sick of it, son! This is going to change!" I snapped pictures of the Native-inspired pieces in the gallery, along with their prices, some as steep as ten thousand dollars, and instead of raising my issue – cultural appropriation and genocide – to these ladies, I chose instead to bring awareness of it to a platform that could reach and teach thousands. The post appeared on my social media outlets the next day, reaching as many as I hoped. The gallery soon issued a public apology and made a genuine attempt to consult with Indigenous representatives.

We left Sedona while a mixture of love and resentment swirled within me. The land called me home in a way that I felt in only a few other places. Yet, the cultural appropriation I saw brought up unresolved issues within me. Cultural appropriation is rooted in the Native American genocide that began with the arrival of Christopher Columbus to our homelands. The truth of Columbus's actions toward the Native peoples he encountered are often left out in school lessons and are far from common knowledge. He is celebrated as the one who discovered America, yet he is truly only the one who opened the door to its colonization, via the authority of the Doctrine of Discovery, at the brutal expense of the thousands of Native American Tribes that already lived there.

The Doctrine of Discovery, particularly its 1493 Papal Decree, attempted political, legal, and spiritual justification of Christian European's claims to lands and waterways found whilst exploring new lands. Even if already inhabited, land could be termed as newly discovered, and therefore claimable, if a flag were planted in its soil in the name of a Christian European monarch. Furthermore, if the people who already lived there insisted on their right to the land, those who "discovered" it could claim that they weren't living on the land according to European Christian standards. Thus, resulting in their acceptable extermination, imprisonment, and assimilation along with the seizure and possession of their lands. The Doctrine of Discovery has been used against the Indigenous peoples of America, Africa, New Zealand, Asia, and Australia in the name of ruthless Christian European land pursuits.

Bartolome de las Casas, a monk that traveled with Columbus, wrote a book called *A Short Account of the Destruction of the Indies,* describing his first-hand experience of the first contact with "Indian" Tribes. Bartolome described the Natives as "Indios," meaning they were "with God." Thus, how the description of "Indian" came to describe Native people. It was a compliment from this man who became known as the "first Indian advocate." He refused to take Native slaves as Columbus implored him to, and instead presented compelling evidence to King Charles V of the atrocious acts committed against the Native people. However, his voice alone was not enough to stop the destruction heading to the shores of Great Turtle Island, the original name for "America."

As more Europeans arrived on the shores of America, laws backed by the Doctrine of Discovery were put into effect that legalized the murder of any Indian considered to be a threat to the settlement of the land, be it man, woman, or child. Often the "threat" was simply their existence. The Indian Removal Act of 1830 pushed nearly all the Southeastern Tribes west of the Mississippi River, and eventually further constrained them, opening their fertile land to the unchecked colonization of settlers, and eventually to the slavery of thousands of Native Americans and millions of Africans via the cotton industry.

To end the ruthless slaughter of their people and make peace with settlers, countless Tribal leaders were forced, under duress, to sign over five hundred Treaties that were drafted by the U.S. Government alone. However, not a single Treaty has been honored to this day, even though it is written in federal law that Treaties are "the supreme law of the land." The push to "Honor the Treaties" has become a prominent issue amongst modern day Native American activists.

The physical genocide of our people faded only after millions died, roughly 90% of the entire population. Any Tribes that weren't wiped out by famine, war, or the diseases introduced by colonizers, were forced onto Indian reservations – lands deemed unsuitable or undesirable for settlers. The buffalo that once numbered into the millions, and upon whom numerous Tribes relied upon almost entirely for sustenance and shelter, were slaughtered by settlers and left to rot on the "range" in the hopes that they'd eventually be driven to extinction, and along with them, the Nations that depended on them.

Figure 1. This gruesome mound of buffalo skulls waiting to be processed as fertilizer demonstrates the extent of the buffalo slaughter committed by American colonizers. Circa 1892. Image source Wikipedia.

Native American children were then forcibly removed from their parents and placed in boarding schools. Their hair was brutally cut, Traditional clothing and names permanently removed, and Traditional Teachings strictly forbidden. In this extremely traumatic manner, these young children came under the control of Christian missionaries and/or military personnel who beat and severely punished them if they spoke their Native language, practiced their Traditional Culture and Spirituality, or acted in any way deemed "Indian" or "savage."

Everything these children knew and loved was removed and replaced with an Anglo-American supposedly "superior" substitute, designed to "kill the Indian in him, and save the man." These words, delivered in a speech by U.S. Cavalry Captain Richard Henry Pratt during the opening of the first off-reservation boarding school in 1879, the Carlisle Indian School, reflected the sentiments of the U.S. Government's approach towards the forced assimilation of Native peoples. The bodies of little Indian children are only beginning to be exhumed from their graves underneath these boarding schools, revealing the truth of the horrific conditions these children endured. Recounts of severe physical, sexual, mental, and emotional abuse are just beginning to emerge from boarding school survivors who are bravely coming forward to share their stories.

Native American parents did not gain the legal right to refuse to send their children to boarding schools until the passage of the Indian Child Welfare Act in 1978, which still has loopholes that allow many Native children to fall through to this day. Even my father and grandmother went to boarding schools. In my family, my generation was the first not to attend, however, I don't feel like my upbringing was far removed from the boarding school environment at all!

It remained illegal for Native peoples to practice our Ceremonies until 1978 with the enactment of the American Indian Religious Freedom Act, which was passed just four years before I was born. In other words, for half of my father's life, for most of my grandparent's life, and for all of my great-grandparent's lives, they could be imprisoned and severely punished for participating in a Sweatlodge Ceremony, attending Sundance, or even for burning sage and praying in their Native tongue – all Ceremonies or spiritual practices which today are freely practiced by groups of people like James Arthur Ray, who lack the understanding, proper protocol, or genetic connection to fairly do so. Their actions marginalize the original teachings of the culture from which the practices originate, spread massive misinformation about the meaning behind these Ceremonies, and make an outright mockery of a sacred way of life that has only recently been returned *legally* to its people who have already endured so much.

Thus, when I first visited uptown Sedona, filled to its maximum with bustling tourists from around the world, and I passed by an "authentic" Native American art store with Dakota-style Headdresses for sale, I couldn't help but feel anger, resentment, and sadness. I felt alienation in looking at the poorly made imitation art of a Ceremonial item, that when Traditionally made, is only bestowed upon a Chief or a particularly distinct woman who has earned, over a lifetime, the right to wear it.

Every eagle feather of their Headdress told the story of their path, of an honor bestowed, and of a long and humble journey as the warrior of the people that they truly were. It was never bought or sold, but was bequeathed, and worn only on special occasions. Yet, here was its replica hanging in this store, with an "authentic" label, misinforming those who didn't know – nearly everyone – that these Headdresses are apparently made from turkey feathers, can be worn by any person, and most deplorably, can be bought and sold!

I looked upon the thousands of people who took in this imitation art, with an "authentic" label stamped above its pricey sales tag, combined with a flat-out lie of a sales pitch about its legitimacy recited by a store worker, and I shuddered as I remembered how much our people have struggled to remain alive and to preserve our Traditions. I stood there, as a survivor after generations of genocide, looking upon the mockery and sale of our Traditions, and I realized the magnitude and insanity of the cultural genocide we still endure! We left Sedona then, confused, but heavily affected by her beauty, a pull that would eventually call us back in.

Directly after our first visit to Sedona, my son and I spent a month in New Mexico to film an episode I'm featured in with *Skindigenous*, a thirteen-part documentary television series that explores Indigenous Tattoo Traditions around the world. It was the first opportunity I was given to share information about the Traditional Tattoo customs of my bands, the Dakota, and Lakota Sioux, to such a large audience!

Our first day of filming featured Beau, aka Riding Thunderbolt, a "tamed" white buffalo we planned to be the star of the scene where I shared the prophecy of White Buffalo Woman. As we pulled into the LaMont farm, Beau was the first sight to greet us. The entire fenced part of the front yard was reserved for him, and his looming body stood alone in it, an unlikely scene for such an incredibly wakan, or sacred animal. I wondered how it was possible to tame a buffalo, especially a bull! I didn't like where my imagination led me.

Monte Fastnacht, his handler, enthusiastically greeted us. After exchanging the basics, I told him that I wanted Beau to roam in and out of the scenes as he pleased, rather than being handled, or forced, to take part. I asked if he could remove the halter from Beau's face. He did, and I saw that Beau was completely bald beneath the halter – a sign that it was never removed!

We planned out the scenes, then started filming. It went well until Monte interrupted us. He was heading out and claimed he had "something we were really going to want to see" before he left. So, we stopped shooting and followed him. He opened the door to a large trailer, and within it stood an enormous taxidermy black buffalo bull! Rendered speechless, we uncomfortably reached for something to say. "Wow!" was all any of us could muster. He tried to sell it to us, or anyone we knew, and then left.

We returned to our set, now confused and a bit angry. I gave the benefit of the doubt to this man as a Keeper of a white buffalo, but now I saw major red flags of yet another case of cultural appropriation in which our sacred buffalo were used to fill this man's pockets! We returned to filming, but were interrupted again, this time by his wife Lana. "Ok kids, time's up! I'm leaving!" We looked at each other in shock, as her husband *just* told us we still had all afternoon to finish our set. We reminded her of this and told her we only needed about another hour to finish our scene, but she insisted that we leave immediately. Reluctantly, we agreed.

Figure 2. Beau, the tamed white buffalo of LaMont's Farm. Photo credit Sara Ben-Saud of Skindigenous.

As I gathered my things and my child into my car, she pulled hastily out of her garage and nearly backed into us. She did not apologize but remained inches away from my car, with her brake lights on, until I moved. Now all doubt was removed from my mind, and I was certain of their cultural appropriation and exploitation of an animal they *knew* was sacred to our people because it represented the fulfillment of a prophecy connected to our entire Ceremonial culture and history! Disgusted by them both, I promised Beau that I'd share his story.

The director of the episode told me later that she had to go back and forth with Lana in emails to settle on a price to "rent" Beau out for the shoot. Lana kept insisting that their offers were too low and demanded more and more. In the end she wasn't satisfied with the final offer but accepted it. Hence, why she must have felt entitled to kick us out hours earlier than we expected!

After completing the documentary in New Mexico, my son and I returned to Sedona, this time in hope of making it home. A stunning, serene spot opened for us after a long week of searching, and we finally moved into our own place for the first time in three years! My Ojibwe spiritual brother, my mentor for over ten years, messaged to congratulate me, to warn me about the "New Agers," and to share some vital information with me: Sedona has been a Ceremonial gathering space of Native peoples for many generations. Even my bands, the Lakota and Dakota, traveled to Sedona for Ceremony. Furthermore, the land was considered so holy that the warriors left their weapons far outside of the Ceremonial space before entering.

Sedona has been known as "the Place of Healing" by Native peoples far before it was inhabited and overrun by New Age "gurus" like James Arthur Ray. Long before outsiders bastardized our Ceremonies and misused them for profit, we came to that sacred land for Ceremony, which was not contained within a single purchased experience or weekend retreat, but was, and remains, a beautiful way of life filled with sacrifice and responsibility that strengthened our relationship with Mother Earth. I realized that I had a direct ancestral connection to Sedona, through the prayers and energy my ancestors left behind. It was my own ancestors who must've led me there and encouraged me to include it amongst the few places I've considered "home."

Sedona is most recently Yavapai territory, and before that, was home to the Sinagua people, who mysteriously vanished. While the Sinagua might have left by choice, the Yavapai were forcibly removed from Sedona in the late 1880s and subjected to the same physical and cultural genocide all Native Americans have endured. Forced to relocate from the homelands they lived upon for generations, the Yavapai were moved to a foreign land and held as prisoners within reservations. Their absence made it easy for settlers and goldminers to colonize "Sedona."

The permanent presence of the Yavapai is mostly gone in Sedona, except for the few local inhabitants and visitors who are descendants. Yet, just like the presence of my ancestors, their spiritual existence stays imprinted upon the land to which they still belong. We believe that we do not own the land, but instead belong to it – creating a bond that cannot be broken, even by generations of forced physical separation.

I didn't forget this when I looked around my home in gratitude, and left offerings to the land. But I noticed who did as I saw the million-dollar Sedona mansions reserved for the "elite," or when I gawked at the exuberantly high prices of everything in Sedona, especially anything "Native American!" I laughed when I heard that a local tattooist tried to patent "vortex dirt" tattoos as his original idea, when Native peoples from the Dakota Sioux to the Yavapai have been using the red dirt from Sedona, and similar areas, in their Traditional Tattoos and paints for countless generations before this guy supposedly "discovered" and "created" it! The disconnection was most obvious as I spotted tourists and locals alike hiking on Bell Rock, a Sacred Site to the Yavapai, who don't walk on it outside of Ceremony, because of their deep respect and understanding of its power.

There were many such distasteful experiences I endured every time I ventured outside my home while there, like micro-aggressions that piled up on me, and for this reason I chose to mostly stay home, finding peace in the solitary hideaway created by the trees, birds, creatures, and running creek in my back yard, who were also coincidentally dealing with the effects of encroaching settlement, industry, and pollution that threatened their future survival. We had much in common, and that space became the place where I channeled my thoughts and experiences into this book, in the hope that it would make a difference in such matters, if not in my lifetime, then in that of my children and the generations to come. For these reasons, my time in Sedona became extremely bittersweet.

At the center of my observations, which have culminated over my entire life, I see that misinformation and separation prevail amongst the masses. I see blissful ignorance and greed overtaking the majority. True sacred connection and Ceremony have been replaced with disconnection, instant gratification, and inauthentic spirituality, which result in a blatant disregard for Mother Earth and her creatures. I pray that this world will change, that the truth will finally be revealed, and that the true caretakers of the land will rise again into positions of positive leadership and environmental stewardship. In fact, I foresee it, through the prophesies our ancestors left behind for us to fulfill, and whose omens are already showing.

I must admit that I went to Sedona filled with expectations for my new life. I thought that I'd have many clients for Handpoked

Tattoos. Instead, my client level went from entirely booked when I traveled to my clients, to an average of five a month when they instead had to come to me – giving me the space and time I needed to recharge. I expected to join with the man I believed to be my partner, but instead remained single – giving me the time to clear my energy. I expected to be involved with the local community, but instead stayed home and felt quite agitated when I did venture into the crowds – I had to realize my ancestors were protecting me. I hoped to jump right away into building a tattoo studio and healing center, but instead found that I was ushered into a private home where few were allowed to enter, and where I instead underwent my own intensive healing – thus how I was led to begin this book!

Everything I imagined would become my experience there proved untrue, except for the serenity I found in seclusion and Nature, and in the stability I knew it would give us. I discovered that Zeke loved to climb mountains and rocks, and that we both had an affinity for climbing the peaks, and then running, sliding, and jumping down the mountains as fast as we could! I can see in retrospect, that after a lifetime of traumatic experiences, I needed a safe space away from others to heal and even play in, so that I could finally face my past. When one is alone and can go deep within, healing is given the opportunity to arise.

On May 13, 2019, I took my boy to the community park. While he played with other kids, I basked alone in the sun. When his friends left, he joined me, and soon became captivated by a caterpillar that fell at our feet. I bent down to inspect its unusual markings, and then stood up to put it back in its tree. As I lifted my arm, my vision blackened, my arms and chest tingled, and my body shook as I swooned uncontrollably. I wondered if this spell, the worst yet, would be the one when I finally passed out! But after a few moments, it passed, so I told my boy, "It's time to go. We must need to eat!"

We ate, relaxed and after a while I put Zeke to bed. I settled in too, but soon received extremely troubling news. My spiritual brother Rah (Raniera) Tamati passed on a few hours earlier, around the same time I blacked out at the park. I was devastated to hear it. He was the sort of person that lit up any room with his joy, and now, just like that, he was gone! I cried myself to sleep, and tossed and turned through the rest of the night. The next morning, I found out that he took his own life.

Rah's larger than life energy, positive attitude, and Māori-based spiritual therapy practice made a powerful impact. Thus, his suicide was unexpected and especially disturbing to his friends and family. His tragic passing brought my own experiences up from the depths. I found myself questioning my take on life. Was there something I could've done to help him? Why couldn't he overcome it? What hurt him so badly that he was driven to end his life so despondently? I wept often, remembering what it's like to be in that state, where it seems the only way to end the pain is to take your own life. I felt horrible, knowing that he was lost in that agony just before his death. I cried for him, and for all of us who've felt that way, and more than anything, I understood.

Later that afternoon, I left the house to divert my focus from the loss of my friend, but it didn't work. I still broke out in tears. On the way back, a tourist tailgated me incessantly, and as I slowed to pull into my driveway, he honked rudely and almost drove his car into mine! I snapped, calmly threw the car in park, hurled the door open gracefully, and took an Inigo Montoya stance. I declared to my new mortal enemy, "Hello. My name is Stephanie. You killed any fucks I have left. Prepare to die!" I didn't care that he was a man, and I a woman, as I challenged him to a duel. He was going down! But instead, he inched around me and sped off, leaving me in my frustration with no relief.

As I broke down again, I analyzed the separation. People commonly spill their hatred onto others. Compassion for others is mostly for show, rather than a constant state of mindful action as it ought to be. The man that attacked me from the safety of his car didn't care if a young child was in the car, or if the person in front of him was just barely holding it together while doing their best to survive an extremely difficult day. He only cared about getting two minutes faster to his destination, so he pushed and shoved the entire way. His actions helped me understand that Rah reached his own limit of other's insane behavior on his final day.

I finally composed myself enough to go back inside. Heading directly to the solitude of the backyard, I sprawled on the deck and cried, praying for help. I've been in this place often, driven into a deep depression because of the chaos and insanity in our world and the havoc it reaps upon the Earth. I felt sick to my stomach. For a moment, I found myself imagining death again, but my thoughts always returned to my son. I'd never willingly leave him to face this world alone. I had to carry on, for his sake.

Hours passed in this way, until I watched an inspirational movie to remind myself of our connection and purpose. It finally dried my tears and reminded me that there's always a light at the end of even the darkest tunnels. Furthermore, in our most tumultuous moments, we build the strength that awakens our highest potential! I was reminded that the power of forgiveness is "for giving," and that first, I needed to give myself compassion and take it easy.

I prayed before going to sleep, picturing everyone in my life that hurt me, and let go of my attachment to the suffering they inflicted. I felt a huge weight lift off my shoulders. I let go of my desire for a relationship, money, or for anything that projected itself as a "need" to fill a void – a sense of emptiness that is channeled to humanity through the programming machines of society that lead us to believe that we aren't enough. I reached into the negative programming of my childhood and filled it with love. I touched the moments when I nearly took my own life, and stood above myself, showering myself with compassion and encouragement. Then, I finally fell asleep.

I slept peacefully for the first time in months and woke with a dire need to share my thoughts on suicide. How would I share? With a social media post? No, not enough. A video? Again, no. And then I realized. It was time to write my book! To share my story. For years, I didn't want to remember. Unfortunately, it took me losing another loved one to suicide to finally find the courage to transform my pain into this poignant story of resilience, reconnection, and empowerment.

This is the story of what kept me going, like a Thunderbird Phoenix's rising, despite wanting to take my life when sadness and grief overcame me. I detail how I found safety, serenity, and life in miraculous ways. I explain my understanding that a common thread exists between all natural people and beings, despite the chaos and insanity that seems to prevail. I also warn that we are in the depths of a spiritual battle between the natural and unnatural that is waged both on Earth and in the Stars; a psychological war that targets the mind. Therefore, we must learn to shield and protect ourselves and others by acknowledging our true history and allowing justice to be served. It is up to each of us to go within and uncover the truth of who we really are, and what we came here to do at this pivotal point in history. Once we come to truly know ourselves, we can begin to break down the illusion of separation that allows us to hurt ourselves and others, then accept the responsibility of mending our broken relationships with each other, Mother Earth, and our Universe.

CHAPTER TWO

IT BEGAN IN HAWAII

From the moment of my conception, I was challenged to grow stronger. It began in the womb, when my twin brother and I, considering our personalities, clearly dueled for space and resources. I admit that he won that round as I was pulled from my mother's stomach as a four-pound preemie, and he, three minutes later at a much stouter six pounds! We joke about how mad this must have made me, my first loss, as we look at our baby picture. In it, I pin him down and stick my tongue out in his face like a Kiss rock star, while he just laughs like a chill Buddha baby!

Our entrance into this world took place on the warm evening of the 18th of February, through the Tripler Army Medical Center, a military hospital in Honolulu, Hawaii. This gave us the same day of birth as our father, and even more interestingly, one of the most grueling endurance races of all time, the Hawaiian Ironman Triathlon. This race was introduced to Honolulu on the same day just four years before us! Was this a foreshadowing of our lives to come? We both think so.

We were born to our Santee and Lower Brule Lakota and Ihanktonwan Dakota Sioux father, and to our Nordic and Irish mother, making us therefore, iyeska – the Lakota term for "mixed blood." My mother has some Indigenous blood, traces from the Inuit and Iroquois, but nothing she was ever able to distinctly claim in terms of knowing our relatives from those Nations. Both our parents served in the military, my father for the Marines, and my mother for the Navy and Air Force. I'm thankful for their service, especially because it took them to Hawaii for our birth. I've been told that a person carries the energy of their birthplace with them for their entire life, which explains why I feel so at home around the ocean, in the sun and heat, and especially when I'm surfing – the original pastime of the Native Hawaiians!

I can't imagine how difficult it must have been for my mother to care for and breastfeed newborn twins, while also raising our older brother, who was then only eighteen months old. "You were always a demon child!" she joked, recalling that I always woke up to feed only moments after my twin beat me to it. I wailed in a hunger rage until I passed out, and she woke me up later for my feeding.

For a while, I took being called a "demon baby" personally, yet as a mother myself, I know how challenging it is to raise just one newborn at a time. I can see that she must have been incredibly overwhelmed with caring for three little ones at the same time. My crying must've driven her insane! I choose to give her the benefit of the doubt rather than hold it against her anymore. On the other hand, my brother won again in the fight for resources, and I laugh to myself! No wonder I stared at him with huge eyes while he was just happy and chill!

Despite my empathy for her as a young mother, her inability to meet my needs marked the beginning of a deep divide between us. Our bond weakened, and my trust in her faded. My mother, who is now an OBGYN physician, helped me piece this together when she told me of a study that proved babies "need more than just a feeding and the proper hygienic conditions to survive." This study was conducted at several orphanages where babies died, despite being provided with all their basic needs – food, water, and the changing of their diapers!

Initially a mystery, their deaths were eventually connected to a common pattern: they lacked the same things – being held, rocked, comforted, and loved on demand. A breakthrough discovery, it scientifically revealed that an essential part of human development and survival depends on having our emotional needs met, especially as infants. I wonder what it did to me to be left for so long without comfort as a hungry infant. I cried myself to sleep, passing out from my own discomfort, from the beginning. Yet, it didn't sadden my mother. It only made her angry at me in her overwhelmed state as she took my cries personally.

I was, however, my father's favorite. My mom said he used to carry me everywhere. I was his "little princess." She attributed his fondness of me to my likeness of him with my darker skin and Native features. It was obvious that we really loved each other, and because of this, I was extremely attached to him.

Although my father had moments of being present, most of the burden of caring for us fell on my mother. She complained that he even refused to change diapers, and confessed she tried to change this by throwing a used diaper at his head! I burst out in laughter as I imagined that. She also came home after leaving us with him to find us locked in closets, or in our bedrooms, for hours! He disappeared for days, leaving us to fend for ourselves while he took the car and all the money.

My mother stayed with my father long enough to have one more child with him, my little sister, who was eighteen months younger than us twins. A carbon copy of my mother, with curly hair and lighter skin, she quickly became my mother's favorite daughter. My mom often told stories of the "angel baby" she was – the one who never cried, and over the years, the one who never cried out, or spoke out, against anything on her own. They still have a strong relationship.

When I was three years old, my mother taught me the difference between "good" and "bad" touches. As she explained "bad" touches, I said, "Oh! That's just like the way my daddy touches me." When confronted by my mother, my dad admitted it, finally destroying their relationship. They divorced, and I was removed from my biological father and his side of the family – my connection to my Native heritage – for the next twenty years. From this point on, my head was filled with the opinion that all Native people are mean drunks that are "good for nothing!" This extremely negative viewpoint of my "Indian" relatives was firmly instilled within us kids based solely on my mom's experience with my father.

I hated the color of my skin, which was the darkest of my siblings, and dreamed of having curly hair and lighter eyes like my sister, instead of brown eyes and straight dark hair. Perhaps then my mother would fuss over my hair like she did my sister's. Maybe she'd like me more. Maybe I wouldn't feel so out of place. I showed the racism I was taught towards my own people; towards myself. I spent the rest of my childhood denying being "Indian" if anyone asked and wishing with all my heart that I was entirely white!

I was raised completely separated from my Lakota and Dakota heritage and culture, and my mother was unable and completely unwilling to pass on any Traditional teachings or knowledge from her side. It wasn't until I was twenty-three, when I reunited with my father, that I found out I was specifically "Lakota and Dakota." Before, I only knew that I was "Indian," and that being Indian meant associating myself with "good for nothing drunks." I had no positive examples in my life that encouraged me to be proud of that part of my DNA. I was only led to believe it was something that I should be ashamed of, and better stay far away from for my own safety.

Thunderbird Rising

After leaving my father, my mother met the man who later became my stepfather, Steven Howard Newburg. A counterintelligence agent in the Air Force at the time they met, a college graduate, and a charismatic charmer, he was intelligent, successful, and well put together. He didn't seem to mind that my mother already had four children, and quickly became involved in our lives. They married soon after, and he adopted all of us kids by the time I was seven. One of my earliest memories of him is when he picked me up, suspending me above his head. He shouted in my face and then slammed me back down. His grip left purple bruise marks on my arm.

Shortly after marrying him, my mother enlisted in the Air Force, beginning an over thirty-year commitment to service. The Air Force paid for her medical school education, and for most of our childhood, she became heavily engrossed in her studies while Steve, who was honorably discharged by this time, took over most of our care. She eventually graduated as valedictorian of her class from John Hopkins Medical School and earned her bachelor's in nursing. Soon after, she returned to school to pursue her doctorate.

For the first nine years of my life, I was a full on "military brat." We traveled all over the world! I became accustomed to quickly making friends and having to just as quickly say our goodbyes as either they, or we, moved on when one of our parents were stationed at another military base. My fondest memories are steeped in the exotic places my mother's military service took us to. Always close to an ocean or forest, there were countless days that I took off with my dog to explore the beaches or woods for hours on my own. Twenty years later, my mother sent me a box of poems that I wrote during grade school. They were filled with my forest adventures, and secrets the trees whispered to me. I wondered what happened to this little girl when I read those poems, for what seemed like the first time, years later. Where and who was she?

I used to get in trouble because I broke out of the house, alone and bare-footed, anytime I wanted a Nature exploration. A part of me deeply needed it, so the risk felt worth it! During one of these expeditions, I crossed a creek by hopping across the old wooden boards that floated over it. I jumped in reckless joy but fell into chaos as I landed with full force on an old rusty nail that pierced straight through my foot! I can still hear my flesh rip as it resounded awfully in my ears and can still feel the searing pain that followed!

I screamed in terror, successfully alerting my mother, who rushed out to find me. She dragged my contorting body back up the steep hill to get me into the house and furiously cleaned my gushing foot. "We *were* going to go to the beach to have fun all day, but now we have to deal with your foot," she complained, "because you just can't stay in the house like everyone else and do as you're told!" After this, I finally stopped breaking out of the house to explore, after having to endure the cleaning of the wound, the ensuing tetanus shot, and the long, painful period of healing that followed!

Around this time, my mother filed the paperwork that allowed my stepfather to adopt us kids. My biological dad, consumed in guilt over what he did, readily signed over his parental rights, and thus the adoption process went forth without difficulty. The adoption removed his name and replaced it with my stepdad's name. Furthermore, my "American Indian – Sioux" heritage was changed to "Caucasian" – further disconnecting me from my Native heritage, but I didn't mind at the time due to the discontent I was taught to have towards it.

Furthermore, since I was born in Hawaii, which is a "sealed document state," the adoption order closed the records of my original birth, preventing them from being opened again without a court order. This later proved very frustrating for me when I tried to retrieve a copy of my original birth certificate – the proof of my Native heritage – after my copy was stolen. I was informed by the State of Hawaii that they couldn't provide me with one, even as an adult, due to its "sealed status."

Native Americans, and Native Hawaiians, must provide proof of their Native blood quantum/percentage, to claim any benefits entitled to them by the U.S. government, such as land claims, Treaty entitlements, and even the right to practice some cultural customs. Therefore, legally sealed adoption records work in the Government's favor, especially because Native children historically, were intentionally removed and adopted out to Euro-American families. It is impossible, without extreme determination, to obtain sealed-document pre-adoption records! I didn't rectify this in my life until thirty years later, when my real dad and I restored our biological connection on paper, via an adult adoption. It is extremely difficult to undo what the adoption of a Native child causes once it's been done!

After we were adopted by my stepfather, my mother was re-stationed to Andrews Air Force Base just outside of Washington D.C. Here, she attended John's Hopkins University, and eventually earned her nursing degree while simultaneously serving as an officer for the Air Force. We kids were enrolled into Mount Calvary Roman Catholic Church and School. Steve, now our newly adopted "father," was hired as the school's religion teacher.

However, he behaved more like a Nazi concentration camp brigadier that controlled our every action, and supervised every peer conversation, rather than the "faithful servant of the Church and God" that he promised to be! My first attempt at suicide reached its peak effect during one of his classes, when the pills I ingested successfully produced extreme nausea and lethargy but didn't cause death. Thankfully, I knew nothing about lethal dosage at my age, so I simply slept it off.

What is a child to do when the person who is in the position of "mommy," or "daddy," and is the "authority," begins to violate and molest the most intimate and sacred part of that child's innocence? A child is simply not equipped with the tools to handle such sickness from the person they are programmed to seek attention, love, guidance, and protection from. Thus, their inappropriate actions suck from the child's life-force, lessening the child's vitality, while feeding the pathogen of darkness that lives in the soul of the violating adult. These types of predators are the most dangerous and diseased of all, which explains how their infection is so easily spread due to the level of shame, guilt, and despondency their selfish actions produce in their victims.

I entered a suicidal state of utter misery, because I was secretly dealing with the devastating trauma of the first experiences of my stepfather forcing himself onto me in the middle of the night, when I was only eight years old! I was old enough to know that something particularly important was being taken from me, but not old enough to know how to defend myself, or to even define what was happening.

I kept these violations of my sacred space a secret because of the shame and embarrassment I felt, and furthermore, the only one that I would have told, my mom, was already far removed from my trust. We hadn't been getting along for years. How could I trust her enough to tell her something as horrible as this?

I used to have these recurring nightmares when I was seven years old. I was smashed by this huge thumb. I wanted desperately to wake up but couldn't no matter how hard I tried. I screamed inside of my dream at my body to move, to make a sound, to wake up! I cried out to my parents for help, but no one heard, no one came, and I just couldn't get away. The dream overpowered my body, even though my mind was awake.

Thunderbird Rising

When I look back on those dreams, I realize they foretold the long, dark period before me, when I'd have no freedom or say over the sexual, mental, emotional, and physical oppression I was about to endure. No one would hear my cries, and there was no escape. There was only the nightmare! I've always had dreams that later came true. Some as soon as the very next day, and some taking years or decades to culminate. This recurring nightmare foreshadowed the entire next twelve years of my life.

Every night, my stepfather let us kids watch a movie until we fell asleep. He put everyone to bed except me. Instead, he kept me downstairs with him, and while I slept, he pulled my pants down and groped me using his grotesque mouth and fingers. I woke up in shock, having no idea what was happening to me, but knowing that he was doing something that made me feel ashamed, terrible, and uncomfortable. I had no idea how to react. I was terrified to give away to him that I was awake, and tried my best to hold my breath, which uncontrollably seized in terror! I tried to freeze my body while he did this to me, confused and fearful of what might happen if he knew that I was awake. Of course, he knew, and my fear and confusion only fed his sickness. It never stopped until he satisfied himself.

He became my living nightmare, teaching me that I was to suffer for his pleasure, and that what I wanted or needed – sleep, security, and most definitely not sexual assault – held absolutely no standing compared to his desire to satiate his sickness. My mother didn't have time to notice and didn't miss his absence in their bedroom due to their already beginning separation.

During the day, he initiated sexual contact through "the tickle game." He took me into his bedroom, closed the door, and said, "Let's pick different spots on each other to tickle!" It was his turn first. "Tickle my elbow," he commanded, and like any child who loves to play, and especially get tickled, I delightedly did so. It was my turn, so I picked my foot. Eventually, he asked me to tickle inside of his pants, placing my hand on his erection. The first time he did this I screamed, ran away, and told him from afar that I knew he was doing something awful! But eventually, this master of manipulation convinced me that "this is what two people who love each other do." Thus, I entered the miserable ten-year period of my life where I was manipulated into being my stepfather's underage sex slave.

At this time, I developed severe Urinary Tract Infections (UTI's). I don't remember any of this, but years later, my mom told me that she used to take me in as a little girl to military doctors, so they could inspect and fix me. As an adult, I know that UTI's in girls, along with certain other behavioral red flags, are obvious signs of sexual abuse.

My mother admitted some twenty years later that she suspected "something was happening," but with no hard evidence, she dismissed her suspicions. This was probably easy for her to do. First, no sane mother wants to believe their partner would sexually abuse their children. Second, my stepfather babysat all of us while she worked and went to medical school. Coupled with his master manipulation skills, my mother believed that we were better off under his care, and so, he eventually took full control of our lives and especially, our minds!

I had no idea that he was "molesting" and "raping" me. I was so brainwashed that I thought it was normal, and happened because he "loved" me, even though it made me feel terrible – so terrible that I fantasized about my death, or his death, every day! I slowly warped from an innocent child deeply connected to Nature, into a despondent, isolated, unsure, and socially awkward child that internalized every violation. I lied for my stepfather, never telling anyone the truth of what he did, because he convinced me that he needed protection, while I suffered the most of all for what I was misled to believe was "love."

In the meantime, my stepfather became a "servant" of the Roman Catholic Church, and a teacher of its religion. He encouraged me and my brothers to serve the Church too, thus, we became altar kids. How ironic it was that my twin Christopher bore the cross of Christ every Sunday morning along with my older brother Shawn, and they were both about to endure their own horrific abuse at our stepfather's hands. How eerie it was that it was my role to kneel, and ring the bell at just the right moments, to signify the importance of the healing words of Christ as they poured over us through the voices of the priests. I learned that sins against anyone could be easily rectified every Sunday with a confession and fifty subsequent Hail Marys.

One day, a priest held my hand with the crustiest appendages I ever felt! The insides of his hands rubbed mine like coarse sandpaper and grit. As he held my hand, he asked, "Why don't you do anything fancy with your hair? You'd look so much prettier if you put it up on top of your head." He tried to fondle with my hair while still holding my hand with his sandpaper grip, so I pulled my hand out of his. He sickened me, and I avoided him like the plague after that. At least I was allowed to stay away from him if I wanted to. My stepfather was an entirely different story.

At the Catholic school we attended, my siblings and I went to a math class taught by an old woman nicknamed "the crazy math nun." Instead of teaching us, however, she used our class time to share inappropriate stories about her life. Once, she confessed that she caught a bad case of tapeworms after she ate food she found in a dumpster. Then, she explained how she got rid of them – by slowly looping them around a pencil until they fully exited her butt!

One day, I told her how beautiful her hair looked, and she screamed back, "It's not my fault that my hair was burned off and I have to wear wigs!" This was her normal behavior. However, she was never let go because she was a "faithful servant of the Church." She reminds me of another group of "faithful servants" the Church keeps in positions of power over children, despite the horrible and tragic proof of their crimes against them!

Quickly, I formed a disgusting view of the vile, two-faced behavior of certain "servants" of the Church. However, the healing words and prophetic messages of God and Christ had such a powerful impact on me, that for a short time I aspired to become a nun! This was far before I swore off the Church and the messages of God entirely after the events that followed in my life, which caused me to lose the entirety of my faith and hope to the point that I became an atheist. For how could there be a God when all I knew was suffering, abuse, and pain? Furthermore, if there was a God, why would he let me suffer so badly under the hands of one of his own "faithful servants"?

Although pain and confusion characterized much of my childhood, countless electrifying experiences made up for it, many thanks to my mother's military service that took me to places I otherwise wouldn't have seen in my lifetime. Right before my ninth birthday, my mom was stationed to a four-year term at Clark Air Force Base, on Luzon Island in the Philippines. Here, the Filipino ladies treated me like I was one of them, and an unusual sense of pride and belonging surged within me that I was quite unaccustomed to.

My mother hired Vilma, an Indigenous Filipino woman, to make clothes for us, along with her exquisite Traditional foods and beverages. Each time she graced our kitchen, I experienced the most delicious and exotic cuisine I ever tasted. She fed and looked after us kids like we were her own, and so, we quickly came to love and admire her. Her daily presence in our home introduced me to the Traditional Indigenous hospitality that I have come to understand is a common theme amongst most Indigenous people worldwide – a kindness, generosity, and honor given especially to guests.

Otherwise, my memory of the Philippines consisted of searing heat, the bananas and pineapples that grew like weeds in our backyard, and the lush jungles of the island. We also stayed mostly on base due to safety concerns. Most of the locals disliked the American soldiers, who were not considered guests, but were instead seen as unwelcome invaders. Soon, things would change for all of us.

On June 10, 1991, our family received emergency orders to immediately evacuate our home. Mount Pinatubo, which had slept peacefully for over six hundred years, suddenly spewed its volcanic gases, ash, and deadly debris high into the air! At just eight miles away, we had a front row view as we joined the long caravan of cars slowly evacuating the base to take shelter at a nearby naval base. We watched in awe as a massive mushroom cloud swelled violently over the angry volcano. The eruption marked the beginning of our last days in the Philippines, cutting the military's four-year plan for us short at just four months.

I recently learned that the Indigenous Filipino people, many of whom gathered outside the gates to eagerly watch us leave, demanded for years that the American military leave their homelands, but to no avail. However, after the eruption of Mount Pinatubo, the military was forced to leave due to the annihilation of its infrastructure by Mount Pinatubo's volcanic forces. The volcano delivered its own justice!

This powerful childhood experience connects the dots to recent events where I've stood with my own people against the military's presence on our ancestral land during the Standing Rock Movement in 2016. No matter how peacefully we tried to enact our sovereignty and right to protect our homelands, fully armed military forces and law enforcement officers used brutal force to obtain their objective – to enforce the construction of the Dakota Access Pipeline through reservation lands.

One day, however, a wicked thunderstorm arrived in perfect timing. While hundreds of us released *lilililili's* and war whoops, lightning crashed, chasing terrified law enforcement officers back into their vehicles, just after they tried to invade our stronghold. These soldiers did not care that we stood our ground as the protectors of the people's water, or as the protectors of the burial grounds of our ancestors. They didn't care about the harm befalling our homelands, but only cared about "following their orders," a sentiment that has become an ominous issue amongst Indigenous peoples worldwide as they try to protect their homelands, resources, and sovereignty from invasion.

Mount Pinatubo's destruction of Clark Air Force Base, and the arrival of the thunderstorm that helped protect our stronghold at Standing Rock, are instances where I was given a first-hand experience of the Earth's supernatural power to protect herself and her people. It was a clear message to all involved that the most powerful force on Earth is the Earth itself. We are a part of the Earth, and we are sustained by her. When we step out of bounds, she does have the power to deliver justice.

Once we reached Subic Bay, we were housed with hundreds of other military families that also evacuated from Clark. We slept on cots, and while awake, we kids did nothing but play! Our biggest excitement came from the glow sticks we were given to provide light after the power went out.

None of us realized, as children hardly ever do, that we were close to death itself. We also didn't know that we wouldn't return to our jungle home, that we'd never see Vilma again, and that everything we left behind would be given back to the land as it was swallowed by a storm of volcanic dust! As Mount Pinatubo blew her top, Typhoon Yunya simultaneously wreaked havoc upon us. The days turned to night, the wind howled as the buildings groaned and creaked, volcanic ash rained down from the sky like a toxic monsoon, and the earth quaked beneath us relentlessly.

After three apocalyptic days, the winds finally died down, the typhoon passed, and the earthquakes stopped. The brutal aftermath was utterly shocking, even to us children! The lush, tropical, flowering jungle we knew before the eruption was no more. In its place sat a cover of goopy, grey, volcanic ash. Buildings collapsed. Roofs caved in or were ripped from their foundations, and trees heavy with the weight of ash fell on newly pancaked cars. Most shocking of all, monkeys who before were cloaked by dense jungle vegetation, now stood completely exposed as they desperately rummaged through the ash for nourishment. We were fortunate to survive, considering that roughly eight hundred other people and countless animals became sacrifices of this historic natural disaster.

Despite my shock, I was extremely excited to ride in a helicopter for the first time as it airlifted us aboard the Naval USS Abraham Lincoln Aircraft Carrier, our transport for the final stage of our evacuation back to the States. The highlight of the rest of the trip, which was from that point on uneventful, was seeing the octopus that surfaced while we looked down at the waves. It was the first time I saw an octopus in the wild, and I've never forgotten it! Through everything I endured, my fascination and connection with Nature and her creatures remained a huge influence in my life in both times of light and dark.

Several months before Mount Pinatubo forced us out of the Philippines, my mother and stepfather began arguing constantly. We kids listened in fear, wondering if they were going to break up. We also assumed that it was our fault if they did. Their relationship continued its demise after we moved to Tampa Bay, Florida. My mother became further engrossed in her studies and work demands, while my stepfather took significant control over raising us. Meanwhile, I withdrew drastically as the sexual abuse increased. I even dressed in boy's clothes, trying to hide my femininity and newly developing body.

I found my only joy in chasing the lizards that lived on the cactus in our front yard, playing with my little sister, and caring for my pet birds, a pair of budgies. I adored their company, and I thought they adored mine, but when they escaped one day, I was forced to accept the truth. While I hopelessly chased after them, I realized quite reluctantly how happy they were to be free! I took it personally at first, because I took good care of them, feigning a special connection with them. I thought they were content to be with me, yet it became clear that their freedom was stronger than any form of entrapment, no matter how humane. I had to let go of them after it became clear that I'd never catch them. They were finally free and chose to fend for themselves. Yet, their escape opened the door to an enticing hobby, one that I continued for the rest of my life!

I returned to the empty cage filled with sadness. With no idea what to do with the leftover birdseed, I lifelessly spread it on the ground outside as a final send-off to my birds. Incredibly, I soon noticed that it attracted flocks of wild birds! From that day on, I kept the ground filled with birdseed, and as more birds came, I learned how to identify them. I stared out the window for hours, fascinated by their differing sizes, colors, and personalities. I never tired of their company. Over the years, I became an avid birdwatcher and birdfeeder, establishing a lifelong relationship with birds that never involved placing one in a cage to force its company ever again! I earned and cherished it from that point forward.

One sizzling summer day, my sister and I played a lazy game of catch. She clumsily threw the ball into the bushes, and I skipped to retrieve it. I stretched my hand down and clutched the ball but froze when I realized that a diamond-back rattlesnake was coiled up right next to the ball! If I extended my finger, I'd touch it! Yet, it didn't shake its rattle at me or take an aggressive stance. It simply peered calmly into my soul. I gasped in excitement and made a choice that I quickly regretted. I told my mom and stepdad about him.

They called animal control, and while he waited for them to arrive, my stepfather poked the snake with a stick. The snake was naturally agitated and shook its warning rattle before it took a few strikes at my stepfather. I begged him to leave the snake alone, but he wouldn't listen. I wished the snake would bite him! Animal control arrived, and in absolute horror, I watched as they quickly captured the snake, then cut its head off with a shovel.

To this day, I shudder when I think of the way they handled that animal that did nothing to provoke them, and who spared me all harm. This was a hard lesson for me to learn, but one that taught me that one's existence alone can be such a threat to others, that they'll kill them over it, even if they were in the place they belonged, and where they had every right to be! I never let another snake or animal die in such a way because of me from that day forward! I became an avid protector of my relatives in the Animal Nation, and I mourned that snake for years to come.

Meanwhile, the fighting between my mother and stepfather reached its climax, and they filed for divorce. My mother explained years later that she believed she was "doing the right thing" when she gave full custody of us kids over to my stepfather, and soon enough the day came when we pulled off in a fully loaded van after saying our goodbyes to her. We moved to Indiana with him, while she stayed in active service and pursued her doctorates degree. She remarried shortly after.

Without my mother around to interfere, my stepfather secretly claimed me as his "girlfriend" and as "the love of his life." He said he fell in love with me, because I comforted him during their separation, and thus feigned his entitlement to enact his sexual attraction towards me every time we were alone, with or without my consent! Over the years, he threatened that if I told anyone about what happened, that he'd go to jail – placing the blame for him having to be held accountable for his actions on me. Furthermore, he concluded that we kids would go into the foster care system, further placing the potential devastating effects of separating the family on my shoulders if I said anything about the abuse.

He isolated us in countless ways. First, he turned my mother into the enemy. Then, he strictly regulated our choice of friends. Our exposure to all sorts of movies, music, literature, and social events were strictly regulated. My eighth grade and high school years were akin to serving time in a federal penitentiary, except the prison was erected around my mind, body, and spirit. Nothing was up to me, nor belonged to me. It was as if every part of me belonged only to him, and if I tried to resist, the punishment was severe.

When we first moved to Indianapolis, we stayed in the basement of his mother's house. It was equally fun there, as it was horrible. It became the place where he stole my virginity, but also the place where we kids spent countless summer days swimming in the huge pool that swallowed the backyard. We knew heaven because of that pool as much as we knew hell because of our stepfather. It was interesting to watch how popular he was with his family. He always made them laugh, and although he did unspeakable things behind closed doors, in the open, he was exceptionally likeable and charismatic.

I adored his mother, Judy, but she didn't like me much. She used to tell me that I had "too much of a mouth on me," and that I should be quieter, and more like my sister. A skilled pianist, she took my sister under her wing, giving her daily piano lessons, an experience she never offered to me. So instead, I taught myself to play. I loved the sound of the piano! Over a few months, I taught myself how to play quite a few songs such as "Moonlight Sonata" and "Für Elise" by Beethoven, and my favorite, "Memory," from Cats the Musical. I could read the music well and built a repertoire of songs I was proud to handle. However, I felt instantly nauseous the day I overheard Judy tell my sister, "Don't worry, she's not that good and she's off-beat." She never offered to correct me but was instead quick to offer backstabbing criticism.

Despite this, I still loved her and desired to please her. So, for her 65th birthday, I selected what I believed to be the perfect gift. I told my sis she could go in on it with me, and I'd say it was from both of us. However, after we presented our adopted gramma with her gift, I heard her in the other room whisper to my sister, "There's no way that gift could've come from Stephanie. You must've picked everything out. She wouldn't choose something so nice." I didn't hear my sister say anything in return.

My step-grandmother taught me that some people will not like you no matter how hard you try to earn their favor. Sometimes it's simply the way you look, or the way you talk, or the way you breathe, that will earn their disfavor. Therefore, you must learn to love yourself despite what anyone else thinks about you. My little sister taught me that it is worth it to earn another's hatred for being true to oneself, rather than to earn their love at the expense of your own integrity.

My step-grandmother's husband was an interesting fellow. He was a firefighter that usually kept to himself. He loved to retire to his den when he got home, a place I rarely ventured into because it made me extremely uncomfortable. John Wayne statues, posters, and lamps decorated the entire lair. It was as if John Wayne himself entered that room as gunshots blasted through the television screen and took down hundreds of Indians every night! Even though I was as far removed from identifying myself as "Indian" as I could possibly be, I subconsciously felt the attack and wished that I could scrub off my brown skin and curl my long dark hair.

I scored my first paid job around this time as a babysitter for my neighbor's kids, one of whom had muscular dystrophy – a neuromuscular disease characterized by gradual muscle loss and increased weakness over time. He was about thirteen years old but still hard to understand when he talked. He was confined to a wheelchair, spoon-fed every meal, and aided with each drink.

He was bullied in school for these reasons, and I stood up to defend him. I clearly understood him when he told me that he loved me, and I was "his angel." I loved him too. He made me feel special in a time when everyone else made me believe I was quite un-special. His drive to overcome his degenerative disease was an inspiration. His determination was so strong that he eventually learned how to run with braces, and even joined the soccer team! I swelled with pride to see his success despite the odds. His heart was bigger than most, which led him to overcome incredible challenges.

After about a year in Judy's basement, we finally moved into our own home, just in time for my twin and I to enter our freshman year of high school. Now fully isolated from the observance of any family members, we kids came under the complete insanity of the control of our stepfather, thus beginning the darkest stage of our collective childhood experience.

After we got home from school, an hour or two would pass before he arrived home from work. In that time, my mind fantasized about his death in a thousand different forms. "Please let him get hit by a car! Or struck by lightning! Or die of a heart attack! Please, anything..." but around the same time every day, he still managed to walk through that door.

First, he went through my backpack and my sister's, looking for any evidence of communication with boys. If he found any, or if he even felt through some sort of osmosis that we did, then he screamed in our faces, called us names, and slapped us until we promised to never talk to a boy again. Although I hardly ever did, not because I made a promise to him under duress, but because of my own shyness, I did dream of one nearly every night.

His name was Joey Z, and he played on the football and rugby teams. I saw him several times a day on the way to orchestra or lunch, and during soccer practice. I thought he was so handsome, and I saw him in my dreams, so I believed that our connection was more than just physical. I felt like he noticed me too, yet he never approached me. For four years I crushed on him, but we never talked, and even if we did, considering my home situation, it wouldn't have gone far, but feeling such a profound attraction for him that was never resolved or even initiated made me feel horrible! I wondered if he didn't talk to me because he thought I was too ugly or too stupid. These were the things that my stepfather called me, and I began to believe it.

Things most teenagers begin to explore as they transition to adulthood, like dating, spending more time with friends, and going to prom, were either completely prohibited, or severely restricted. It wasn't until I turned eighteen that I finally met a boy that my stepfather allowed me to date. However, during a private meeting with him, my stepdad told him embarrassing things about me to separate us.

Later, my boyfriend told me that my stepfather acted more like a jealous boyfriend than my "dad." He thought it was weird and asked if there was something going on that I wanted to talk about. At that time, I didn't know, even though I was eighteen years old, that I was molested and raped by my stepfather, and I was too ashamed to admit anything was wrong! So, I said no, everything was good. Shortly thereafter, mostly due to my stepfather's constant interference, and my inability to admit the truth of my reality, we broke up.

I otherwise had a well-rounded academic and extracurricular experience in high school. We attended an upper-class school on the north side of Indianapolis, with the children of professional football players, lawyers, scientists, and otherwise materialistically successful people. Our sports teams, student orchestra, band, and science teams consistently placed in the top three tiers in state-wide and national competitions. I took mostly advanced placement courses designed to prepare me for college at prestigious universities like Harvard and Stanford. Quite a few of my classmates got accepted into those universities to continue their education. Although I performed consistently well during my freshman and sophomore years, my grades, along with my ability to care about anything, soon plummeted.

I became increasingly rebellious against my stepfather, fighting with him through the afternoons and nights rather than submitting to his sexual advances out of fear and confusion like I did before. The more I fought with him, the more he pressured me and forced himself on me. I went to school the next day with extreme fatigue while in a complete state of despondency. Sometimes, I just gave in to him so that I could at least go to bed at an earlier time and get more rest. More often, I fought because I hated him and his touch so vehemently that I couldn't stand it anymore! One time, I became so angry at him that I threw glass all around my room, at the walls, and directly at him, smashing him in the face. He told me that I scared the shit out of him, and for the first time, I realized my power!

My hatred for my stepfather and the situation he forced upon me manifested itself in mystery illnesses, which the doctors couldn't explain, as well as in chronic bouts of strep throat. I used to have severe digestive issues, most certainly caused by being trapped in a constant spiritual, emotional, and physical fight with my stepfather for the right to control those aspects. I used to get excruciating pains in my chest that felt like getting stabbed with a knife! The doctors told me on my eighteenth birthday that if I got strep throat one more time, they'd have to remove my tonsils. My body was breaking down before it was even eighteen years old! However, there were vital aspects of my life that served as a lifeboat while the rest of me nearly drowned.

I played violin for the school orchestra. I loved playing my instrument and became especially adept at it. My skill level placed me as the second chair violinist. Our conductor, who previously lived in Oklahoma, shared stories with me about the Indian children he once mentored there. I always wondered why he told me because I clearly didn't care! He tutored me with private lessons after school, and often commented on how many scholarships I could get because of my Native American ancestry, but I always coldly warned him, "I don't care, I'm not Indian. So, stop saying anything about it!" He replied, "You are an enigma!" I rolled my eyes with a smile and replied, "You have no idea!" If only he had known, maybe he could have helped me.

I also played striker for our school's varsity soccer team. The striker is the only player who runs the entire field, switching back and forth between offense and defense as needed. I was fast, aggressive, and had a knack for scoring goals from half field. I also didn't hesitate at all if another player stood in between me and a goal. One time, during a breakaway, it was just me, the goalie, and the goal. She stood her ground as I approached her rapidly, skillfully dribbling the ball with my toes. I smashed into her as she tried to grab the ball and knocked her out! I took that opportunity to kick the ball into the goal, scoring the winning point for our team. I didn't care that she was carried out on a stretcher. Because of what I was going through, I had quite a wicked streak and loved to take it out on the field.

On an especially frigid day during the winter break of my sophomore year, my siblings and I headed out to go sledding, despite the warnings to stay inside except for emergencies due to the blizzard-like conditions and dangerous cold. To us, that was a clear invitation to go party! We walked about a mile away with our new snow tube to check out the steepest hill we knew of. It was marked with a clearly visible sign: "No sledding." Undoubtedly, we found our spot! On this monster of a hill, some remarkable kids before us foresaw our arrival and built an ice ramp into the hill! We screamed in unison, "AWESOME!"

My little brother was the first one to try to conquer the ice ramp with the snow tube. I observed his launch and descent like a scientist on a field mission, taking notes on his bloody landing. "Well," I theorized, "he let go of the tube, which resulted in him landing on his face and bleeding, therefore, if I hold on tight and don't let go, I'm certainly going to nail the landing!"

My turn was up! I climbed onto the magic carpet ride and held on for dear life. I pushed off and flew down the hill, quickly gaining incredible amounts of exhilarating speed. I curled over, then up the ice ramp, and shot straight into the sky like a rocket! I didn't let go, even as the snow tube turned completely upside down. I held fast! I descended from the sky like this, holding on tightly to the snow tube, which now rode me, rather than me riding it, and that's when I nailed the landing on the ice ramp – with the back of my head! I remember almost nothing from that point forward, but my brother relates the story well.

Everyone burst out in roaring laughter and continued to guffaw as I slid the rest of the way down the hill of freezing snow. Their deep belly laughs resounded through the hills, until they noticed that once I reached the bottom, I neither stood up nor moved. I just lay there, my body contorted like a discarded ragdoll, still face down in the snow. They joined in my silence for a moment, then ran down the hill after me. My twin turned me over and gasped! My face was a purple and blue mess as my eyes rolled back into my head, and my breathing ceased. He immediately ran back up the hill to get an ambulance. A few minutes later, I sat straight up, screamed hideously, and vomited, terrifying my sister.

The ambulance arrived about a half hour later, unable to get there any sooner due to the hazardous road conditions. The snow was so deep that the ambulance couldn't reach me directly, so the EMT's had to trudge through quite a bit of snow to help me. They positioned a brace around my neck, nudged me onto a stretcher, and transported me awkwardly back to the ambulance. About the only thing I do remember is when they cut off all my brand-new Christmas clothes so they could hook me up to the heart machines and monitors. I remember this because I was thinking, even while concussed, "Really!? You gotta cut through *all* my brand-new clothes!? That's Abercrombie and Fitch. Fuck my life!"

Every few minutes of that long and cold ride, I whispered, "Sorry, but I have to throw up again!" The EMT's then quickly turned the gurney I was strapped to so that I could vomit over the side. It took a considerably long time for us to reach the hospital as the blizzard reduced travel to one treacherous lane. The EMT's had no choice but to hurl open the doors and try to force cars out of our way. Thus, my bare skin was exposed to the dangerous winter weather.

I finally arrived at the hospital, still fading in and out of consciousness, vomiting incessantly, and now in a state of hypothermia. Suspecting that I might have permanent brain damage, or life-threatening bleeding in my brain, I was delivered at once to the radiologist who channeled me through a CAT scan to determine the effects of the concussion on my brain. The doctor forced me to stay awake to my avail. "Why is he so rude?" I thought. "Why can't I sleep? I'm so tired!" I had no idea that if I went to sleep before they eliminated their suspicions, I might have slipped into a coma. Miraculously, I had no permanent damage or bleeding in my brain, although it was badly bruised and extremely swollen from the "hit" landing.

I was hospitalized overnight and released the next day to continue my recovery at home, which took well over a month. To this day, I can still feel the cold much more than others and have dizzy spells that nearly cause me to pass out. I also quickly get motion sickness from the slightest uneven motions and have some significant memory loss. These effects are welcome compared to the options of permanent brain damage, and even death, that I faced on that cold January day. Yet, even during my recovery from this near-death experience, my stepfather continued to force himself on me, further reinforcing the notion that his "needs" far outweighed mine!

I was not the only one who endured horrific abuse at the hands of my stepfather. My little sister and I were close growing up, practically best friends. She trusted me enough to confide that our stepfather also touched her inappropriately, and that our older brother Shawn liked to burst in on her when she was in the shower and yell, "Show me all you've got!" I held counsel with them, genuinely believing that if I called them out, they'd stop. They both promised they would, especially my stepfather. I found out years later that of course they hadn't.

Obviously, Shawn was repeating the cycle of abuse he was taught. He targeted my little sister for years. I do remember a time when we were little when he tried to crawl on top of me. Years later, I put the pieces of the puzzle together and realized that Steve must've also been molesting Shawn. Shawn, however, never came out about his abuse. He simply buried it and instead became a perpetrator, echoing what he endured. However, he never tried to approach me sexually when we were older. Instead, he and I were engaged in a relentless round of mortal combat. We were the exact opposite of one another and fought constantly!

My little brother Joe was the only biological son of my stepfather. I have no idea if Steve molested him too, but I do know that Joe still carries the scars on his back from being beaten with a belt by him. Steve's best friend, Victor Macri, moved into the basement of our home not long after we moved in. He and Joe took a liking to each other and spent an incredible amount of "alone" time together in Victor's room.

I was oblivious to it at the time, but years later I had a dream that Joe showed me the things they did in that room, for instance, how Victor prepared him for penetration by sticking tampons in there when he was only nine or ten years old! My twin recently confirmed this, as he recounted the time he walked into the living room, and saw Joey, who was around eleven at the time, straddling Victor, while Victor had his finger in his butt.

My twin said that as soon as he walked into the room, Victor stopped, and that he didn't say anything at the time because he'd certainly get his ass beat if he did by our stepdad! All of us were in a state of absolute chaos that never ended. Furthermore, Joe used to "tell" on my twin, often making up lies about something he did, just so he could watch our stepfather beat the living shit out of him. My twin was in no place to make a stand against Steve's best friend! So, Victor continued to do whatever sick stuff he wanted to. I'm under the impression now, that child molesters like to stick together.

My twin received an equally devastating amount of abuse as me, but in a different form. I used to feel powerless when my stepdad would get that belt out and take it to us, especially my brothers. My twin received the brunt of that. Our stepfather obviously abhorred him, and he tried to make the rest of us do so too. He used to hold meetings with all of us, a living room "gathering," where he isolated my twin and announced all the "terrible" things he did, trying to make him an example to the rest of us of how not to behave, how not to breathe, and how not to exist. He attacked him physically, emotionally, and psychologically every single day.

I must admit that I bought in for a time to my stepfather's manipulation and isolation of my twin, and I avoided my twin in school. I took part in the isolation of my own flesh and blood, and I spent years feeling extreme guilt for falling prey to his tricks. My twin and I are still repairing our relationship from the effects of this childhood abuse.

I usually retreated to another room when my stepfather beat my brothers. Occasionally, I tried to stop him, but there was nothing I could do. It was normal to us. He beat us since he came into our lives, and he'd whip me too with that belt if I got in the way like he already did many times before. He was so much bigger and more powerful than all of us. So, I tried my best to block it out, just like everyone else blocked out the arguments they could hear between him and I in his locked bedroom.

My brother later shared stories with me of the details of the abuse he endured. Along with thrashing him daily with the belt, starving him as a frequent punishment, and isolating him, he used to take him into the bathroom and waterboard him with the toilet. My twin shares some of his experience in his own words:

"All I ever wanted out of my father figure was a 'good job.' If I got straight A's, he instead told me I sucked at sports; that I needed to learn how to touch my toes. I was going to go to hell and all the other kids were gonna go to heaven. I deserved to have my head flushed down the toilet. I remember passing out as an altar boy once. Every one of my relatives and friends checked on me to make sure that I was ok, except for him. All I could think was, 'Fuck! What was he gonna do?' Sure enough, when we got home, I got one of my many 'private sessions.' Instead of a pep talk and some much-needed self-confidence, I got a beating on my ribs, lower back, and ass that no one would see. Didn't make it easy to walk the next few days. I've never actually talked about these 'private talks' we had before. I figured my sisters went through enough. I didn't need to whine about anything. I was convinced I deserved it."

We kids were also required by our stepdad to completely avoid "Black" people. When we drove through a "Black" neighborhood in Indianapolis, he told us not to "look them in the eye," and to look down so they wouldn't see us. How cowardly and utterly racist is that? I had a good friend in high school that was Black, and I had to keep our friendship a secret from my stepdad to avoid punishment; but he still found out about him because my friend said "hi" to me when I walked with my stepdad thru the school to attend a parent-teacher conference. He struck me later for this while calling me a "whore" and a "Black lover."

The high school we went to was of a mostly white demographic, where I and one other girl were the only visibly brown kids. We became friends for a while simply because we felt accepted by one another. Otherwise, my intense shyness and restricted social capabilities allowed room for just three other friends for my entire high school experience. They were a group of all-white, upper-class girls, whom I loved at the time, but who also stopped communicating with me after I confessed to them what happened to me while we were in high school. Can't say I blame them. It's heavy stuff to deal with!

Throughout all of this, I find it incredible that my brother and I survived the fourteen years of abuse we endured from our stepfather. Many who have been, or who are, in our situation, do not. I can attribute most of my survival to my ability to maintain high enough vibrations to simply become numb. I was so engrossed in music, sports, birdwatching, gardening, and Nature that I managed to just barely keep my head above water. I am extremely thankful for those influences, which became my coping mechanisms. Although the abuse lingered with me for all my life, so too have the positive aspects, which have been far more powerful in terms of keeping me connected to myself. I don't think I would've survived without them. I would've become another suicide statistic.

I can, however, find certain things our stepfather instilled within us that were extremely beneficial, such as the time he encouraged me to read the *Autobiography of Malcolm X*, who afterwards became one of the biggest influences on my life and my perception. He also taught my sister and I to sing while he played the guitar. He bought us many pairs of rollerblades to ensure that we went for our twenty-mile rollerblading sessions every day after school. I had an entire repertoire of tricks up my sleeve that I performed on those blades! I felt like a superhero, like I could fly when I reached top speed. I could fantastically spin and jump over walls and stairs in them. Can't say I miss those days, but I do miss those blades!

In my junior year of high school, I stopped working at the place I worked for years, where my stepdad managed. I begged him for permission to work somewhere else so I could make more money and get my own car, which I quickly did. I really wanted to work as a server, and after convincing him to give me a little bit of freedom, I got hired on at TGI Friday's as a hostess.

As I went into my senior year, I finally became a server at Friday's, but soon wanted to leave because I couldn't stand their requirement of having to be so fake happy all the time. I couldn't do it! So, I got hired at Victoria's Secret inside the mall instead. I loved it there. Secret things were my specialty, and I quickly became one of the top saleswomen.

Eventually, my manager was offered a new position at a men's suit store, where she made more money. She asked me to follow her, and I too made huge commissions every week by super-selling suits to professional young men. I started socializing with other men besides my stepdad, especially these Italian guys from the pizza shop in the food mall. They gave me free pizza and made me laugh.

I also befriended an ecstasy dealer. Wanting to feel anything other than the despondency I knew like the back of my hand, I experimented with his product at least three times a week. School soon became obsolete. I skipped classes constantly and stayed nights away from the house without my stepdad's permission. I went wherever I wanted to because I had a car and an exciting new hobby. The high of ecstasy produced an extreme feeling of "love" within me, and I felt an instant connection with everyone I met. I never felt this way before! But the feeling didn't last long, and recovery soon took up to three days. All my dopamine was depleted, and I felt even worse than before I took it. After a few months, I quit cold turkey and almost never took it again!

Then one day, while working at the suit store, I met Izz, who was friends with the Italian guys from the pizza shop. He invited me over to his place. I accepted, and soon he became my first real boyfriend. We started living together almost immediately. With only two months left before my high school graduation, I dropped out and moved in with him at just eighteen years old. He was twenty-eight, and I was infatuated. I lost all interest in school, and furthermore, my stepdad was hunting me down, trying to force me to come back to the house and under his control. But, like the budgie I once kept in a cage, I found my freedom at last, and there was nothing he could do to make me come back! Thus, I spread my wings and flew out of his house, blindly venturing forth upon the first path that enabled me to escape from his oppression and invisible slavery forevermore.

CHAPTER THREE

"ADULTING"

I never wanted to leave Izz's house. More than anything, I had nowhere else to go, and I certainly wasn't going back to my stepfather's house! Plus, I believed that I loved him. I fell for him so quickly. I was absolutely starved for love, having been used against my will for my body and love for most of my life. I was reckless, lost, in desperate need of help, and in an even deeper need of real love. Izz stepped up to help with some of that, but not very happily, nor with much integrity. At the time, I thought it was wonderful that he was eleven years older than me. I was already forced to be with a man over twenty years older than me for so long! Izz was younger, and he wasn't my "dad" in any way, so for the first time I felt free to express my love genuinely.

So, I stayed with him, blindly loving him, even as he told me after I professed my love for him, that "he loved me, but wasn't in love with me." I stayed after he confessed that he was still in love with his ex and therefore, emotionally unavailable. I stayed when he told me that I wasn't nurturing enough, yet he nicknamed me "love sponge," a term for a person that is completely in awe of their partner and who caters to their every need. I stayed after he repeatedly tried to "get rid of me" to other men. I stayed as he compared me to other women, and while he indulged in his porn addiction at least three times a day.

I felt the searing pain through my breaking heart over and over, and still I stayed because I never knew what "normal love" was. It took me many, many years to figure that out. Name calling, abusive, condescending, and narcissistic behavior were normal to me. I forgave him every time, but the fantasy of "him and I" that I built within my mind died a little more each time.

We did a lot of talking, about all sorts of things. And we smoked a lot too. The first time I smoked marijuana was with him. I remember how good I felt, yet how weird and giggly it made me at the same time. I liked it, and it became a daily ritual for me for many years to come, becoming both my healer and my number. It helped me ignore the ugly things buried within my past, and the current things Izz said and did to me. It pacified me, allowing me to just float through life as I tried to get a grip on who I was, and what "adulting" meant. I had no idea what I was doing, but I went for it!

Izz, who was half Jamaican and half Italian, introduced me to reggae, which quickly became one of the biggest and most positive influences on my life for the next two decades. He also introduced me to authentic Italian food, jerk chicken, and Jamaican beef patties. I think the first time I put hot sauce on chicken was when I ate it with Izz. I never wanted it plain again! We had plenty of laughs, but also plenty of arguments. I came from a broken place, and so did he. He was openly sharp-tongued, mean, and critical, yet charismatic, loving, and genuine when he chose to be. He was different from my stepfather in this way, who instead appeared to be a saint, but behind closed doors, was a monster.

Izz already had two young children when we met. I was intimidated by them, having no idea whatsoever how to parent, and having no desire to. I never wanted to have children. There was nothing that convinced me that this was a good place to bring them into, this world with all its problems. Why would I want to subject my offspring to that? But, after a while, I got comfortable with his kids, and we hung out and played whenever they were around.

Their mother, however, loved drama, and Izz liked it too. She used to call him on the phone, and they argued loudly about me being there around her kids. She wanted to challenge me to our own phone argument, and I always thought, "What the fuck for? I don't give a damn about you and bring no harm to your kids." Yet, Izz still put me on the phone, so I listened to her scream and thought, "What the fuck is going on!?"

My eighteen-year-old traumatized self stood no chance against this master of baby-mama drama, and I didn't care to. I didn't know what her problem was to begin with! There was no need to defend my presence. Yet, after I handed the phone back to Izz, he told me how much better his ex – who was their age – was at speaking up for herself in the same situation. Over time, I realized he should have manned up and fought his own self-created "battles," rather than including anyone else in them, especially his partner.

Eventually, our arguments intensified as my resentment grew over the way he mistreated me. Once, he shattered my beloved Van Gogh "Starry Night" painting right in front of me. It was his answer to my demand that the name-calling end. I collapsed in a corner and sobbed, deeply hurt that he intentionally broke something I loved, simply because I defended myself. I couldn't stop wailing, so he slapped me like Batman slaps his enemies with a loud "*Thwack*!" He claimed that I needed it so I could "snap out of it." The day he put his hands on me violently, my love for him left, but still, I didn't leave. Truth is, I didn't think I had anywhere better to go.

On our manageable days, I opened up about the things my stepfather did to me. It boiled within me, so I could either release it, or explode. But when I told Izz about it, he tore me down, claiming that he couldn't understand how I "allowed that to happen," and that "something like that would never happen to him" because he was "too strong." His victim-shaming stunned me. So, I called my twin instead. My concerns over my little sister's safety weighed heavily on me.

"I remember the phone ringing," my twin recalls. "It was an old-style phone, still attached to a wall. I was eighteen years old and about to head to college on a full-ride scholarship for my rugby skills. A starter for our team that placed third in the nation that year, my future looked bright, but my spirit was about to be crushed."

"It was my twin sister," he continued. "She moved out a few months before because of our stepdad and wondered how I was dealing. Then she asked about our little sister – was she still sleeping in our dad's room? I said yeah, thinking it was normal. She took a deep breath, then disclosed that he had molested them both since they were little, and that something had to be done to protect our little sister."

I finally revealed my biggest secret to the right person! My twin immediately called our stepdad for an emergency conference. Together, we confronted him, and he admitted everything while looking down, never meeting our glares, in a state of shame and humility neither of us had seen before. He begged us not to call the police; to keep it in the family. We disagreed, accusing him of ruining our lives. So, he fled while my twin called our mom to tell her the truth. She too wanted it to stay within the family, so we made our own decision.

Minutes after calling the police, they arrived, and I confessed to the investigator everything my stepfather did to me that I could remember. Her encouragement moved me deeply. She told me that I was brave to tell my story, and that now the healing could begin, even though it would be an arduous process. She asked if I was willing to testify against him in court, and I quickly said yes. So, a warrant was issued for his arrest. He didn't show up at the house again after our meeting, but instead escaped to his mother's house, who took him, along with our little sister and brother, into her "protection."

His entire family, the only family we had known for the last ten years, completely turned their backs against us, except for our Auntie Kay. She counseled and encouraged us throughout the entire process. Everyone else accused us of lying and refused to let us see our little sister and brother when we came for them. They even refused to talk to us for a while. This was the first time we experienced betrayal from such a large unit at once. It was enlightening to say the least!

Despite this, I cooperated fully with the prosecution process. In the meantime, our stepfather disappeared with our little sister in a desperate attempt to escape his fate. She later told us that he tried to commit suicide with a combination of pills and alcohol. Eventually, he manned up for just a moment for the first time in our lives, and turned himself in. He was taken into custody, but pled "not guilty" to all charges, manning-down once again, forcing me to take him all the way to trial. Then, he tried to claim temporary insanity for what he did, denying any responsibility for his behavior because he suffered from a "sexual addiction."

The judge didn't buy it, especially after the prosecuting attorney revealed his psychological test results as psychopathic! A person with this disorder cannot admit wrongdoing in their behavior, or express remorse for it, but instead continuously deny their actions, placing the fault on everyone but themselves. He was also confirmed as a "malignant narcissist," a term first coined by the social psychologist Erich Fromm in 1964, who described it as a "severe mental sickness" representing "the quintessence of evil [that is] the most severe pathology and the root of the most vicious destructiveness and inhumanity."

I took the stand against him in the courtroom, testifying to the unspeakable things he did to me in secret for ten years. He stared at me coldly in his revealing stripes and handcuffs. My face reddened with shame, and my eyes turned down to the ground, but I spoke, defying everything he once programed me not to do! On November 29, 2000, my stepfather, Steven Howard Newburg, was convicted of two felony charges, Sexual Misconduct with a Minor, and Child Seduction. He was sentenced to nine years in prison!

My attorney gave me the biggest hug when we walked out of that courtroom, and I felt something release within me as justice took favor upon us that day in recognition of the fifteen years of torment my siblings and I endured under his hand. Over time, I convinced my sister to open her own case against him, for her own sanity, and three years later, he was handed an additional nine-year sentence for the crimes he committed against us! For the rest of his life, he legally became known as a "sexually violent predator," and his status and crimes are registered on all national sex offender databases.

I believe that by speaking out, I helped to protect an innumerable number of other children from falling prey to his insanity. I also think that speaking out about abuse helps break the cycle. Those who bury their experiences are most often the ones who end up repeating them. My older and little brother never talked about the abuse they endured, and I know that my older brother became a perpetrator because of it. I encourage all victims to speak up. Exposing our abusers, despite the shame and embarrassment it causes, enables us to protect ourselves and others. Then, healing can truly begin. No one deserves abuse, and no predator deserves protection!

After the house cleared, my twin was left alone to deal with his pain and shock. He turned to the huge cabinet filled with alcohol that our stepdad left behind. Unable to deal with the emotional burden, my twin's best console became that cabinet filled with every kind of liquor, wine, and beer he could ask for. He drank until the pain was gone, or at least temporarily forgotten, and kept drinking. He and I lost touch for a few years because his alcoholism and the effects of our trauma didn't make things easy between us. Furthermore, Izz persuaded me to isolate myself from the remaining family I did have, especially my twin. He thought my twin was "weird" and didn't want him around.

I still dreamt of my twin even though we didn't see each other. I saw him as a military soldier with many other men under his charge. That dream rotated constantly through my mind, and a few months later, I reached out to him because of it. Turns out he *was* a Marine soldier that led the physical training portion of his battalion. My prophetic dreams were back, and I was learning to listen to them!

My health was, however, questionable. I still experienced stabbing pains in my chest, usually right over my heart. One night, I struggled in pain, incapacitated on Izz's couch. My heart seared. I could hear it pounding, one beat racing to meet the next. Everything went numb as I struggled to move. I cried out, "I don't want to die yet!" while Izz recommended that I "calm the fuck down." I couldn't, so he eventually called an ambulance. EMTs soon strapped me into a gurney, and for the second time, I was taken to the emergency room by way of an ambulance.

When my heart rate stabilized, the doctor assigned to my case nonchalantly informed me that I survived a heart attack! Briefly, she described the effects of cocaine use on the heart and condescendingly suggested that I leave it alone. Too weak to talk, I couldn't defend myself as she dismissed me with no further consultation or follow-up. Without testing any blood or urine samples, she assumed that the heart attack was induced by cocaine use, but I never used it before. I can only assume now that her assumption was based on my appearance, which often causes others to react based upon negative stereotypes.

Years later, I learned about my father's genetic heart condition. I realized my heart problems were most likely passed down from him. Shortly after finding this out, my heart was evaluated by an EKG machine, which monitors the electrical system of the heart and detects any potential problems. The results revealed an abnormally low heart rate of twenty-three to forty beats per minute, way below the normal average, but did not reveal the cause of my heart attack at such a young age. I am certain, however, that enduring chronic trauma is devastating to anyone's health and can cause extreme physical reactions, like a heart attack, with or without any pre-existing conditions!

Meanwhile, I struggled to earn the money I needed to survive as my bills increased from "adulting." I sold my precious violin for a few hundred bucks that didn't last long, severing my relationship with my instrument forever. Meanwhile, Izz somehow convinced me that dancing in strip clubs at night, and slanging wings at Hooters during the day, would more than solve my financial issues. So, I tried out amateur nights, then got hired on. Hooters was a breeze to get into as well. Although I entered the doors, I never made as much money as the other girls because I wasn't willing to "meet up" with men outside the club or restaurant, and I didn't put myself out there for lap dances or tips. I realized much later that a man's purpose, in the Lakota and Dakota Traditional way, is to protect his woman. Izz was doing the opposite of that when he encouraged me to sell myself out sexually and to carelessly place myself in realms where women are aggressively preyed on. It took me a long time to learn that my body and spirit are sacred, and how to treat myself with respect.

In the meantime, we saw some disturbing things in the times we spent together. One night, as we sat in his car in front of my apartment, a grotesquely misshapen being resembling a human with greyish-green skin, a Quasimodo-like hunchbacked shape, and horns emerging from both sides of its head, appeared from the side of the building. It rolled a tire before it, and awkwardly entered the building. It then lopsidedly hobbled into the apartment across the hall from mine. We stared at each other, questioning the reality of what we saw! What in the actual fuck was that? Did we just see a demon!?

A week later, I was out of that place! My roommate was using meth and lost her mind. She thought I turned against her, so she locked me out, and my possessions in. I banged on the door, demanding to get my stuff. She didn't answer, so I easily let myself in through the back window and retrieved my belongings while she stared in horror. An extremely unhealthy energy pervaded that building, and it was a good thing that I was no longer welcome.

Shortly after, I moved into my first solo apartment. It was a tiny studio with an itty-bitty kitchen in a high-rise building, with a musty smelling, Gandolf-looking manager, but I loved it, mostly because I finally had a safe space that I was in complete control of. I gained much-needed time alone for the first time in my life! It was here that I dreamt for the first time of my Native ancestors. An older relative in a Headdress came to give me hugs, softening my heart towards that part of myself. Inspired by these dreams and the kindness my ancestors bestowed upon me, I finally researched who we really are and found out that we have a beautifully rich culture and history.

I swelled with pride in my Native ancestry for the first time. At this point, I still didn't know that I was Lakota and Dakota. I only knew I was "Indian" and therefore studied whatever I could find. Thus, I was introduced to the romanticized idea of Indian Chiefs and Medicine Men, and I believed that all my relatives must be like this! Regardless, being exposed to more truth about my people gave me more confidence and a positive direction to channel my budding spirituality. For the first time, I saw more of the worth within myself. Nonetheless, I still had an epic road to travel.

The holidays neared, so I drove out to California to visit my mom, little brother, and sister. They became an inseparable trio after my stepdad was unmasked. The first night there, I slept in my car beside the ocean and had a vivid dream. I stood on a tall cliff overlooking the Pacific Ocean from the Northern California coastline with my mom. Suddenly, a massive group of all kinds of sea creatures appeared that traveled together from the north towards the south. Sea turtles, dolphins, sharks, hundreds of species of fish, whales, manta rays, jellyfish, and more passed. Most poignantly, I saw orca whales swimming with their bellies tuned to the sky. On each of their bellies, a human stood.

In awe, I watched them pass, clueless as to what it meant. Then, with absolutely no warning, a huge tsunami appeared over the ledge directly below us, instantly washing away the people who stood on it! I realized with horror that multiple waves of tsunamis, each bigger than the one before, rapidly approached! I screamed and turned around, clawing my fingers into the earth, running like an animal as fast as I could away from the shore. I woke up then, and after processing the dream, realized that I was given an especially important message: to follow the animals at any cost, without fear, for it could one day mean the difference between life and death in the Earth changes that are descending upon humanity!

I returned to Indiana as this dream weighed heavily on my consciousness. In the meantime, Izz and I spent more time alone. When he did come over, we usually fought. His condescending remarks and utter lack of respect took a toll on me. We got into a particularly intense argument because of it, and he announced that I was "at the bottom of the totem pole of all the women he was ever with." He stormed out, and in my solitude, I finally decided that I could take no more.

So, I left him a message. I didn't want to see him ever again. We were through! At nineteen years old, I finally realized that I deserved better. He, however, finally realized how much he loved me, but it was too late! I was done. Yet, as fate would have it, I soon felt nauseous and extremely tired. My moontime was late. I took a pregnancy test, and it was positive. I accepted my fate and called to tell him the news. We were having a baby! The pregnancy brought us back together. He apologized profusely for the way he treated me and promised that this was our new beginning.

I quit Hooters and the club immediately and got a job as a server at Santorini's Greek Kitchen instead, where I worked on and off for the next five years. This place had the most delicious Greek food, and I made more money working nights there than I ever did as a stripper! On Friday and Saturday nights, Traditional Belly Dancers entertained the crowd. I learned how to belly dance by watching them. After a few years, I quit serving and started belly dancing for the restaurant. I made even more than I did as a server, thus marking a shift in the realization of my talents and passions. I absolutely loved dancing!

Meanwhile, as my pregnancy progressed, I abandoned my cute studio apartment and moved into a "fixer-upper" with Izz, which was too generous of a description for this house. It had no working kitchen or bathroom, and each room featured walls with collapsing fragments. After too much work, we managed to make the living room and dining room livable, so we just subsisted out of those rooms for a while.

That house was incredibly haunted and terrifying, and living in it produced terrible nightmares within me. One night, as I dreamt, I entered a murky world. The ground beneath me was shaped from skulls and discarded human bones. Horrified, I ran as fast as I could but realized something hovered behind me. I peered over my shoulder to see an enormous demon-bat that hunted me. It soared behind me effortlessly with its gruesome fifty-foot wingspan. I screamed and ran for my life as fast as I could, waking up just before it consumed me.

Every night I continued to have these nightmares while living in that fixer-upper. I dreamt of walking, or running through hell, while demons attacked me, and I could not find my way out. It got so bad that I finally turned to prayer, even though I was a staunch atheist for years up until this point. During a particularly angry thunderstorm, I ignited my Sage Medicine mixture, and prayed with all my heart to God, if there was a God, to show me now. "Please help me!" I cried. I couldn't handle the ghosts I felt in the house during the day, and the demons that chased me through hell all night! I was losing my mind, and it felt as if my soul were trapped somewhere that I just couldn't escape from by myself no matter how hard I tried.

A day after giving my prayers to that incredible storm, a giant dog that lived down the street appeared in our back yard. The biggest boxer I'd ever seen, he was more the size of a bullmastiff, and most certainly an alpha. We had a boxer and bullmastiff mix named Rio. She was an alpha herself, but when he showed up, she yielded her food bowl and aggression at once. He was a boss, and she knew it! His owner showed up later that day and tried to take him home, but he bit his owner, refusing to leave.

It soon became clear to me why he came. As I slept that night, I again found myself wandering through hell in another fitful dream. I tried desperately to find my way out, but it was hopeless. I was lost. Suddenly, the giant boxer showed up in my dream! He calmly stood there in hell with me. He talked to me and told me to climb onto his back. So, I did, holding tightly to his neck. He rushed off and swiftly carried me out of hell like a knight in shining armor!

I'm not sure if I would have ever found my way out on my own. Because after this, my dreams of being trapped in hell never plagued me again. He answered my prayers by becoming the *personification* of them! He returned me to my belief in something greater than myself. I remembered that God, or the Creator of our souls, did exist, and that I really wasn't alone! I learned, over those few days that giant boxer spent with us, that prayers have real power, and that angels can come in many forms! After this dream, he went back home and never returned.

Tears flow from my eyes in joy as I write this, as I remember this pivotal shift in my life where "man's best friend" was sent to free me from the place my soul was trapped within for who knows how long! In my understanding of these things now, I realize that part of my soul dissociated as a little girl and was lost in a dimension that it could not escape from on its own. I didn't reach out for help through prayer because of my despondency and disbelief caused by decades of continuous suffering and abuse, and thus, these forces continued to feed on me because I couldn't protect myself. The only act that could save me, or free me, was the activation of the power of prayer. As soon as I humbled myself and acknowledged that I couldn't save myself all by myself, and thus *asked for help,* Creator sent one of his animal angels to my side in one of the most obvious and miraculous ways I have ever been blessed to hear of or experience first-hand! My life and my dreams transformed from that point forward.

Soon after the boxer came to my rescue, Izz's mom bought another fixer-upper just down the street. She invited us to move in on the condition that we pay rent and help fix it up. It still needed work but was in much better condition than where we lived. At least it had a working bathroom and a kitchen! I was six months pregnant and happy to prepare the new space for my first baby.

Izz, however, returned to the same belittling behavior I tried to escape from before I found out about my pregnancy. He also quit his job around this time, leaving me to carry the load of supporting both of us. Things at work were stressful too. My boss came from a culture where pregnant women didn't work but stayed at home. He accused me of being "too slow," and claimed I was "getting in the way" as my belly grew larger by the day. I stayed on anyways until a week or so before my baby came. I knew my rights; he couldn't fire me just because of my pregnancy, and I wasn't going to let him push me out with his demeaning comments.

Izz and I began fighting again, further increasing my stress. One day, he threw me down on the couch and strangled me while my bulging belly loomed out before me, foreshadowing the dark era that was coming for me and my future children. He never apologized for his behavior, but instead acted like it was my fault, and even worse, like nothing even happened a few hours later. Thus, a vicious narcissistic cycle ensued that repeated itself for years to come, where I was labeled as "too emotional," or "too focused on love," when I called him out for mistreating me, and was called every degrading name in his vocabulary as I held my ground. He showed absolutely no remorse and never accepted responsibility for his atrocious behavior and abuse.

I didn't leave because I thought I had nowhere to go. I was close to having my baby, and extremely vulnerable. I was also conditioned to believe that a woman had to stay with her partner, especially if they created life together. My belief systems kept me put, even though he was violent, condescending, disrespectful, lazy, and unsupportive. He had some good qualities too of course, but his negative aspects far outweighed the positive, and I heavily resented and abhorred him.

Thirty-seven weeks into my pregnancy, the doctors told me that there was an issue with the growth of my baby girl inside the womb. They informed me that I needed to be admitted that day to induce, or force, the birth of my child. Once admitted, a gel was placed on my cervix to "ripen it," which would prepare me for induction, but that, they assured me, would not cause me to go into labor. They gave me something to help me sleep, but I told the doctors, nurses, and even Izz that I felt like I was in labor. I felt those contractions!

They laughed at me, and alleged, "No, we've only ripened your cervix. You won't go into labor until we induce you in the morning!" Then, they left me to sleep. Izz was with me for a while, but soon claimed that he needed to leave to let the dogs out. I begged him to stay! I knew I was going to have the baby soon, but he didn't listen and left anyways.

So, I passed out, sleeping through most of what I knew was my labor. I awoke a few hours later with the need to push with all my power. I buzzed the nurses, and they came right away to check. My baby girl's head was visible! A few minutes later, I brought my baby girl into this world! I watched the miracle through a mirror, which was also the last time I'd do so. Although it was awesomely beautiful, it was just as incredibly grotesque and graphic.

Izz missed it all, but I hardly cared as I held my first baby in my arms, the tears flowing down my cheeks. The doctors and nurses told me that I did very well and furthermore, that it was their first time watching a woman give birth without complaining or screaming. "Instead," they remarked, "you smiled through the entire process! Amazing!" My future labor experiences weren't all that way for me, but this one was, and I beamed with pride as I stared at my beautiful creation in absolute wonder!

CHAPTER FOUR

CREATING THE NEXT GENERATION

I fell in love with my baby girl! Little Star. A new baby with the name of an old soul. However, my adoration of her couldn't hide my extreme exhaustion and stress. All of her care fell on my shoulders, including earning the money to provide for our new family. At this point, I had no idea what healthy boundaries were, or what an equal give and take scenario in a relationship looked like. Normal was as foreign to me as outer space. Therefore, I accepted a situation that would normally be completely unacceptable!

I borrowed as much money as I could from my mom to make ends meet, but I never felt good about it. My mom never liked lending me money, understandably, and it was humiliating to ask. I wanted to provide everything but caring for a baby was much harder than I imagined.

When Star was about three weeks old, she woke up as she always did in the early morning for her feeding. Izz didn't help prepare her bottles during the night, so I woke up in the usual fog, and carried her fussing little body with me down the particularly steep stairs in our house. I always put my flip-flops on because a layer of dust perpetually sat on the floor from the aged walls and ceilings which still needed refinishing. As I carried her down, my flimsy shoes slipped, and both of us flew into the air! I crashed down hard, hitting my elbows directly on the corner of the stairs. My hands opened uncontrollably in a jerk reaction, and my little baby's body flew the rest of the way down the stairs. She landed hard, hitting her head.

I screamed as she did too. She didn't stop for quite some time. I sobbed as her head swelled and she turned red from crying. I took her to the doctor, and thankfully she was okay! But Izz never stopped insulting me for it, like I slipped and dropped her on purpose. "You suck as a mom," he complained. I suggested that he try to understand that it wasn't my fault; that I needed his support more than anything. Furthermore, if I weren't so overly tired from taking care of her on my own, I wouldn't have fallen in the first place!

Endless arguing circles like this became our way. I felt like he never understood me, no matter how hard I tried. Eventually, he resorted to name-calling, until I finally gave up and left the room. There was no reasoning with him! It was the argument he lived for, and I slowly learned that silence was better than taking part in his merry-go-round style of debate. I dreamt of leaving, but my fear of being alone encouraged me to stay in the chaos.

Our time together wasn't always unpleasant. We had our moments of serenity, laughter, and peace, but those moments were far overshadowed by the suffering and struggle that became normal. I remember the heated arguments more than anything. The shouting, the cursing, the name-calling and blaming, and the violence. He never beat me in the way my stepfather beat us, but he did slap and choke me and break the things that I cherished.

He also had this way of comparing me to other women that made me feel insignificant. Like I could easily be replaced, and I wasn't quite attractive enough to keep his full attention. It became his excuse for retreating multiple times a day to satisfy his porn addiction in solitude.

He often pointed out how crooked my nose was, claiming that all I needed was "a nose job" to be "pretty enough." When I sang to express myself, he compared my voice to Aretha Franklin. It was clear to him that I'd never be as good as her. Yet, I knew deep inside that even she needed years of practice to reach her pinnacle of expertise. When I danced, he critiqued me, claiming I was nowhere near as good as him in his breakdancing days. To him, I was perpetually "not good enough," and always barely "average."

We might as well have been polar opposites! Turns out astrologically, we were. I started studying astrology and soon learned how to calculate my birth chart. I realized that my twin and I are zero-degrees Pisceans, not the Aquarians we before thought we were. My understanding of myself instantly expanded. We sit exactly on the cusp between the two signs, meaning we carry both Aquarius and Pisces traits, but with Pisces taking the lead. It helped me to learn a lot about my characteristics and shadow aspects, but also helped me to understand that I could learn how to control both my negative and positive tendencies and use them to my advantage.

Furthermore, I realized that Izz was my exact astrological opposite, on *top* of being a natural jerk, the latter which had nothing to do with astrology. He lived fully in his shadow aspects. Therefore, what was light to me was dark to him. What was fun to me was a waste of time to him. I lived in a dreamy world, and he lived in a practical world where nothing was good enough if it didn't come from him. We clashed constantly because we saw the world as if we lived in, and were even from, two separate dimensions. I lived for love, and he lived for what "made sense," or what was practical, and we kept trying to make it work despite the deepening chasm between us.

His inability to see what was important to me, or even consider it – which had absolutely nothing to do with his astrological chart, but everything to do with his character choice – caused me to lose my trust, love, and respect for him over time. I'm not sure if he ever respected me, and love was never his motivation, so the baby became the only thing that held us together. Our loveless relationship created a deep well of emptiness within me. I kept hoping that he'd fulfill the role of my loving partner, but he was incapable and had no desire to.

The real problem was that I looked to him to fill a void within me, which no other person, no matter how compatible, could ever do. I was so damaged and broken inside that I accepted this extremely dysfunctional relationship that made me feel dead inside. I didn't know how to love or respect myself yet, thus my relationship with Izz reflected that. But there was still something beautiful to hold onto – the relationship with my daughter. She kept me going through it all. We loved each other deeply, and in her I saw the promise of a better cycle that could start with my own offspring.

When I was twenty-two years old, I was given a dream that I'll never forget. In a dark forest surrounded by tall mountains, I ran towards a destination, but also for my life. Hideous grey-colored beings chased me. I couldn't outrun them, so I had no choice but to stop and fight. Each time I won, but it cost all my energy. I became so exhausted that I knew I could no longer fight alone. I sat down, hunched over the earth, desperately trying to recover. I looked up and spotted a pack of huge white wolves in the distance, silently watching me!

Without hesitation, I cried out to them: "Please help! I can't do this alone anymore!" Immediately, they surrounded me, and my strength returned. I stood up and ran again, this time as the wolves surrounded me in a completely protected circle. The grey beings still attacked, but the wolves fought them for me. Eventually, even the wolves lost their power against the constant onslaught of greys. As our strength and ability to fight diminished, we prepared for death, solemnly acknowledging that we did all we could to reach our destination.

Suddenly, a woman's voice came from everywhere at once, its omnipotent force making itself clear as it resounded loudly throughout the mountains. "Do you dare break the Sacred Code!?" she threatened. Immediately, the grey beings receded far away, beyond the limits of the mountaintops. All they could do then was watch, as they peered out with their yellow, fear-filled eyes from beyond the mountainsides. The wolves and I stood tall as our strength returned. They gathered at my side, and we ascended the hill before us towards a light that emanated from beyond its peak.

As we walked up the hill, many forest animals gathered in a line on both sides that extended to the top of the hill. Rabbits, deer, moose, elk, squirrels, birds of all sorts, mice, and even lions were amongst those of the Animal Nations that came to participate. Their heads bowed. Although I still didn't know what was happening, I felt it, and the wolves and I acknowledged each of our relatives with deep respect as we passed.

Finally, we reached the peak, where the source of the light emanation was finally revealed. A beautiful woman dressed in a shimmering buckskin dress walked towards me. She too was accompanied by huge white wolves. Shrouded in a beautiful golden light that now illuminated the entire hilltop, her hands stretched toward me, and within them, she held a large Pipe. It was beautifully carved, and from its stem hung large, spotted eagle feathers. Finally, she stood right before me. She smiled and asked, "Do you accept the responsibility?" I smiled back and held out my hands, "Yes I do!" She placed the Pipe gently in my hands. Immediately, the dream ended.

I woke up forever transformed from this dream, one of the most profound and vivid visions of my life. I had no clue what it meant. At this point, I still knew nothing about my Native culture, especially our prophecies and teachings, but I still knew something huge transpired! I shared the dream with Izz, but he shrugged it off and told me I shouldn't attach any importance to it. "It was just a dream," he claimed, and therefore there was nothing special about it. So, I tucked the dream into my heart, allowing it to become the awakening guide it was intended to be.

Over time, I realized this dream was a gift from my relatives in the Spirit World. It showed me why I must never give up and was a promise that help would come when the battle became too much to handle alone. Most importantly, I must never forget that the day would come when those who attacked us would be instantly neutralized by a more powerful force, a force that would restore balance to not only myself, but our people.

I came to understand that certain people in my life, especially those that I held close relationships with, were manifestations of the grey beings in my dream, who relentlessly attacked me and nearly succeeded in keeping me from completing my mission. The dream instructed me to follow my intuition, rather than listen to the misguidance and naysaying of others. It inspired me to honor the connection I always had with Nature and the Animal, Plant, and Elemental Nations. This dream, not any person in my sphere of influence, became my deepest inspiration to find out about, and embrace, my Native American heritage.

Through such incredible visions and dreams, my ancestors counseled me via my subconscious mind, showing me the truth of who I was. They knew my conscious mind was already too far gone to pierce. My trust was so far gone from any human that nothing but a vision could sway my perception or crack the thick shell I built around myself. This was the dream that really sparked my interest and reshaped my entire thought content and perception. It became the true beginning of a deep connection with my inner self, and the first poignant moment when my ancestors and spiritual guides gave me a vision that impacted me so deeply that it continued to guide and inspire me for the rest of my life.

Soon after this dream, I again felt inspired to leave Izz, but instead found out that I was pregnant for a second time! Thus, I stayed, and eventually brought my first-born son, "One Who is as Brave as a Lion," into the world. While on my hands and knees, he entered the world with the help of a midwife. She fully supported me having as natural a childbirth as possible, thus it was an exceptionally beautiful birth experience. Lion must have needed it because he too, like me, was brought into this world as a sensitive and dreamy Pisces.

After a month, I went back to work at Santorini's, while Izz watched the kids. I felt like I had no choice because he refused to work, and we desperately needed the money. He said he was proud to be a "stay at home dad." Although I enjoyed a bit of a break from the kids, I didn't enjoy coming home to a house that was always trashed, to Star being put to bed by the television, and to Lion always having a bottle propped up to his mouth rather than being held for his feedings. Izz's parenting style and his refusal to work became increasingly disturbing.

One day, I finally said, "Enough is enough!" I came home and announced that I quit Santorini's. I declared that it was Izz's time to work and my turn to stay home and take care of the kids and the house. I refused to work a dead-end job any further that took me away from my kids. It was his turn to provide, and it was my turn to follow my dream of creating my own business while keeping my kids at my side. I wasn't budging on it! Despite this, he didn't even try to find a job. He claimed he was "overqualified" for this job, or didn't want to work at "that place," or was "too good" to even donate blood in exchange for twenty bucks. I finally lost it the day he declared he was "better than those homeless people" he'd have to sit by in the clinic to give blood!

I screamed, "How dare you sit at home all day using the last of our money to buy yourself cigarettes, instead of providing for the kids before yourself! You aren't any better than anyone! You're sitting on your ass and mooching off me, my mom, and your mom, and you act like we all owe you! You need to go and work or I'm leaving and taking the kids!"

I decided to take a break for a bit. I contacted my twin and little sister and convinced them that it was time to reconnect with our side of the family on the reservation. My brother was hesitant, but my little sis was along for the ride, so eventually all sides agreed. We turned it into an incredibly fun road trip. My twin had just gotten a brand-new Mustang that he pushed to ridiculously fast speeds. If there was no other car to race, we figured we might as well race the speed of light itself. Fuel stops were a frequent occurrence, but we sure did have a blast!

It was a peculiar feeling to see our dad again, for the first time in decades, in a murky prison visitation room, as he served time for his fourth DUI offense. We weren't new to the idea that our father had problems, especially with substance abuse, a far too common issue in "Indian Country." Regardless, I was elated to see him again! My sister was too, but my brother remained standoffish, and understandably so.

I gave thanks that most of everything we endured as children happened at the hands of our stepfather, rather than potentially at the hands of our biological father! At least it gave me the chance to see him objectively and to forgive him easily. I wanted to know who we truly were and where we came from, more than anything in the world.

We spent about a week together at our grandmother's house on the Ihanktonwan Dakota Oyate, or Yankton Sioux "rez." I was awestruck at the rolling hills of the Plains, which were left untouched for countless generations. The unspoiled beauty of Mother Earth can still be felt and seen on many Indian reservations. We've always practiced minimal alteration and interference with Nature. She's better off being left alone, and so too, are we.

Our grandmother showed us pictures of us as little babies with our father, and of our aunts, uncles, cousins, and relatives. For the first time in my life, I felt whole! We had a huge family there that we were kept from for twenty years, and they seemed to really love us as they embraced us with open arms.

We returned home, and after my dad was released from prison, I came back to the rez with my daughter to visit again. My dad, uncle, and gramma took me to my first wacipi, or powwow. I was fascinated by the women's Fancy Shawl Dance and told myself that one day, I'd dance like that! As I looked around at all the brown-skinned, dark-haired, and sharp-featured Natives that surrounded us, I felt extremely proud of these same features I had. Before, I was ashamed of them because they were looked down upon in the white world I was raised in.

I returned home with a newfound sense of pride in my heritage and a much better understanding of who I was, and where I came from. I had a long way to go, but that visit activated something deep within me. I began to identify with my Dakota and Lakota heritage more than any other part of myself. Nothing felt more connected to my inner nature and outer reflection.

Coming back to Izz challenged my new-found empowerment, so I called off our engagement and sold my wedding dress. I resented his proposal anyway, which was no more than, "We might as well since we're together," rather than the romantic profession of true love I always fantasized about.

I earned enough money from selling my wedding dress to move into a house with my little sister. Soon after, I realized that I was pregnant again! But, this time, I wasn't going back. So, baby Leone was coming, along with the intimidating reality of becoming a single mother. But I was soon given an encouraging dream that showed me that he was a miracle baby, no matter what my relationship with his father was.

One of my closest friends at the time had an unwanted pregnancy and a subsequent abortion. Soon after, I dreamt that I found a baby dove that was torn to shreds by a hawk. I picked it up and stroked it lovingly. Suddenly, it came back to life and flew away. A guide who stood with me in my dream told me that I would now carry this spirit with me. I soon found out that I was pregnant! Years later, my friend shared that if she carried the baby, and it was a boy, she would've named him Leone! We both felt that the spirit of her baby was transferred to me to carry because she was emotionally not ready, but the child needed to come through for an important purpose at that time, so I was chosen as the vessel to give him life despite my life's circumstances.

My little sister and I were both newly pregnant and single at the same time, so we helped support one another. We shared the house, and she helped me care for the kids. It marked the beginning of the first steps towards having the courage to stand on my own. It was also the first time I lived in a peaceful situation since the babies came along, and I hardly communicated with Izz at all.

In my serenity, and far away from his daily influence, I realized that I'd rather be alone than be with a partner who constantly drained my energy, counteracted my efforts to raise the kids in a more natural, healthy, and balanced way, and who, most importantly, did not honor, respect, or love me. I dreaded physical contact with him for years because I didn't love him, and the way he treated me made his touch repulsive. He didn't respect my right to be left alone, but instead adopted the same habit my stepfather once had – to force me to comply sexually, or fight with me until I tired and gave in. Izz further believed that "I owed him sex, and it was my job to please him at least three times a day." We fought profusely about that, as I countered that it was his job to love me and earn the sharing of my body!

However, when I was around eight months pregnant, I developed intense chills, a fever, and uncontrollable shivering. It came and went though, so I ignored it, thinking rest was all I needed. But every night, it kept getting worse, until I began vomiting uncontrollably. So, I finally asked my sister to take me to the emergency room, where I was diagnosed with a severe kidney infection. If I waited any longer, I would have miscarried the baby and possibly even died! Izz visited me in the hospital and took care of the kids while I recovered. He was so convincingly caring and supportive, and I was so vulnerable with the coming of the new baby, that I surrendered my new-found liberation and moved back in with him, giving him one last chance to be the partner I always hoped he'd be.

Soon, baby Leone arrived via the longest and most painful labor yet, but still I didn't falter, denying the epidural when it was offered. I wanted to feel the full power of bringing my baby into this world. He was born with these incredible blue eyes that seemed like a miracle to have come from two brown-eyed parents. In my later biological studies, I learned that he inherited recessive genes from both of us that made it possible. Over the next few weeks, his against-the-odds blue eyes transformed into a beautiful emerald green, the hue they've remained to this day.

Shortly before Leone was born, my twin called me from jail. He needed my help to continue his college degree while he was detained. I jumped on it and subbed in for him on all his online courses. I really enjoyed it, and did well, earning "A's" across the board on all his assignments. Leone came into this world on a weekend, so I returned home just in time to continue my twin's classes without a lapse. I sat with newborn Leone in one arm and typed one-handed with the other. In this way, I continued to earn my bro "A's" on all his assignments until he was released and resumed them on his own.

Five weeks after giving birth to Leone, I received shocking news from my mom about my older brother. "Shawn's been in a motorcycle accident. He's in a coma and might not make it." Her words changed my life like a swift bolt of lightning. I cried and sobbed for my older brother often, thinking of the pain he must've been in. A few hours before, as he rode his motorcycle home, a truck pulled out in front of him. He had no time to react, and at about sixty miles an hour, he t-boned the truck. His body catapulted off the motorcycle and flew head-first into the truck. Even though he wore a helmet, the impact broke every bone in his face and forced him to bite his own tongue off. Without the helmet, he would've died instantly. Most of the bones in his body were horribly smashed. He was utterly unrecognizable in the hospital, and it was extremely disturbing to see him.

I tried to process this as I cried alone in the back yard, while Izz came out and announced that Shawn was fine; he was going to pull through. He didn't say it kindly, but condescendingly, as if I was trying to invent a reason to be sad. I told him to just leave me alone. I didn't feel good about it. Something wasn't right. Even though my older brother and I never got along, I still loved him, and his accident unhinged the long and dark past we shared together.

That night, I was visited by the future Shawn in my dream. He walked a little lopsided, and spoke with a bit of a slur, but miraculously, he survived! He laughed and smiled at me with the same crooked grin that was unmistakably his. I knew, given his fierce grit and determination, that he of all people could pull through, if only he were given the chance. The dream gave me hope, and a glimpse of his future if we all supported him in his recovery.

However, my mom called about five days later to tell me that Shawn's wife, Amy, was pulling the plug on him! She booked me an emergency flight, and I needed to leave early the next morning to make it there to see him for the final time before his "departure." I never got that chance. We arrived late at the airport, just ten minutes late to check in my bags, and they refused to let me through no matter how much I begged! I felt my heart rip out of my chest, and I sobbed the entire way home.

I did, however, make it to his funeral. I brought baby Leone with me, who was then just six weeks old. My mom, twin, little sister, little brother, and I stood united in our pain and sorrow. None of us could hold it together for long. There was some comedic relief however, thanks to baby Leone. During the long moment of silence held in honor of my brother and his incredible achievements, Leone released the loudest and longest newborn fart I ever heard! I'm certain my brother Shawn was laughing his spirit head off and saying, "Now that's my nephew!" My brother was a huge fan of lewd jokes and was notorious for climbing on the counter to fart on everyone's food during our childhood. We hated it as kids, but now laugh nostalgically about it.

My brother's Navy comrades showed all of us incredible respect and honored my mother by presenting her with the flag that was folded over his coffin. My twin and I remember how, during one of the most emotionally difficult parts of his Navy funeral, a tall White Egret landed right outside the window and stared calmly at us, ensuring us that everything was going to be all right.

We then left to follow Shawn's body to the funeral parlor, where we were treated remarkably differently by his wife and her family, as if we were outcasts and criminals, rather than Shawn's closest relatives. They looked at us as if we were the ones who put him in that coffin! It was the most absurd behavior I ever saw, the way they intentionally isolated us, and furthermore, it was disturbingly eerie that they placed pictures of our stepfather all over the reception room as if that man were the brightest light in our lives!

It was extremely triggering to us, to see pictures of the man who tortured all of us for our entire childhoods, staring at us from those pictures with those cold, blank eyes, while we freshly mourned the loss of our big brother. Amy's family even hired security guards to ensure that my twin and I wouldn't give a eulogy before he was placed into the earth. I stared at her in utter disgust. She didn't shed a single tear but instead stared blankly ahead as if she was lying dead with him in that coffin. We listened to our mother when she asked us not to make a scene, even though we both wanted to tear her to shreds!

So instead, I took my written words to my big brother and placed them on his coffin before they threw the first piles of dirt onto it. I told him that I loved him, and I knew that I'd see him again. Travel well, brother! We cried rivers that day, as old wounds that were buried deep within us from our childhood came spilling out to the surface. No one could understand what we were feeling but us.

We focused our initial anger on Amy. We knew that she decided to pull the plug on our brother because the Navy informed her that if he died, she'd get a $500,000 life insurance check! It was obvious to us that she cashed in the years of care she'd have to give him to aid in his recovery, for this quick lump sum. It's why she deliberately outcasted us because we knew the truth. We despised her and everything she stood for, and we felt sorry that Shawn had obviously chosen a wife who did not love him, but instead loved the materialism that came with his hard-earned success. It cost his life for this truth to be revealed.

A few days after Shawn's funeral, and after baby Leone and I returned home, I was visited by Shawn in another dream. He cried to me after watching everything Amy did. He was devastated that the woman he thought was the love of his life, turned him in for a cash-out. It was difficult for me to see my brother so distraught, so I told him, "I know brother, and I'm so sorry! We would've helped you. I know you would have made it. I love you brother!" Then, I woke up.

Shawn was born on September 19 (9/19). After his death, his number, 919, became a significant sign to both my twin and I of the guiding presence of our brother from the Spirit World. When we saw it, we knew that we were either on the right path, or that a path presenting itself before us was a good one to follow. A stark correlation between the number 919 and good luck, fortune, positivity, affirmation, and confirmation became undeniable in both our lives. For many years to follow, we both knew that when we saw the number 919, our brother was guiding us, and we needed it. We sought it desperately!

We both vowed to follow in his footsteps of extreme success and achievement despite the odds that were stacked against us. Shawn achieved so much in his twenty-five years that we had a lot to live up to, and it seemed that whenever we needed it, there was his number, guiding us! This number and its affinity to our older brother also connected us to the Spirit World, helping us both to understand that there was more than death; that life continued somehow, and that there was much more to life than could be felt, seen, or heard with any third-dimensional sense.

Meanwhile, things between Izz and I spiraled faster downwards. The temporary honeymoon feelings I experienced, which misled me into returning to him and his house just before Leone's birth, quickly faded. He was still the same emotionally abusive and unsupportive man I always knew him to be. He again forced me to have sex with him or fight, and I was extremely triggered that he repeated what my stepfather did to me for the last ten years of my childhood.

Sometimes, I watched his face morph into my stepfather's while he loomed over me and forced me to do something I had no desire to do. I started to hate myself again, I deeply abhorred him, and I loved only my children. There were countless nights that I slept outside, trying to escape his overbearing presence. My daughter usually woke up in the middle of the night and joined me. It was so pleasantly peaceful, just the two of us on that cozy swing sleeping deeply, while only the crickets and cicadas buzzed.

I stayed with Izz because I believed I had to. We had three kids together, and I felt hopeless. Society, organized religion, and other influences taught, or rather programmed me, to believe that I needed to stay in this toxic relationship "for the kids." It took me many years and especially, poignant guidance from the Spirit World, to understand that this was not beneficial for either of us, or for the kids.

Children exposed to toxic fights between their parents receive programming that instills a skewed perception of love. They either repeat this dysfunctional pattern they've been taught or spend many years healing from it to overcome it and break the cycle. Our dysfunction left little energy from either of us for the kids. Our patience was drained, and our ability to bring them up in the most coherent manner possible was impossible when we surrounded them with the dysfunction and hate generated between us. We modeled the epitome of a narcissistic, codependent, and loveless relationship.

It takes an incredible amount of courage and strength to break out of this cycle, and to leave a relationship with someone you have invested so much time into. We were addicted to our codependency, and even though everything in me wanted to be anywhere but with him, I stayed because something outside of myself convinced me that I had to stay to be considered a "good woman" by others.

One day, during a rare occurrence when Izz unexpectedly left the house for a few hours, I took the opportunity to clean up and organize the garage by myself. I wanted to make a play area for the kids, but every time I suggested it before, he declared that it was "a waste of time." So, in his absence, I quickly went to work, sweeping, dusting, re-arranging, and throwing away piles of trash.

I needed to move a large trailer that stood in the way of the intended play area. It was so heavy, but I tried anyway with all my might, until I heard a loud pop. A searing pain raced up my spine! I could no longer stand up straight but had to hobble into the house bent into a ninety-degree angle. I pulled my back out – an injury that would act up for the next seven years. Izz returned home to find me in agonizing pain. He didn't sympathize with me, but instead told me that I "wasted my time" and furthermore, that "I was really stupid." I felt like the only stupid waste of my time was him!

Soon after, a friend of mine from Santorini's introduced me to the woman who later helped me transform my life, Shell. An enrolled member of the Cherokee Nation, she introduced me to my first experiences of "the Powwow Trail," our Traditional Ceremonies, and the world of Native entrepreneurship. Her willingness to live outside the box helped me to understand that as women, our intuition, empowerment, and courage are important aspects to nurture to successfully leave an abusive partnership, and to raise our children on our own without falling into another codependent relationship. She introduced me to natural methods of healing and birth control thru herbs, and to Earth-friendly products, thus encouraging a shift in my perception towards a more conscious connection to the Earth and the divine feminine.

Shell casually adopted me as her spiritual daughter, a customary practice in Indigenous communities, and I felt blessed for many years to have this woman in my life who introduced me to a more appropriate mother and daughter relationship, and who fully supported my quest to deepen my Native spirituality and roots. Inspired by her example of entrepreneurship, I took a short class on making wire wrapped jewelry, and soon spent my days making pair after pair of earrings to sell at her soap booths during upcoming powwows.

After spending an entire day locked away in a room filled with the flow of my creative force, Izz came in and wiped the smile right off my face when he asked, "What the hell are you doing that for?" He told me once again that I was "wasting my time," and that the earrings I made "would never sell." Regardless, I loved what I was doing and kept at it despite his constant naysaying. I fully committed to no longer working to build other's dreams, but instead to doing only the things that brought me a deep sense of satisfaction and joy. Despite his nagging, and our quickly dwindling finances, I refused to leave the house to work another dead-end job simply because we needed the money – thereby giving Izz the opportunity and responsibility to step up as the man and father I gave him seven years to be. He never did.

Continuously, he refused to sacrifice his ego in any way to provide for us, while I, in the meantime, unceasingly researched and designed an entire business plan for the organization of my dreams – "One Oyate," or One Nation. Through it, I wanted to help inspire and encourage unity through the synergy of the artistic creation of two, to billions, of people! This vision was inspired by the dream with the beautiful woman in buckskin who handed me a C'anupa, or a Sacred Pipe, along with a responsibility.

On my twenty-fifth birthday, I returned to my birthplace, Honolulu, Hawaii, with my mom and daughter. It was the first time I returned to the islands since our family left when my twin and I were only babies. As soon as we landed, I felt a deep connection to the land. I could tell this place was special. I slept outside one night, on the patio of the high-rise oceanfront hotel we stayed in, so that I could listen to the waves as I slept with my daughter wrapped snuggly in my arms. I'll never forget what happened next!

I dreamt of an iridescent purple star being that floated in front of me. Behind him, for as far as I could see, a line of stars just like him spiraled into the Universe. Each emanated their own source of light, just as the stars do when one gazes upon them through the black cloak of night. He spoke to me with a soothing voice, "A time of chaos and confusion is coming. In this time, you'll have to find the ones who love you, and the ones you love in return, and be with them at all costs, for it will be the only way to survive what's coming!" As soon as he said this, I awoke.

The dream imprinted profoundly upon my psyche and changed my entire perspective on relationships. I learned how to question everyone in my life based on the life and death conditions the Star Nation presented to me, and once I did, it made it quite easy for me to make decisions to either leave or stay based upon their warning. Everything was now passed through this filter: If this were a life-or-death situation, would this person stand by me? If my heart and their actions said "yes," I stayed. If my heart and their actions implied "no," I'd leave without hesitation, no matter the cost!

This dream became the final push in my choice to leave Izz forevermore and continues to guide me through life. I learned how to pass everyone through the screen of true love the Star Nation gifted to me. Even if I genuinely loved a person, but they didn't love me in return, or vice versa, I'd end the relationship because I knew we couldn't waste any time together. It's been fourteen years since I had that dream in

Thunderbird Rising

February of 2007 and now, in 2021, it's obvious that we are in the time of chaos and confusion the star beings warned me about.

As we enter the sixth mass extinction event in recorded history, massive amounts of species are facing extinction, and more are in danger of it with each passing day. Climate change and global warming are now upon us and can't be stopped. Catholic priests and Hollywood stars are being exposed for child molestation, rape, and child pornographic rings. Children are being forcibly removed from their parents in mass numbers and detained in deplorable conditions at the American and Mexican border. The Standing Rock Water Protector Movement was born, and after a two-year stand, was squashed by weaponized military forces, who forced the Dakota Access Pipeline through Oceti Sakowin burial grounds, Sacred Sites, and reservation land.

Donald Trump, an extremely racist, narcissistic, and misogynistic man, was recently President of the United States, and developed a cult-like following. The Black Lives Matter Movement arose in response to the recorded death of a Black man by a white officer. The Movement challenged continued racial issues embedded in American society. The coronavirus wreaked havoc upon the world and changed everything as we knew it, and now, its vaccine has become a political and social issue that is turning people against one another. The bodies of thousands of Indigenous children are just being unearthed underneath Canadian boarding schools, revealing the truth of the atrocities the Canadian government put the Original people through. American boarding schools will also soon be exposed for their dark truths. Finally, the storms, fires, droughts, earthquakes, and floods of Earth are increasing and bringing death and utter destruction to entire communities in ways humanity has never experienced before! Our world as we once knew it is crumbling. The chaos and confusion are upon us! Soon too, will come the time when survival can only be found within the tribes we've formed, tribes made of those who genuinely love us, and those we genuinely love in return.

My birthday fell on the last day of our trip to Hawaii. Mom wanted to get me a fancy guided horse tour, but the one she wanted to get felt too commercialized and routine, so I asked instead for the privately guided tour that took us through the Lava Fields overlooking Molokai Island. An Elder Native Hawaiian man guided the trip. We instantly connected as he shared the history of a once-free Hawaii that came illegally into the possession of the United States government through the theft of the land and resources, and the oppression of its people. Diseases were introduced, as they were with us Native Americans, to intentionally weaken and thin out the Native Hawaiian population.

He said that nowadays, the invasion continues to spread through tourism. As we looked down on the island of Molokai, he revealed that he was one of the activists working hard to protect it from tourist infrastructure. To that day, there were still no motorized vehicles on it, and he wanted to help keep it that way. The government once quarantined Native Hawaiians with leprosy on the island, so it remained sheltered from industrialism. He became the first activist I met, and I was inspired by his genuine leadership fueled by his love for his people, land, and horses.

I also met with a Hawaiian seer. She told me straight up that Izz was "a real jerk," and that I had to set boundaries with him; that the best thing I could do was to "tell him no." She also thought I was "a million-dollar babe," which was one of the first times I heard positive encouragement about myself from another woman. Her words became my personal affirmation countless times over during the many years that passed. Whenever I felt down, or lost hope, I looked in the mirror and told myself that I was a "million-dollar babe" and I had this! Eventually, I believed it!

Despite feeling on top of the world because of the beautiful vision I received, and furthermore, because of the reconnection with my mother, a conversation with my twin revealed that my mom complained that I was "bothersome and irritating" during the entire trip. I felt the stab in my heart, reluctantly realizing that everyone has their own perceptions. I couldn't force anyone, even my own mother, to enjoy my company, or to change, if they didn't want to. She helped me learn that lesson many times over.

So, I returned to my other children, and to my life with Izz, but our fated end soon arrived. I awoke that day to the discovery that he spent the very last of my money, which I saved for diapers, on cigarettes for himself. I lost my cool and shouted at him that I was done! "I'm leaving and taking the kids!" But he blocked the door and wouldn't let us leave. So, I took the kids and sheltered in the upstairs bedroom. He followed us and broke down the door with a bat, forcing his way in. He choked me in a fitful rage in front of the kids. Star screamed as I fought to push him off me.

I finally decided that I was done for good and asked Shell to help me leave this long seven-year relationship filled with narcissistic dysfunction and abuse – which I didn't realize the reality of until many years later. The problem with being raised in dysfunction and abuse is that it normalizes that behavior. You don't realize that it's *not* normal until you get far away from it and have plenty of time to heal. This is how suicide becomes an enticing escape for people in this situation because they have no idea there are other options, and the misery and depression are so deep that the thought of ending it all to escape is extremely compelling.

My childhood was steeped in misery, and my relationship with Izz was no different. Therefore, I tolerated his abuse and narcissistic behavior because I didn't realize that I deserved better. I didn't even know what "better" looked like, felt like, or that it existed at all! I learned by following my intuition, and by receiving guidance from my dreams, from Shell, and from a seer, that it was more than acceptable for me to leave this horrible situation.

Shell gladly agreed to help me and connected me with a Native American organization that granted me a scholarship to aid with the first month's rent and security deposit of a new home! I gathered the children and our belongings, while Shell watched, so that Izz could not interfere, and left for the third and final time.

CHAPTER FIVE

REMEMBERING

It was incredibly liberating to be in my own space with my children! I finally had the time to focus on my own dreams and healing, and to raise the kids in an environment that aligned with my heart. We were free from the constant arguing and drama that was before the daily theme, and for the first time, I accepted that we deserved it.

In the meantime, Shell and I became a team of weekend warriors on the Powwow Trail. While she sold her handmade soaps, I intensely watched the dances. She encouraged me by gifting me with my first shawl, a beautiful cobalt blue shawl with blue fringe and two giant bear claws sewn onto it. Inspired by her gift, I joined the Fancy Shawl Dancers for the first time. Something opened within me, and I flitted across that dance floor as if I'd done so a thousand times before!

A woman excitedly approached me afterwards and asked, "How long have you been dancing?" "It was my first time!" I replied. Her jaw fell to the floor. She introduced herself as a Fancy Shawl Dance teacher and congratulated me because to her it looked like I was already a seasoned dancer. I beamed with surprise! After she walked away, an Elder approached me with his hand held behind his back. He acknowledged my dance and pulled his arm out, revealing the eagle feather he concealed. With it, he invited me to dance at his upcoming powwow. I gratefully accepted, and thus, my Tradition as a Fancy Shawl Dancer began and continues to this day!

Figure 4. My only Fancy Shawl Dance competition in 2009. From this point forward, I only danced for Tradition.

Meanwhile, the kids and I adjusted smoothly to our new life with me as the single provider and caretaker. Due to the violence we experienced with Izz, I refused to communicate with him or allow him to see the kids. Star was also waking up every night, screaming, "No, Daddy! No!" Her nightmares showed me that she endured a lot of trauma because of him, and I didn't want that to be repeated. If life worked according to my plans, the kids would never be in his care again, but as I've learned, life does not usually go according to plan!

Shell and I teamed up in the soap shop. I worked early in the mornings, bringing my kids with me while I wrapped soap. I earned enough money each month to pay my rent and take care of my little family. In the afternoons, I was free to work on my own projects while the kids played. Shell showed me that it was possible for me to run my own business doing something that I loved, while simultaneously raising my children on my own. She helped to empower my career and shift the paradigm of what I was capable of as a single mother and as a Native entrepreneur. I spent six months intensely working with her and on my own dreams, while building my self-confidence and feminine power as I reconnected with my culture. It was a powerful new beginning!

Then one day, while standing in line at Wal-Mart with my kids, I noticed a brown-skinned, strikingly handsome, and muscular man with waist-long black hair standing behind me. I was too shy to say anything to him, but wow, did I notice him! I finished paying for my items and walked out. He noticed me too, because he ran out after me to introduce himself, then asked if he could take me and the kids to lunch. Thus, I met Tonio. He was half Mexican, and half Aztec, and we fell deeply in love almost at once! From that day forward, we spent every day together for the next two years.

Tonio almost immediately wanted a baby from me, in fact, he prayed for it every day. He became a wonderful father figure to my children, especially Leone, who was just a toddler at the time. They became best friends, and Tonio took care of my children as if they were his. He absolutely loved them, and I knew that he genuinely loved me. He also supported my explorations into my culture, coming with me to every Powwow, and watching over the kids while I danced. It wasn't too long before I carried his child, and as soon as he found out, he proposed to me. I accepted, although we never did get the chance to take it all the way.

My life with Tonio ended my work relationship with Shell. Tonio was a very hard-working entrepreneur himself. He owned a roofing company and always had contracts to fulfill. He had plenty of money, thus, I no longer needed to work. He took care of me and the kids completely! Soon, he received an offer he couldn't refuse: to replace roofs in Kentucky after a series of tornadoes devastated the area. Thus, we moved to a new place for all of us. For the first time in my life, I was engaged in a healthy and loving relationship, where I was free to simply be a mother to my children and to take care of the home. I loved it for a while, but soon felt myself being called towards something more.

While in Indiana, I researched conspiracy theories, discovering that the government told many lies to the people. I also uncovered the truth about what happened to my ancestors, and to nearly all Indigenous peoples around the world. I felt a responsibility to become more involved in spreading the truth, and there was little I could do in that world as a stay-at-home mom, even though I was grateful for Tonio and all he did for us. The calling gnawed at me, while my belly continued to grow with new life. Tonio respected my point of view but wasn't called in the same way that I was.

He was content with just working, coming home to us, and enjoying his Coronas – another habit that gnawed at me deep down. If he had only one downfall, it was his drinking habit. Although he never acted out against us because of it, he often drank until he passed out, and it reminded me of my father and his substance abuse issues. I didn't think I could continue to accept it, but I tried, because I loved him so much and every other aspect of our lives was beautiful. We had a lot of fun with him! We played with the kids on the trampoline, and traveled often for fishing excursions, camping trips, and Powwows. He really loved the kids, and they loved him deeply too. There truly was no shortage of love in our family.

Tonio went to work every weekday from sunrise to sunset. This gave me lots of alone time with the kids that led to me noticing disturbing behavior coming especially from my two oldest. One day, I walked into their room to find them sexually "exploring" in a manner that felt completely abnormal. They were too young to have natural sexual urges on their own at just five and six years old! Several more incidents occurred where my daughter showed over-sexualized behavior for her young age, and I noticed she was the ringleader.

Thus, I took the time to explain to her what appropriate and inappropriate touching was and asked if anyone ever touched her like that. She disclosed that her dad touched her inappropriately "one time." So, I contacted CPS to report my suspicions that Izz may have molested her. They interviewed her and reported that the case "could not be confirmed," and therefore the investigation against him was closed, with no charges pressed. So, I moved on with our new lives. There was nothing more that I could do except give my kids the best life that I could.

Finally, the day came when it was time for our new baby to arrive! I gave birth to a healthy little boy. Tonio and I chose his name together – Cuauhtémoc – in honor of an Aztec warrior that was a fierce legend amongst his people. As soon as Tonio's family heard that I went into labor, they came out to help, and in fact, they helped so much that I was almost uncomfortable with it! Through this experience, I learned how a woman and her new baby are really meant to be supported. They showed me what a healthy family behaves and looks like!

I had some of the most fun, secure, and happiest times of my life during my relationship with Tonio. He loved me, and his family embraced me, but after we moved to Florida to accept the new job opportunity he was offered, his drinking suddenly became a problem. We moved into his friend's and coworker's home until we could find our own home in the area. It was stressful having to live in a home with his friends, as our six-person family was now confined to one room! I realized then that I needed my own space to live happily and in balance. Tonio's friend also liked to drink and their influence on each other led to Tonio drinking himself to the point of passing out every night. He was useless in that state and gave us less and less quality time.

I was quite different from all the other women, which left me feeling alienated. While they cooked in the kitchen at gatherings, they generally kept themselves separated from the men. I, however, abandoned "my place" after a few hours and joined the men in their soccer game. I aggressively scored goals and kept up quite well with them, to their surprise. No matter how hard I tried, I just couldn't be like all the other women. I often asked them why they didn't join in on the fun. They just said it was "the way it always was," and they never thought to act differently until I came along. They never did join me, but just watched curiously from the sidelines.

One night, I was guided to look through the history on my laptop's search engine. My heart broke as it revealed Tonio's excessive porn consumption, which ensued every night for weeks, while I slept alone with the kids. After my experience with Izz's porn addiction, and my abusive stepfather's similar obsession, I no longer had any tolerance for this behavior. I knew it was a sexual disease that created extreme dysfunction in relationships and thought patterns. Thus, due to my mounting stress of needing, but not having my own space, the feeling of not belonging, and the issues that correlated with Tonio's increased drinking habit, I packed up the kids and drove from Florida to Fairfield, California in two days, leaving my once perfect life with Tonio far behind.

My mother, who still served in the Air Force, was stationed in Afghanistan at the time. She gave me permission to move into her home with the babies. Of course, I missed Tonio deeply, and the issues we had no longer seemed as pressing. So, we made plans to reconnect, after Tonio promised to control his drinking and to find a job closer to me and the kids. No matter how much I still loved him, I knew nothing would change if I came back to the situation I left, so it was up to him to show me that he was going to join me responsibly to make a better life with us in this new location.

However, just a few weeks later, I received an upsetting phone call from him. He was detained in U.S. Border Patrol custody. His ten-year visa recently expired, and he hadn't renewed it yet. There was nothing he or I could do. He was being deported back to Mexico and wouldn't be able to return for at least ten years! In shock, I realized in an instant that I was now forced to be solely responsible for the babies. I was devastated and shocked that he'd be gone for what seemed like forever, and my heart was terribly broken. However, after I accepted this reality, I was thankful that I moved away from him, because now it was clear that he was going to be taken from our lives one way or the other! The pain of our separation, therefore, wasn't as deep as it would've been if he had been taken from us too suddenly. I knew that I had to walk this new path alone, so I sent up a bittersweet farewell to one of the healthiest partners I've ever had.

My twin and little sister also lived with me at my mom's house, which had plenty of space for all of us. Our migrations from Indiana to California were now complete, and our mom's home in Fairfield became our introduction to the West Coast life. After recovering from the harsh loss of Tonio, I connected with Doj, a local Native activist I met via social media. Through him, I was introduced to the local Movement scene at D-Q University. My twin and little sister offered to watch the kids, while I explored Indigenous activism with Doj. My siblings knew that I was discovering an important part of myself through my involvement with the Movement, but also that the activist environment wasn't the safest place for the kids, so they were happy to help me. They enabled me to have some time to find myself by answering the calling to become involved in something bigger.

D-Q University is California's first all-Nations Tribal college. Before it became DQU, it was a surplus Army telecommunications center. It is written within the Fort Laramie Treaty of 1868, established between the U.S. government and the Oceti Sakowin, that its signatories would be given first consideration to attaining surplus military lands. Armed with this knowledge, and with months' worth of previously filed legal paperwork that attempted to procure the land for the establishment of a Native American University, Art Apodaca and a group of Native UC Davis students bravely jumped the fence. They initiated an occupation of the abandoned military base, successfully holding it in their possession until a permit for the land was given to officially establish DQU. It was 1971, and a major Indian Civil Rights Movement and Native cultural resurgence were underway. D-Q University became an important hub for both.

Major Indigenous activist organizations such as The American Indian Movement, Indians of All Tribes, United Native Americans, The Brown Berets, El Movimiento Chicano, and similar Indian and Chicano groups held a strong presence during the peak of DQU's days from the 1970s until 2005. Movement leaders such as Dennis Banks, Russell Means, John Trudell, Floyd Red Crow Westerman, Winona LaDuke, and more either attended school there, lectured, or were involved in campus activities. Murals on the walls celebrated Indigenous sovereignty, power, and leadership. The campus provided a safe and all-inclusive space for Indigenous students of Northern Tribal and Southern Tribal origin (including Mexican, Chicano, and South

American) to learn, live, and practice Ceremony in a more Traditional manner.

Figure 5. *Art Apodaca explains the founding of DQU, 47 years after he and several UC Davis students jumped the fence to occupy the surplus Army base, enabling the establishment of DQU. Photo credit Jason Sinn, 2017.*

DQU unfortunately lost is accreditation in 2005 due to financial mismanagement issues, lack of federal funding, and its inability to meet other accreditation standards set by the Western Association of Schools and Colleges. Students complained of the embezzlement of their financial aid by several members of the D-Q Board of Trustees. The scandal created a faction between certain Board members and the Movement-dedicated students and Elders. A group of Elders and students refused to leave campus, and the grounds became a student-Elder occupation that was repeatedly attacked by the Board of Trustees, which attempted to force them off the campus grounds. I joined the student-Elder occupation at this time, and instantly became a target.

One woman in particular, Consuelo, focused her assaults on me. She often threw slanderous insults, accusing me of being a "whore" because I had many male occupation friends. On one occasion, she stole the keys to my car while I was away on a walk with my kids and refused to return them. It quickly backfired as she nervously watched me break into my own car, call a locksmith, and have the key replaced. Another time, she swerved her car at me and my young son Cuauhtémoc, trying to hit us, but we quickly got out of the way. There were many times that she called the police on me, accusing me of trespassing, but because one of the Elders signed over the use of his trailer home to me, the cops took my side, telling her that I had "more legal right" to be there than her. She lived in a tent, which my trailer "trumped." They warned her that if she wasted their time once more by calling them out against me, they'd arrest her instead for trespassing!

Despite many dangerous or just ridiculous run-ins with people like her, my experience at DQU was otherwise exciting, illuminating, and empowering. I received intensive training about sovereignty and Treaty Rights and was exposed to the ugly truth about the genocide of our people and the theft of the land by the U.S. government. The more truth I awakened to, the angrier I became.

I also took immense pride in my Native heritage, which was reflected in my clothing and attitude. I wore moccasins and beautiful skirts and dresses every day. Feathers adorned my hair, and I danced proudly any chance I was given. I even started singing, and some of my close friends nicknamed me, "Bluebird Woman", for my singing talent. I was transforming into a powerhouse Indigenous activist and was no longer afraid nor ashamed to embrace my lineage, my voice – both singing and speaking – and my identity as a Dakota and Lakota woman.

The first Sweatlodge, or Inipi Ceremony, that I took part in was held at DQU. It was a mixed Sweat, meaning it was held for both men and women, and was packed to the brim. This Sweat, filled with young DQU warriors and Elders, became my introduction to our Traditional Ceremonies. As empowering as it was challenging, it marked the opening of the Ceremonial and activist path that I embarked upon from that moment forward. There was no turning back! It was 2008, I was twenty-six years old, and I was finally stepping foot onto the Red Road that was my destined path of service to the people, Wakan Tanka, and Unci Maka, or Grandmother Earth.

I was taught that the Inipi Ceremony brings us back to Mother Earth, and through her we are reborn and reconnected in balance and harmony to our intended place within her. This Ceremony was one of the Seven Sacred Rites given to us by White Buffalo Woman, who came to the Oceti Sakowin nineteen generations ago to seed Great Spirit's prophecy in the hearts of our people. I learned about her for the first time during my experience at DQU, where a painting of her was suspended over the first room that I slept in. I began to believe that she may have been the beautiful woman who came into my dream seven years before to hand me a Pipe and a responsibility!

I met several Elders at DQU who had a powerful influence on my life. Harry Riverbottom was the first. An Ojibwe polo player, tipi maker, and wool-saddle blanket maker, he taught many of us younger ones his crafts. He was remarkably positive, so when we ran into obstacles, he cheerily said, "Well, things will be clearer in the morning!" Then, he peacefully carried off to bed. He taught us that we had to keep creating no matter what, and through our creative energy, we'd always overcome any challenge we faced. An avid cultural horseman, he shared the meaning behind his last name, Riverbottom, that told the story of how one strain of Native horses emerged onto the land from the bottom of a river. His teaching was the first time I heard an Indigenous perspective of how our people obtained horses. Western history teaches that all horses originated from Europe, which turns out, is not true. Modern archaeological evidence supports Indigenous Oral History and is finally retelling this story. Horses instead originated in Great Turtle Island and populated the rest of the world. There are several strains of original Indigenous horses that have always been in the "Americas," including the wild horses at Theodore Roosevelt National Park, Sitting Bull's strain in North Dakota, and the Ojibwe Spirit Horses.

Harry also had a dream to organize an all-Native polo team that rode Sitting Bull's horses. Many of us were excited to join, but it never happened because we were so busy with the "conflict" at DQU. Harry passed away soon after we all disbanded and left campus. I will always honor his positivity, creative entrepreneurship, and "Medicine Wheel" horsemanship. I find his encouraging words echoing through my mind often during challenging times, still a hugely positive influence from the Spirit World, where Harry now lives on.

The second Elder was Mazatzin. Of Kickapoo and Chichimeca First Nations descent, he joined us quite often at DQU to share the Aztec calendar teachings, and Aztec Cosmology of which he is recognized as a Tonalpouki of – a Keeper and interpreter of the calendar count. He stood with us as a supporting Elder against the frequent DQU Board attacks, and because of his teachings, we learned much about our inherent strengths, and how to overcome our challenges based on the energy that each day and astrological transition offered to us. His teachings had a profound effect on my re-connection to my identity through the teachings of the calendar system. Just recently, I learned that our family also carries Aztec heritage. No wonder his teachings resonated so deeply with my soul!

The third was an Elder named Standing Elk. His influence was not as positive as the others yet was a vital introduction to the internal issues that plague "Indian Country" – a term that can describe the modern interactions, happenings, issues, and more affecting Tribal peoples after decades of colonization. Walking in two worlds, that of the Traditional past that we hold on to from our ancestors, and that of the modern world in which we deal with the issues of genocide, forced colonization, and assimilation, creates an internal and external struggle that all of us face as Native survivors of the largest unacknowledged genocide in history, which is often quite difficult to navigate.

Standing Elk epitomized the colonized mentality. He was a Lakota spiritual leader who used to run the Sweatlodge Ceremonies at DQU. When our brothers from the Zapatista Mexica Resistance arrived, most of us welcomed them with open arms. They immediately got to work, building bamboo structures around the Ceremonial areas of D-Q that blocked the harsh winds. They also improved the fire pit area, helped to prepare and cook food daily, and offered the beauty of their culture through their song, dance, and art. They were powerful allies.

Yet, Standing Elk and a group of his followers attacked them, declaring that they were not welcome at DQU because "they were from Mexico." He refused to welcome them into the Sweatlodge. They even went so far as to tear down the structures that our Mexica brothers built. This made my daughter cry because she helped raise the structures and thus developed a close friendship with these brothers. Standing Elk taught me about the internal racism and lateral violence that is prevalent in many Native communities today – a direct effect of generations of colonization and genocide.

Long before borders were imposed, trade routes ran all through Great Turtle Island, what is now known as Canada, and North, Central, and South America. Traders from the Tribal Nations of these areas peacefully traveled along these routes to trade goods from their own lands, for food and natural items like shells and wood from other lands. They valued and honored what other Nations had to offer and acknowledged that we are all connected and of equal value no matter where we originated. But colonization and assimilation enforced separation for the first time. Reservations created isolation between Tribes and a fear of outsiders, and the morals and teachings of the ancestors were intentionally replaced with the mentality of the colonizer, who implanted fear, hatred, and separation in the minds of young children at boarding schools. Violence, tragedy, and abuse took hold in our communities, while our connection to one another and the original teachings started to fade away.

This reality struck harshly as we watched Standing Elk and his crew aggressively dismantle the structures built by our Zapatista brothers. Somehow, they felt they were doing the right thing by ripping the structures down because of who built them! I also experienced this internal racism directly when some California Natives came out to DQU and claimed that I shouldn't be there, because "I was Lakota." They said, "It's California Tribal land," so, in their eyes, I didn't belong.

They all missed the point of what the "D-Q" in DQU stood for! Named for two influential leaders before the era of European contact, Deganawidah-Quetzalcoatl University is normally referred to as simply D-Q University, out of respect for the Iroquois leader whose name is meant to be spoken only in the proper spiritual context. Also known as "The Great Peacemaker," he was influential in creating the Iroquois Confederation, which united the Iroquois Nations and whose governance the Declaration of Independence was later based on. Quetzalcoatl, or the Feathered Serpent, is a spiritual leader and deity originating from the Mexica, Aztec, Mayan, and neighboring Nations.

Thus, D-Q University was meant to include and unite all Tribal Nations from pre-European "America." It is written in its name, but that clearly was forgotten, as we watched Standing Elk's crew viciously tear down the structure our relatives built. That was the day that many of us made our final decisions to leave the occupation of D-Q University for good. It had become a war zone, where Native people fought mostly amongst themselves. Although it took a few weeks for us to completely abandon the grounds, our hearts just weren't in it anymore.

Several months passed since I first joined the Movement at DQU, and I underwent a powerful transformation because of it. I was growing spiritually and awakening to the intense truth of our collective plight. I'd never again be the same timid young woman that once ached to fit in where I didn't belong, and who yearned to lighten the color of my skin and eyes so that I'd be accepted by those who surrounded me during my childhood. I finally embraced my identity through my voice, dance, heritage, and budding discovery of my people's beautiful culture. I would never allow myself to be separated from that again, or to alter who I was inside to suit the opinions of others.

My mother, who never knew this side of me, soon returned home from her deployment. Her negative opinions of my father and my Native side of the family were made clear to me since I was a little girl. Thus, my involvement with the DQU Movement did not sit well with her militarized mind. Quite frankly, I was an embarrassment to her, and it soon became obvious that she no longer wanted me around. My mother stood for the military, and I represented the Movement. Of course, we clashed like lightning and thunder!

I was at DQU one night soon after. I hired a babysitter for the kids for part of the night and arranged for my twin and sister to pick them up and watch them for the rest of the night. It was all good between us. However, my mom found out and threatened to call CPS because I left the kids to go there. When I got back to sort it all out, she announced that I was no longer welcome to stay at her house, and that the kids and I must leave at once!

In shock, I packed up our belongings and moved into my car with my four young kids. Occasionally, we spent the night at D-Q, but it became too dangerous for the kids due to frequent law enforcement raids and Board attacks. I had nowhere to go, and no money to get there. I was suddenly under an incredible amount of stress. I had to find a way to give my kids a better situation. So, after a huge internal struggle, and after exhausting all other options, I sent my two oldest boys to live with their dad, who still at least had a home that they could live in. It was intended as a temporary solution that would give them more stability until I could get a place of my own, and a reliable source of income. The relationship between my mother and I took a major hit at this time! I didn't speak to her for many years to come.

The times I spent at DQU were becoming quite intense. Strange things happened that I never received explanations for. One day, as I chopped wood for the fire, I rubbed my eyes and suddenly, they burned like fire! I poured water into them, but it only made it worse. No one was there to help me, and for hours my eyes burned and teared until finally it went away on its own, long after I gave up trying to fight the burn. One night, I heard a low rumbling noise and looked up into the sky. A huge black triangle aircraft hovered directly above me! It lingered for about ten minutes before it finally took off. Another evening, I watched a drone-like craft survey the outer regions of the campus with what looked like lasers. I had no explanation for these strange sightings, but it was obvious to me that we were heavily monitored.

As I walked through the campus another day, I saw a juvenile American Kestrel hawk sitting calmly in a tree right in front of me. I gently placed my hand underneath him and gasped as he stepped onto my fingers! He allowed me to carry him around campus like that for a few days! Several members of the DQU Board saw this. However, even though they saw me holding him with their own eyes, they hated me so much that they persuaded themselves into believing that I forced him to sit on my hand with the help of a rope. But the hawk simply liked me for some reason, and only allowed me to hold it. He attacked anyone else that tried to touch him with his sharp beak. A few days later, he flew peacefully away. Our interaction perfectly describes the absolute magic, wonder, and mystery that was the brighter side of my D-Q experience.

Soon after, however, I dreamt of the energy that ended up taking over. As I walked the campus grounds in my dream, I saw a spinning vortex of blackness emerging from the center of DQU's land. I watched as it overtook the entire campus and destroyed everything in its path! None of us could prevent it. This dream encouraged me to stop fighting for DQU. Shortly after, the student and Elder occupation were threatened with arrests in an imminent DQU Board-organized raid. All of us who were involved in the occupation decided to leave.

I followed my Elder Mazatzin and his son to the Los Angeles area. For a short while, we stayed with them in Venice Beach, which itself was an awesome place to be, however, the environment at home created a stark contrast. Their grandmother, who was nice and charming at first, soon openly called Star a "little bitch," and me a "whore." I felt depressed and lost, and so sorry for my little girl that I couldn't provide a safe home for her at the time, no matter how hard I tried. I did my best to dry her tears and explain dementia, but after several long talks, and after watching her heart break time after time, we agreed she too would have to stay with her dad until I could stabilize. My heart broke then, as I had to let her go back to the same person I tried to shield her from for the last four years. Sadly, it was just me and Cuauhtémoc then, and for both of us, the challenges and hardships had only just begun!

CHAPTER SIX
CUAUHTÉMOC

Sometimes, I wonder if we cursed our little boy by giving him the name Cuauhtémoc – the name of the last Aztec ruler who is regarded as a hero of his people because of the brutal torture he endured at the hands of Spanish conquistadors. But then, I collect myself, and I remember that if my son's destiny could have gone any other way, it would have! Such is the nature of the guilt and grief that has tried to eat me alive for the decade that's passed since I now write this chapter. Mourning a child that is still alive is something I do not wish upon anyone. It is the sort of trauma that rewires the way a brain functions, how a nervous system reacts, how one interacts with themselves and others, and how ones' DNA functions. For years, I tried to numb the pain by staying over-busy, with "bettering" myself, and by engrossing myself in my work. However, it only managed to bury the pain deeply within me, and I knew that I had to face these places of darkness within me, or else I'd become their prisoner forever. In the end, the truth shall set us free, and what we've survived will make us stronger. Our resilience is undeniable! Thus, I rewind to 2009....

It was a crisp, star-sparkling night in the late evening, as Martin, Temoc, and I traveled north of Sacramento on a quiet Northern California highway towards the Robinson Rancheria Pomo Indian

Reservation. Martin was an Elder that was involved with the D-Q University student and Elder occupation, one of the only ones that lived on campus during the entire occupation. We lifelessly watched the road as we traveled, entirely exhausted from the dramatic events at campus, but we still jumped out of our seats as we drove over the huge body of an animal that had already been hit by another car. I slammed on the breaks and backed up to check it out. It was a huge mountain lion!

We prayed and left an offering for her spirit, then accepted the gift we knew we were given! Together, we hoisted her on top of my SUV, and she finished the rest of the trip with us back to the rez. Doj, the activist who first introduced me to the Movement, had offered Temoc and I shelter at his family's home on Robinson Rancheria. I accepted, and we soon arrived with the mountain lion in tow.

She became the first animal I learned how to skin! It was humbling to touch her, to honor her, and through her, to intimately realize our place in the circle of life, and our connection to all things in it. She gave us hope, and a glimpse into the power of what is usually unseen and unknown. Martin and I agreed to share her skin. We both tanned her hide and took turns traveling with her. It was an arrangement I thought we were both happy with.

Doj's family took Temoc in as their own, in the way most of us Natives do when little children come into our homes. They showered him with attention. Thus, when I received a job offer at a nearby Medicinal Marijuana farm, I trusted Doj's family with Temoc, accepting their offer to watch him. I got to work right away, excited to have the opportunity to rebuild my stability and to start the subsequent return of my children because of it!

However, one day after work, I pulled onto the rez to pick my boy up. Doj's sister brought him to the car. With a huge smile on her face, she announced, "I cut his hair, isn't it so cute!" I hadn't even trimmed his hair before this! Now, it was spiked into a short Mohawk, and she just smiled at me as if nothing happened. I felt like she slapped me in the face. My first instinct was to beat her down to the ground, but I just grabbed Temoc instead, who lunged for me. Did she not know how disrespectful it was to cut his hair without my permission? Wasn't she Native? Didn't she know that we don't cut our hair unless someone close to us dies? Didn't she know that cutting the hair of a child disconnects them from their mother? The truth is, of course she knew. It was just another blow in the long list of passive-aggressive and disrespectful experiences I was beginning to have with Doj's family. This became the last time I ever left them alone with Temoc, and consequently, the last day I worked on the farm.

One day, I went back to the rez, parked my car in front of Doj's place, and took Temoc with me for a walk in the foothills. When I returned, I realized that someone had broken into my car and stolen the mountain lion skin! I soon found out that Doj's mom had done this "on behalf of" Martin, confident in her right to do so because, apparently, I "stole it from him!"

"Well, how did the lion get torn?" Doj later questioned with an accusatory tone. "What the hell are you talking about?" I demanded. He explained that a huge rip spanned across the entire length of her skin! They assumed that I was the one who caused the tear, but I knew at that moment that it didn't happen until his mom violated my space, and took it from me based upon the rumors, gossip, and misunderstandings they all spewed behind my back! Instead of confronting me face-to-face about the blather, she was so compelled that I wronged Martin, that without any evidence of it, she broke into my personal space to take the skin that Martin and I agreed to share over time.

I was so disgusted by the entire situation that I didn't even fight to get it back, especially after realizing that Martin was complaining behind my back about sharing the skin. They could all just keep it, and the tear that appeared without explanation in her skin showed me that the spirit of the mountain lion was not happy with the way she'd been taken either! Martin instantly transformed from an "Elder" to an "older" in my eyes. In our way, an Elder imparts wisdom earned through a lifetime of experiences upon the younger generation, whereas an "older" is just an older person who instead misleads the younger generation, and who often acts inappropriately and bitterly towards them when they don't get their way.

The final event I experienced at their house that became the final push to me leaving Robinson Rancheria forever, happened the night that I was awoken in the middle of the night to a married man's hands buried deep into my crotch, feeling me up, and literally leaning over his pregnant wife to do so! With all my childhood trauma, in which night after night I was forcefully awoken to a sexual violation like this as a child, I was instantly insanely and deeply triggered! Not knowing what to do, and consumed with rage, I ran to the hills and prayed, begging for guidance. I was told to "tell everyone what happened." Yet, when I did, they did nothing but raise their eyebrows at me!

Instead of helping me, I was blamed for it, and through yet even more gossip, rumors, and misunderstandings, everyone agreed that I was playing the role of his mistress and enabling him to cheat on his wife! Doj was the mastermind behind all this thinking, which I overheard him feeding to my abuser's wife, to his mom, and to his sisters. I became "the whore" who was shamed by everyone, especially Martin, who refused to even look at me as I sought out his counsel as an "Elder" to explain what happened.

After this event, I finally left that place, that huge chaotic shit storm, which gave me the realistic view of what reservation life is really like, and what colonization has done to our people. My romanticized idealism of our people was gone! A few years later, this man that no one believed had violated me, was arrested, convicted, and deported for sexually violating a child. It came as a surprise to everyone but me. "Adi-fucking-os!" I cheered.

While still on that rez, I visited Eddie, Doj's cousin, who lived right down the street. He was also a D-Q University warrior. He was one of the only ones who remained on the grounds, caretaking it, cutting wood, growing gardens, and talking to the Spirits… out loud. I was attracted to him because he consistently demonstrated "action over talk," and I admired his peculiar ways. You always knew if Eddie was around because you could hear him off in the distance laughing loudly and clapping at the birds. I liked to talk to him because he spoke in riddles and mentioned prophetic knowledge often. I didn't realize what a huge impact he'd later have on my life.

Just before I left Robinson Rancheria for the last time, Doj confessed that he and his cousins' gang-raped their own twelve-year-old cousin a few summers back! He asked for my help and hand as he tried to trauma bond with me, but I cursed him and left him on his knees, walking out of his life and all the insanity that came with it!

I received a beautiful blessing shortly after – the opportunity to Fancy Shawl dance during the Reggae Rising 2009 Festival! I danced before thousands of people on a stage shared by reggae all-stars like Steel Pulse, UB40, Capleton, and Rebelution. It was an awesomely empowering moment in my life amidst all the chaos. Pictures later revealed that hundreds of Spirit Orbs floated around us as I danced during the closing Ceremony!

Figure 8. Fancy Shawl dancing for the closing Ceremony of the 2009 Reggae Rising Music Festival. Orbs float all around us!

I also began to perform at local events and record my original music. Because my name was announced on stage, I started to seriously consider changing my name to one which truly reflected who I was. I already carried the "Newburg" name, and the "Newburg shame," for far too long! This false label haunted me every time I was called by it, every time I had to sign my name with it, and every time I read it on a piece of paper. It simply wasn't me, and I hated who and what it stood for – my stepfather who stole everything from me, my innocence, my original last name, even my fucking virginity, along with any chance at happiness, or so I once thought!

I considered changing my last name back to "Neiss," the name passed down to me from my father at birth, but it too didn't feel like it fit, especially after my dad told me he found out from my grandmother that he had a different father than his brothers and sisters, or in other words, we weren't biologically "Neiss's" either! His real father was Teddy Rouillard, and he was an enrolled member of the Lower Brule Lakota Sioux, or the Kul Wicasa Lakota Oyate. He was also half Santee Sioux, or Isanti Dakota. Unfortunately, he passed on before my dad or I were able to meet him, but just knowing about him helped us gain a huge part of our identity as we finally knew who we truly came from!

I traveled out one summer with my dad, when I was around twenty-seven years old, to visit my auntie in Lower Brule. She welcomed us warmly, and hugged me saying, "Welcome Niece! I love you!" She showed us around the rez a bit and took us to see an Indian horse race that my biological uncle raced in. A beautiful, tall, muscular black stallion impatiently waited to take off, and when he finally did, he easily broke free from the rest of the pack and took first place! He was one of the Rouillard stallions, and I felt immense pride to realize that we came from a family of horse racers!

However, as we prepared to leave, my auntie brought my uncle over to introduce us, but instead he spit on the ground before my feet and refused to shake my hand. "You're not a Rouillard!" he hissed at me. Shocked, I shouted back, "Ok, whatever dick!" I climbed in the car with my dad and left. That was the first, and only time I would talk with my "Uncle Rouillard." At first it hurt my feelings, but later something happened to make me thank him for his rude outburst.

I met another one of my relatives who researched a huge part of our family tree. I studied it, and realized that we descended from *Waŋbdí Táŋka*, or "Big Eagle" five generations back on my grandfather's side. This name was passed down for a few generations before the French name "Rouillard" was. Big Eagle and many of our relatives at that time were warriors, freedom fighters, and leaders! Some of them were signatories on the Fort Laramie Treaty of 1868, which was intended to create peace between our people and the U.S. Government. They endured incredible hardships so that their families could survive. Understandably, I felt much more of a connection to them than I felt to this modern-day Rouillard who was now spitting at the feet of his own relative. So, I said to my father, "You know what? That Rouillard man is right! We are not Rouillards! We are Big Eagles!"

A few years later, I finally went through the court system to legally change my name, and that of my youngest son, to carry on the name of our ancestor "Big Eagle." It was my way of reconnecting to the part of my lineage that sought to uphold our Nation's sovereignty and to resist colonization. Ultimately, it was my reconnection to the era of my ancestry that didn't carry the scar of colonization. That trip, and the harsh treatment I received from my uncle, changed my association with my identity and corrected it for the rest of my life, and for generations to come.

For a short while, I dated a man I met during the DQU Movement, Phillip. It was a hurried romance that I fell too quickly into because I mistakenly believed that he actioned the words he spoke as poetry over uplifting and Indigenous-fused music tracks. I soon moved in with him and started performing with him – Fancy Shawl dancing, singing, and drumming behind his spoken word poetry.

Through Phillip, I met John Trudell, who became an incredible inspiration to me! Trudell was the powerful "Voice of Alcatraz" during the takeover of Alcatraz Island in 1969, along with a group of Indian protestors called the Indians of All Tribes. Their takeover of the deserted prison island ushered in the rise of Native American activism in the decades to come. I listened to Trudell's songs constantly, and his logic reprogrammed my thinking. For the first time, I could see the reality of government corruption and the "system" and realized our place in it as "The Original People."

Although Phillip worked with Trudell when we first met, it soon became clear to all of us, even Trudell, that Phillip was verbally and mentally abusive to everyone around him. They soon disconnected over this, but not before I got the chance to hear Trudell scold Phillip about his public accusation that I worked for the C.I.A! Trudell told him that was exactly what happened to Anna Mae Pictou Aquash, an activist who was murdered by her own people, who mistakenly believed she was working as an F.B.I informant. He warned Phillip that he better be careful saying something like that against me; that it was in other words putting a mark on my head, and that was nothing to play around with.

Figure 9. John Trudell and I meet after one of his epic shows.

I'll never forget how John Trudell spoke up for me, and how he calmly put an erratic and overly emotional Phillip in his place, whose only true claim against me was that I caught on to his borderline personality disorder and narcissism and put him in his place often because of it. John and Phillip never spoke again after that, although Phillip often spoke out against Trudell publicly afterwards, also claiming that he was a federal agent for whatever agency fit in the moment.

One day, Phillip, Temoc, and I traveled north on Highway 101 towards Trinity, California to visit our beloved Elder, Standing Bear. My Movement sister, Redhawk, rode along. Although we now traveled through bear country, it was still rare to see one. So, I saw it as an incredible blessing when I spotted a bear lying in the road before us! I slammed on my breaks, parked the car on the side of the highway, and sprinted to the bear. I touched it gently with admiration and was overcome with sadness at its passing. It had just been hit. A juvenile bear, it was still warm from the life it recently lived. Even though we were time restricted, I knew that I had to honor this bear!

Despite Phillip's nagging that we had to go, I dragged the bear to the side of the road. Redhawk jumped out to help, and together we dragged that bear that was bigger than both of us to the side of the road so that I could skin its hide. Before I did, I left a tobacco offering and prayed for its spirit to find its way to Wakan Tanka, Great Spirit, and thanked it for choosing us. I also apologized for not being able to take the entire body, as it was far too large for us to hoist onto the car. I knew in my heart that the bear would be honored because it was the only action that I could take in the moment.

I worked as quickly as possible, skinning that bear as fast as I could, ignoring the traffic that whizzed by. Phillip reprimanded me the entire time, "You're wasting your time! We need to go! What the hell are you doing!?" I ignored him completely and focused fully on the task I was chosen for. Not once did he lift a finger to help me, but he only stood in the way the entire time!

When I got to each paw, I carefully worked the skin away from the meat and the bones, and successfully disconnected the bear's claws and paws without any tears or rips. When I got to the last paw, and when the skin was almost completely separated, a cop pulled up behind us. I kept working anyway. He approached me, declaring that he received a report of "a dead body" and "people standing over it on the side of the road." I laughed out loud and pointed out that it was a bear! Now that the skin was mostly disconnected, the bear did look stunningly like a human. I could see why they thought that.

I told him what I was doing, and what the bear meant to us culturally, but he said that I still had to stop. He couldn't allow me to take the skin; the bear was protected by law. After realizing that I couldn't reason with him, I put my knife away and apologized to the bear. I watched as the cop covered him with a tarp. He wouldn't leave until we did. So, I let go of the bear, knowing that I did all that I could. After a few hours, I realized my heart still pulled towards the bear, so I decided to go back by myself to see if he was still there. He was! I jumped out and quickly disconnected the last paw! I wrapped his hide in a tarp, placed more tobacco and prayers on the bear, promised that I would honor him as best as I could, and then jumped back in the car and whizzed off with the hide. He gave himself to me after all!

However, after Phillip impatiently watched from the sidelines, scolded me, and did absolutely nothing to help me as I took it upon myself to honor the bear, he released a story on social media about how *he* had found the bear, drug it to the side of the road, skinned it, and then took it to his Elder's house to tan it all by himself! When I saw the story, my jaw dropped to the floor in disbelief. I confronted him about it, and he tried to explain that he posted the story as if he did it, to "protect me" because the "cop might be looking for me" after I went back to retrieve the hide. There was absolutely no reasoning with this unbelievably narcissistic guy, who now pretended that he was willing to take the fall for me if the cop did come looking for me, which of course didn't happen!

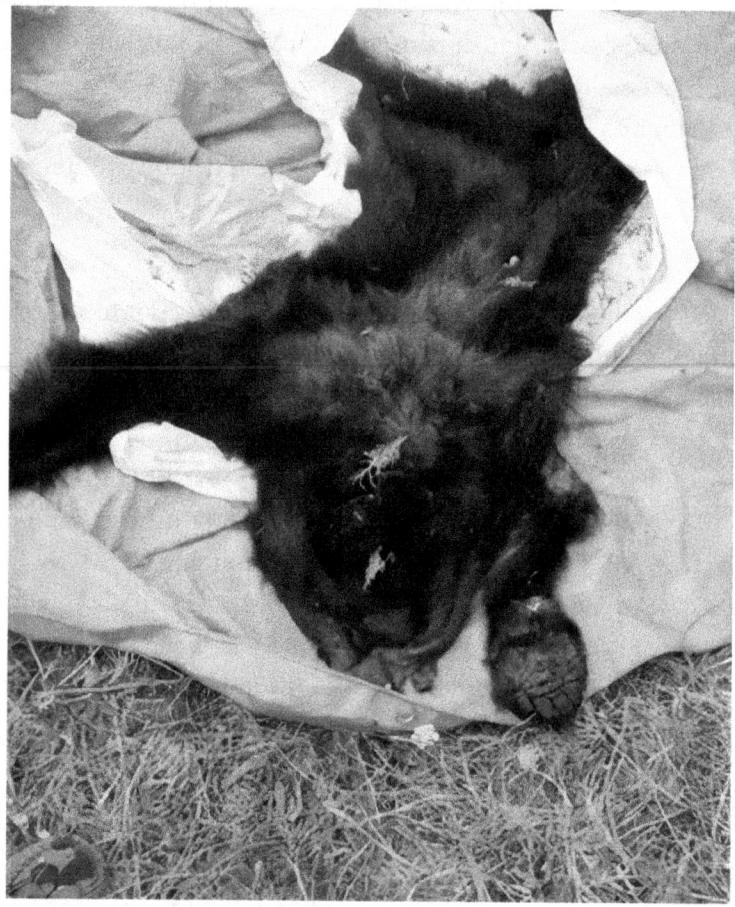

Figure 10. The stunning hide of the juvenile bear. His blood stains the moccasins that I wore while I skinned him (left lower corner).

Over the next few days, I worked from sunup to sundown on that beautiful bear's hide! I called my friend, a Bear Dancer, to tell him what I found. He then invited me to come out to speak to his Elders about becoming a Bear Dancer – a dancer that served the people as a

Healer during Ceremony through the spirit of the bear. Thus, I began the lengthy process of preparing him to work with the people.

After a few days, Phillip and I prepared to travel south for a few performances. Standing Bear invited me to leave the bear with him, promising to look after it for me. I trusted him and accepted his offer. However, a few weeks later, Phillip announced that Standing Bear called and disclosed that he cut the paws off the bear's hide! Somehow, the hide "went bad" and he chose to "save the claws," even though I properly preserved it in salt, which should have kept it in good condition until I could return and continue working on it.

I called my Bear Dancer brother and told him what happened. He revealed that Standing Bear's actions disconnected the spirit from the bear, and that the hide could no longer be danced with! I never returned to that "older's" home after that. I couldn't bear the betrayal, literally! Once again, I had to let go of another hide and accept that the spirit and experience of the bear would be with me for a lifetime, despite another human taking it upon themselves to physically disconnect us.

Meanwhile, the more I stood up to Phillip's outbursts, the more he outcasted me, publicly accused me of working for federal agencies, and emotionally devalued me. He claimed that he could easily perform alone. Remembering the dream the Star Nation gave me about true love and survival, I began to look for an escape route to leave him in the dust. It came in the form of Dez, a Wendigokaan Heyoka – a Sacred Clown in both the Anishinaabe and Dakota Traditions – whom Phillip invited out to record a series of Anishinaabe Ceremonial songs. I was instantly drawn to Dez, who came with a wealth of Traditional knowledge, and who quickly took me under his wing for the next ten years.

The three of us traveled together after Dez recorded his beautiful songs. Dez sat quietly in the back of the car, witnessing Phillip's abusive behavior that he didn't even bother to hide anymore. I finally had enough, and because Dez saw the truth of the way Phillip treated me, he watched protectively over me as I packed up my things and left that day! Phillip tried to stop me, but because Dez watched, there was nothing he could do to stand in my way.

Dez rode along with me as I left, and thus, became a friend and spiritual mentor, teaching me about the Thunderbird and Heyoka ways. He also taught me that I was "Lightning Family." I denied it at first, claiming that I didn't want to be associated with "Clowns" in any way. In our Traditional teachings, a Heyoka, and members of the Lightning Family, are sacred beings from the Sky World above, who are chosen by the Thunderbeings to bring their Medicine and power to Earth. They do things backwards, or contrarily, and by doing so, bring healing and laughter to the people. However, they often have extremely difficult lives. I didn't want this path for myself, even though Dez saw it in me. It took me many years to realize that you cannot escape what life, or these beings, choose for you.

Dez caught a ride back home to Wisconsin, and I stayed in California with my twin brother. Soon, I met Mohawk, an Iroquois descendant, who spoke fluently in his Native language, spent most of his time beading, and often ran Sweats. He also took me under his wing for a bit. I felt comfortable with him and recounted the dream I had years before of meeting the woman who handed me a C'anupa and a responsibility.

He excitedly proclaimed that I was handed the Sacred Pipe of the White Buffalo Calf Woman! As he said this, he grew even more enthusiastic because he saw a rainbow on my forehead. It turned out I was standing in the right place at the right time, as the sun shined through the peephole in the door and created a prism that reflected directly onto my forehead! He saw it as a sign of confirmation. I didn't know what to think. I didn't even know who she was yet. So, he shared her story with me for the first time.

"It was told that next time there is chaos and disparity on Earth, she would return again. She said she would return as a White Buffalo Calf. Some believe, she already has." – Chief Arvol Looking Horse, Keeper of the Sacred White Buffalo Calf Pipe of the Oceti Sakowin. White Buffalo Calf Woman came to the Oceti Sakowin nineteen generations ago, as they lived upon the Great Plains. Several versions of the story are told, but the story has never been forgotten amongst our people and has struck a deep chord of hope since the birth of multiple white buffaloes beginning in the 1990s that continue to this day. The appearance of the white buffalo marks the end of an age, and the beginning of a new age, marked by peace, understanding and harmony.

White Buffalo Woman's story isn't just a legend or folklore but is Indigenous Oral History that has been handed down for generations by our ancestors who received her visitation, and who, from this visit, handed down the Seven Sacred Rites still practiced by our people today. The following is one version of one of the most important origin stories of our culture and history as it happened nineteen generations ago:

Two warriors went out upon the land to hunt for buffalo as the sun rose. They searched everywhere but found nothing. Their people were starving, so they kept hunting. They did not want to return home empty-handed. Suddenly, they saw a mysterious woman filled with light that approached them from far away! As she came closer, it became obvious that she was an incredibly beautiful young woman. She wore white buckskin that was beautifully embroidered with sacred designs that shimmered with radiant rainbow colors.

One of the hunters, a warrior with a pure heart, first saw her as a white buffalo appearing from white light. Then, she morphed into a woman dressed in holy white adornments, with a single eagle feather in her hair. He knew then that she was wakan, sacred, and immediately fell on his knees before her, silently praying for whatever message she was bringing. The other man, who was consumed with the disease of separation, did not recognize her holiness, but only saw her beauty and desired to take that beauty for himself.

As she came close, he whispered to the other man, let us overwhelm her and take her for ourselves! The other warrior warned him that she was wakan and remained on his knees, preparing for her arrival. She carried with her a large bundle wrapped in white buckskin. As she approached the men, she lowered the bundle and gently set it upon the earth to rest.

The sick man lunged for her and tried to overtake her, but a great white cloud descended over him as she spoke the incantations of the Sky Grandmothers. She recognized his suffering and his illness, and thus returned his soul with compassion to Wakan Tanka, the Great Spirit. His body was disintegrated, and his soul given over to the light, as his darkness was released, and his insatiable hunger, which could only be filled by destroying others, was cured! The cloud receded, and the warrior's ashes and bones lay in a pile at her feet. She then sent the good-hearted warrior back to his people, with a message to prepare their hearts for her arrival and for the teaching of the bundle she would bring to them.

The hunters stood for the duality between men. One chose the humble path of the spiritual warrior; the other was infected with the sickness of separation. The sick one could only see White Buffalo Woman as a thing to overcome and take for his own needs, while the other saw her true form and honored her. She returned the sick man to the source and left him as a pile of ash and bones, and the other, she blessed and sent to the Tribe to spread the news. In this way, she brought a teaching to men to not take from a woman what they think they are missing inside their own selves.

A great tipi lodge was built and made ready for her arrival. All the people of the Tribe gathered within it and prepared for her coming as instructed. For six days, she sent a red tail hawk to watch over the people as they prepared for her. On the seventh day, the red tail hawk circled high above her as she approached the camp from the east, and the sun rose behind her. She entered the lodge and walked in a clockwise circle, greeting each person as she passed.

Cedar was burned from the Altar, blessing and purifying the space before she spoke. She removed the bundle from her back, blessed it with the cedar smoke, and raised it with both hands to the Chief. She presented the Sacred Pipe that was contained within the bundle and explained that the Pipe was a very wakan instrument that must always be treated with deep respect, which would deepen their reverence with themselves, with one another, and with all life. She instructed them how to pray with it, and proclaimed that as a people, they were chosen to be Keepers of a path of prophecy for communicating Wakan Tanka's mysteries. She confirmed that she was sent to them from Wakan Tanka because of their prayers to be of service to all beings, and the C'anupa, or Pipe, was the manifestation of their prayers from the sky!

She taught the people that the Earth is our mother, and that the bowl of the Pipe is made from red stone to represent her holy body upon which we live. Praying with the Pipe allows us to clearly hear her voice, and to offer her our constant gratitude, honor, and prayers. Through this relationship, she would teach us how to love her and one another in all ways. The bowl was carved in the form of a buffalo, to represent our connection with all Nations – Plant, Animal, and Spirit – and to signify that they are all our brothers and sisters, our relatives.

Twelve eagle feathers hung from the point where the bowl of the Pipe joined with the stem to stand for the winged ones from the sky above who are our family. The stem was carved from wood to represent the Plant Nations, and when all pieces were joined together, they became one and signified our connection to all our relatives in the sky, on our Mother Earth, and throughout the Universe. Through the C'anupa, we were enabled to pray with and for the entire Universe, and to carry out the plan of Wakan Tanka, the Great Mystery. The stem, standing for the masculine, and the bowl, representing the feminine, united both aspects throughout the entire Universe as the Pipe was joined together, and thus was given to both men and women to carry and to pray with, blessing all through the smoke that passed from the Pipe, which became Wakan Tanka's breath.

White Buffalo Woman taught the people how to pray with the C'anupa, and how to bless the sacred herbs to be used along with the Pipe. She taught them all things were possible using the Sacred Pipe and told them that Wakan Tanka would reveal to them Seven Sacred Rites. These Rites would help guide the people through several ages that were yet to come. Then, she seeded prophecies in the hearts of the women that couldn't be understood at the time, but which would be awakened in the DNA of the generations to be spoken in the future.

She warned that the world they knew at the time would one day change to a world filled with others from other lands who had forgotten who they were. They would be filled with the disease of separation, and would become their enemies, and furthermore, they would take almost everything from them! She said this age – the age we are in at this very moment – would near its end when these same people who were once their enemies, would come to them for the Medicine of the Pipe and the Seven Sacred Rites, to heal their sickness. At first, they would understand almost nothing of what would be said to them, but she instructed the people to look for the questioning in their eyes, and they would know in their hearts that she was coming soon to speak on their behalf!

She promised that she would be with the people through all the ages to come, although they would not see her. She taught that the Pipe would show the people how to find her within themselves, and that they would learn that what is within them can never be stolen from them! The Pipe would carry the people all the way through to the end of all these ages, completing the prayer of Wakan Tanka to cleanse the disease of separation from the hearts of all people!

Then, she would return and physically walk amongst all of us to seed a new prophecy, as the original prophecy she brought to the people reached its fulfillment! At this time, a living C'anupa would exist in the hearts of children from the stars living upon the Earth. They would recognize her voice, and become the embodiment of her new prophecies, freeing the Earth of the darkness of the past ages. Upon leaving this message, she told the people that they would know the end of the coming ages were upon them, and her return was heralded, with the appearance of the white buffalo upon the Earth.

She exited the tipi, and a great eagle descended from the sky and circled above her as she departed from the village. As she walked away, she shapeshifted into a reddish-brown buffalo calf. Looking back at the people, she playfully kicked and tumbled, representing the first age when it was just their people upon the land. Then, she stood up and turned pure white, staring into the eyes of the people, representing the coming of a new people to the land, and the beginning of great hardship.

Her fur then turned black, representing the third age and the disease of separation that would spread across the Earth within the hearts of men. Finally, she shifted back into a white buffalo, and then returned to her form as the White Buffalo Woman. As she walked away, she shifted into light, lightning struck the earth all around her, and she ascended into the sky, returning to where she came from.

I did not learn this detailed version of the White Buffalo Woman Prophecy until 2019. When Mohawk first told me of her back in 2009, I was given an abridged version of her story. Yet, even in its simplicity, it sounded just like the dream I had of the woman who handed me a C'anupa and a responsibility! Receiving the full prophecy ten years later finally helped me realize that my entire life was negatively affected by the disease of separation she warned our people about, which exists in the hearts of those who turned into my enemy through no fault of my own, and whose actions caused almost everything to be taken from me!

It is she who gives me, and many others like me, hope! It is her prophecy and her visit to my dreams that has encouraged me to continue all these years despite the times that I felt like giving up. Her influence helped me realize that there is a pure heart that lives within me that can never be contaminated by the sickness of others! Because of her, and the prophecy that she seeded within our people, which I now carry within me, I have the strength to carry on no matter what I face.

It is also clear to me that having a dream of White Buffalo Woman presenting me a Pipe, doesn't mean that I'm *her* as others have been guided to believe. It simply means that I carry her prophecy within me, and that I hear her voice. It means that I carry a responsibility to pray for the people, for the sickness of separation to leave their hearts, and to honor and protect Mother Earth. It means that she has spoken to me, and therefore, that I am to carry on in the way that she has instructed our people to live. It also means that she knew me before I remembered who I was! She came to activate a part of me that was forgotten and stifled, and that over time, would grow to take over all of me!

In the meantime, after living in Sacramento for a few months, I grew tired of the city energy, so I took a trip back up to Clear Lake for a respite and recharge. As I visited by the lakeside with a group of friends, I was introduced to "Two Wolves" through his brother, a comrade from D-Q University. A half Pomo and half Lakota warrior, we became instant friends and soon made plans to leave California. His family lived in Minnesota, and I wanted to get closer to my kids in Indiana, so, we left together and began a beautiful cross-country journey! We traveled north through Washington, where we jumped into the frigid mountain water to clear the energy of California from us as we embarked on our new paths. We really enjoyed each other's company, and he was a good example for my little boy Temoc.

Once we arrived in Minnesota, I dropped him at his mom's, and I headed for a local powwow, where I met Dennis Banks, the co-founder of the American Indian Movement (AIM). After talking with him for a while, he invited me and my boy to come stay and help at his home. I gratefully agreed! There, I spent my time learning how to make drums, praying in his Sweatlodge, and arising early each morning to prepare healthy meals for Dennis that helped to control his diabetes. I also loved to take the canoe out on the water every morning and night with my boy so he could play on the island across the lake.

It was a good time, until the night Dennis held a meeting with his fellow "Aimsters," and introduced me to them as an "advocate for the homeless" in a mocking way, humiliating me! Then, the next day, he and his buddy took off in my car without my permission, leaving me enraged and feeling extremely disrespected. The final straw came when an acquaintance paid me to take him to Minneapolis. I had no source of income at the time, and desperately needed the cash, so I accepted, without knowing what he was going there for. He just told me he really needed to see a friend, so with some money finally in my pocket, and him paying for all the gas, we took off. We arrived at our destination, he went into his friend's place, while I waited in the car, and then we headed back to the rez.

By this time, it was early in the morning, just before sunrise. I barely made out the shape of two large deer grazing on the side of the road as we approached them. My headlights still lit our path, and suddenly, the deer ran right in front of us! The first to cross our path, now fully illuminated in the flash of the headlights, was a huge *all-white* buck! A much smaller brown doe followed closely behind him. I screamed in joy, abruptly stopped the car, and jumped out to give my thanks for receiving this sacred sign! I left tobacco and prayers of gratitude. My friend saw it too and was just as excited as I was. Neither of us had ever seen an all-white deer before, and we both knew that it was an incredibly special moment that carried a potent message! I was excited to get back and tell Dennis the news.

It was still early morning when we returned, so I carried my boy to our room, and eagerly waited for everyone to wake up, but Temoc beat everyone else to it. Soon, I heard Dennis's son, who was in his late twenties, stomp upstairs and complain to his dad that "this damn kid" was making all kinds of noise that woke him up. I felt really angered by this, a grown man complaining about a toddler! But I ignored it and joined them to share the news about the sighting of the all-white buck.

When I told Dennis, he didn't care, and instead revealed that he was really upset with me because, "That guy you took to Minnesota is a meth dealer, and you probably just helped him out." I had no idea at that time who "that guy" truly was, and Dennis's cold reaction to my miraculous sign totally took me aback. He treated me as if I was plotting with this guy to bring meth to the rez. Nearly in tears, I went downstairs, packed our things, and left without a word! I never spoke to him again due to my frustration and anger.

It took me many years to realize that Dennis was just as exasperated as I was. We were both taken advantage of by a meth dealer, and Dennis's own daughter was an addict. Even though I had no idea what that dealer was really doing when I took him to Minnesota, I learned that keeping the wrong company can bring you down and hurt others, no matter how good your intentions might be!

However, I knew that in my innocence, I was right where I needed to be at that point in time, because I witnessed the miracle of an extremely wakan all-white deer jumping right in front of my car! Life was changing rapidly for me, whether I was prepared for it or not, and I think that deer came to show me that everything my son and I were about to go through was a part of our greater purpose, even if it took me many years to realize it!

My experience in Minnesota, which I discovered over ten years later was part of the original ancestral home of my people before we were forcibly removed and imprisoned on reservations, had come to a sudden and challenging end. So, I called my dad up and arranged to visit him in Omaha, Nebraska. He then took me to my grandmother's house on the rez in Pickstown, South Dakota, and they agreed that I could stay there with Temoc for as long as I needed to until I found my own place to stay, and the means to get it. I used that time to work on myself in any way that I could.

Every day, I put Temoc in a stroller and ran with him up and down the hill that led to the river about a half mile away. During one of these runs, on a perfect summer day, I found three eagle feathers on the ground alongside the water! There they were, just flowing in the wind and gently calling my name! I left an offering and deep thanks to Wakan Tanka for the gift, and then carried those feathers with me for the next few years, until they too, like many other sacred items I found, were taken by another person infected with the disease of separation. What I will always remember and cherish is that the first eagle feathers I received, I found, and furthermore, I discovered them in the land of my ancestors!

One day, I walked along the river, and nearly stepped on a beautiful diamondback rattlesnake that was dying in the street! A gun-toting cowboy pulled up in his truck and tried to shoot it, but I stopped him, shielding the snake with my body. After he left, I picked the snake up and carried it home with me. It died in my hands before I even got there. I offered tobacco to his spirit and prayed for his safe journey home. Then, I skinned him, adding the delicately laced skin and its rattle to my Ceremonial items. I buried the rest of the snake in my grandmother's yard, asking for its spirit to look after her and protect her.

Later that night, a wicked thunderstorm arrived! I stood in it with my hands outstretched to the sky for hours as lightning crashed all around me! The rain soaked and chilled me to my bones, but I prayed with all my heart during that stormy night for the cleansing my soul and heart desperately needed.

Living at my grandmother's house gave me the opportunity to visit with my relatives, and to get to know my dad's side of the family more deeply, who before were nothing more than strangers. I used to hang out with my grandmother quite often when I first moved in with her. She shared entertaining stories about my dad and uncles, and of me and my brother when we were little babies.

Eventually though, she grew tired of our company. I could easily overhear the conversations she had on the phone with my Uncle Ronnie where she called my boy Temoc "a little terror" and "a little shit!" They laughed together, and I realized that he too was saying nasty things about us. She behaved more and more negatively towards us, and soon the toxicity became too much to tolerate.

It hit its peak when my Uncle Ronnie came for a visit and crawled over the couch in the living room to avoid me, rather than passing me like my relative through the doorway! He ignored me repetitively as if I were invisible and worthless. The moment I heard him and gramma in the other room discuss what a "pest" my little boy was, and how I would "never amount to anything," became the opportunity I took to leave my grandmother's house before anyone noticed my apparently welcome disappearance.

A few days before, my friend Eddie from D-Q contacted me and offered to pay for a trip back to California if I picked him up from his rez in Minnesota. I agreed with the stipulation that we pick up my kids in Indiana first. The day before, my daughter called and cried over the line, claiming that if I didn't get back together with her dad, her life was "going to be ruined!" She wouldn't tell me exactly what was happening to her, but I knew it wasn't good. I was determined to get my children, and this seemed like the perfect opportunity to do so.

I picked Eddie up, and our first stop was the 2010 Mdewakanton Shakopee Powwow in Minnesota. Eddie disappeared for three days, while Temoc and I camped out. I danced with my boy at my side, putting my prayers and intentions for my children into that wacipi circle filled with hundreds of beautiful dancers.

Fig 11. Dancing at the Powwow.

Our next stop was the Pine Ridge Reservation, where we met with Alex White Plume, a powerful Lakota activist and leader in the hemp industry who asserted his sovereignty by exercising his right to grow hemp on his land. He used the fibers to build tipi canvases, and even used hemp bricks to build his house – one of the sturdiest and best insulated homes I've ever been in. He showed us his hemp manufacturing "shed" and explained a bit of the process. It was hard but rewarding work, which was often thwarted by the FBI when they raided and destroyed his hemp crop season after season, just before harvest time!

Then, he showed us his huge herd of beautiful and ornery Lakota ponies. I learned how to ride bareback that day after he put me on one of his horses and slapped its butt! It ran off and took me straight out to its herd. I laugh now as I remember how little control I had over that horse! I climbed off it after realizing that, and with nothing else to do, I just sang. The horses stopped eating, pricked up their ears, and quietly gathered in a circle around me, all of them facing me. They stood there, peacefully and attentively holding space with me, through the duration of my entire song! When they realized I was done, they simply went back to grazing.

I thought I better try to head back, so I climbed a tree near a nice-looking horse and climbed on its back. It too, however, didn't go anywhere when I asked it too. So, I just sat there and rubbed its back until I heard the approach of an ATV. Alex pulled up laughing and retrieved me, asking if I fell off the first horse. I just laughed too, climbed off the second horse, and joined him on his much better-behaving electric pony.

We soon left Alex's place to head to Rapid City, and from there, the plan was to head east to finally pick up my babies! However, once we reached Rapid, Eddie suddenly announced that he "had no more cash," and just like that, we were in a bind! I realized in an instant that he gambled all his money away at the Shakopee casino while I danced!

While I waited in the car and tried to figure out what the hell we were going to do, Eddie went into the Safeway before us. A cop car soon pulled up, and I saw Eddie being escorted out of the store in handcuffs! Turns out he stole some soap and toiletries. Suddenly, I found myself on my own in this city where I knew no one and had no cash. I had no choice but to sleep in the car with Temoc. Eddie's family later warned me, "Leave Eddie the hell alone! We have it all taken care of." They treated me like *I* was the one who put him in jail. I didn't expect any more from them after the way they treated Temoc and I during the few months we interacted with them in California. However, it did add to my mounting stress and confusion!

The next morning, I saw an older Lakota man wearing a t-shirt commemorating "The Longest Walk." I knew I had to talk to him then! I learned about the walk during my time at D-Q University – the place where the meetings were held to organize the first walk back in 1978. The 3,000-mile march, which began on Alcatraz Island, and ended in Washington D.C., was led by thousands of Native activists and their supporters from all nations! It served to call attention to the rights of Native people in the United States, and successfully shut down eleven anti-Indian bills introduced in Congress that threatened Treaty Rights. I offered that man a similar t-shirt, plus a piece of art, and he asked immediately if I had a place to stay. I shared my predicament with him, and he invited us to stay with him for a while. He introduced himself as Melvin Miner.

It turns out Melvin was an artist and Traditional historian. He loved to make all sorts of old-style Lakota art and instruments, which beautifully decorated his home. He showed me a large bag of hand-painted Medicine Bags he made and invited me to reach in and pull one out without looking, which would then belong to me! I did so, and pulled out a small white buckskin bag, painted with a yellow lightning bolt, and seven blue dots of hail. I smiled, but he looked confused. He thought it was strange because that Medicine Bag was considered Heyoka and Thunderbeing Medicine, but "it chose you," he explained, "so, it must belong to you." Later that night, I dreamt of a beautiful lightning storm. Thunder boomed, and hail splattered the ground all around me, but I wasn't scared. I just laughed and scooped up the hailstones, eating them like they were delicious little dots of candy! This dream became a recurring one that always brought me joy.

He also remarked on how unusual he thought I was. "Most Lakota women didn't look men in the eyes," he said, "but you do, and your glance is piercing!" He said he would always remember me for that and claimed that I was quite different from all the other women he knew. He taught me how to make tobacco prayer ties and showed me how he made his gourd rattles. Without a second thought, Melvin welcomed me into his home, and taught me about our history and art, without any expectations. He provided a safe, stable, and healthy place for Temoc and I to stay, and didn't ask anything from us, but just shared what little he had. He was a shining example to me of what it really meant to be an ikce wicasa, a simple Lakota man!

Soon, Eddie was released from jail and called me to pick him up. I asked Melvin if he could stay with us, and he welcomed him too. I remember though, after a few nights, that Melvin pulled me aside. He warned me that Eddie probably wasn't too good for me. I didn't listen though and kept Eddie around. I still felt a sense of loyalty to him as a Movement brother, so I remained committed to taking him to California.

Eddie and I spent a week contacting both of our families, desperately looking to borrow travel money, but no one could help at that point on either of our ends. So, we sought out other options. We tried to work with "Labor Ready," a day-by-day hiring agency for various hard labor work, but because I had Temoc to look after, and no one to watch him, I couldn't take that opportunity, nor any other, without adequate childcare. Eddie couldn't find work either because he didn't have his social security card, which was needed to get hired, even if only for the day. Our situation quickly became hopeless in this city, which I soon learned was notoriously known amongst Native people as "Racist City."

Melvin suggested that we go to the churches to ask for their help. At first, I strongly resisted, due to my disdain for the Church that it earned during my childhood experiences, but soon desperation forced me into entering their doors anyway! I sucked up my pride, buried my scorn, and with Temoc perched on my hip, walked into every church in Rapid City that I could find, genuinely seeking their help to get back home.

However, one by one they turned me down, claiming they "didn't help people leave," or that we "had to be members to get assistance," that they "needed to know us," or even most ridiculously, that we should instead "go to the Native church to get help." The lone church that supported us shared $30, which was a start, but only enough to buy Temoc some food! I used up what little I had left to travel to these churches just to get turned down!

In the meantime, I experienced first-hand the rampant racism that existed against our people in Rapid City. I never experienced obvious prejudice like that for being Native before besides what I was exposed to in my childhood. In California, it wasn't an issue, in fact, you were celebrated for having brown skin and Native heritage. Here, you were treated like the scum of the earth for it!

Furthermore, I saw that our Sacred Sites were turned into tourist attractions and given names such as "Sitting Bull's Crystal Caves" and

"Mount Rushmore." Our sacred Black Hills – upon which Rapid City was illegally established, based upon the 1868 Fort Laramie Treaty, which reserved the area for "the sole use of the Lakota, Dakota, and Nakota Nations until the end of time" – were exploited right in front of my eyes by European-American outsiders for profit. I saw gold mining stores that celebrated the gold mining period of the Black Hills, and I knew that this was why our Treaty was broken, and what our people were forced onto the reservations and murdered for! I saw for the first time how truly broken my people were, and who profited off their misfortune, and I grew beyond angry!

Experiencing this racism first-hand was an awakening and triggering experience. Furthermore, the realization that we were now trapped in this place because of it ushered in a feeling of hopelessness and further hatred towards the Church and the colonialist system it served, which obviously fed off our homelands and its broken people, who were now largely homeless and impoverished because of it! I hated to see that so many of my people used drugs and alcohol to numb the pain. It angered me to see that the descendants of those who murdered my people for gold still profited from it, while my people suffered the cost of it, and were treated like dirt in their own homelands!

I was lost in hopelessness, rage, and the insanity and backwardness of it all, and now I was destitute and struggling to feed my son. During all this chaos, I received a disturbing phone call. Melvin suddenly died of a heart attack! I was crushed by his passing, and now realized we had no place to stay. What were we going to do?

In mourning, I helped his family cook and clean during his funeral and paid my respects to this beautiful man who took us under his wing without any judgments or expectations. He was a good-hearted man, and I'd miss him dearly. His kindness and compassion were rare gems to find in an extremely sick world. As he was laid to rest into

Mother Earth, a sun dog, a rainbow around the sun, appeared to perfectly honor the life he used to bless this world!

After the funeral, which was a blessed distraction, the stress continued to mount from the situation Eddie and I found ourselves in. I now desperately begged the churches for help, still to no avail. We pawned anything we owned that had any value, and were quickly down to no money, no gas, nowhere to stay, and no hope of getting out of the situation.

Still, I said, "No!" the first time Eddie suggested that we break into one of these pompous churches, and "liberate" some material items to trade in for cash, so we could get home. I said no the second time too. But when he told me to "warrior up," something inside of me wanted to please him, yet something even bigger wanted to lash out at these churches and institutions that were the embodiment of the downfall of all Native Americans and most Indigenous people the world over – with a book (the Bible) in hand, they took the land!

We were in a desperate situation, and sometimes you must do things you normally wouldn't to survive. It's called duress! Like Tupac said, "I did what I had to do." Finally, after praying and receiving a "yes" from my heart, I agreed. The next night, Eddie and I parked behind Rapid City's Mount Calvary Baptist Church in the middle of the night. Eddie broke a window and crawled in easily. I followed him, while my heart raced, and Temoc slept peacefully in the car.

We quickly "liberated" a television, a laptop, a projector screen, and a DVD player. I tried to stop Eddie when he grabbed a trombone. "Hell no!" I yelled. "Leave that!" I knew from experience the personal connection to one's instrument, but he took it anyway. Finally, I wrote on a classroom board inside the church: "Thank you for your reparations for the breaking of the 1868 Fort Laramie Treaty with the Lakota,

Dakota, and Nakota Nations! As you probably don't know, your establishment has been built upon land that was promised solely to our Nations, for our use as we saw fit, until the end of time. Therefore, you are an illegal and illegitimate establishment upon our land. You continue to profit from our people's misfortune, and your government's lies and immoral actions. This is the next subject you can teach the children – the truth about the land upon which they stand!" Then, we took off.

Over the next few days, we took the items to pawn shops, and Eddie successfully exchanged most of it for cash. Finally, most of the money we needed to get out of there was in our hands! We didn't have any issues until he tried to sell the trombone to a music shop, which promptly refused to buy it. Shortly after we left, a Rapid City police unit pulled us over. My heart then sank into the earth as one of the most heartbreaking experiences of my life ensued.

The police approached our windows and interrogated us. "Did you steal this? Were you trying to pawn a stolen item?" I only responded with, "I am not under your jurisdiction. I am a descendant of the Lakota and Dakota Nations and therefore claim sovereignty upon my Treaty Land via the 1868 Fort Laramie Treaty, which is declared in the United States Constitution as the supreme law of the land." Despite not giving away any incriminating information, they arrested Eddie and required me to follow them to the station for further questioning. Some "liberated" items, like the trombone, were still in the car.

I went in to speak with the detective, and of course Temoc was with me like he always was. While waiting for the investigator, I allowed him to behave as he wanted to, climbing all over the chairs and even the table. Apparently, they watched this on the camera, and when Detective Todd Heinle finally entered the room, he immediately questioned my parenting. "Why do you allow your child to crawl all over everything and not make him sit still in the chair?" I laughed. "I wasn't aware that I was being brought in to be questioned about my parenting. Neither one of us asked or wanted to be here! Furthermore, he is a toddler and that's what toddlers do!" He tried to separate us by offering to have another officer watch him while he questioned me. "No." I quickly refused. "He'll be staying with me."

Detective Heinle rolled his eyes and took a seat. He questioned me about Eddie, asking if I was aware of a robbery at the Mount Calvary Baptist Church. "Did you help Eddie? Did you drive for him? Is he your boyfriend?" I answered each question the same: "We are standing upon Fort Laramie Treaty grounds, and furthermore we are in Rapid City, which is truly known as the Black Hills. The Black Hills have been especially reserved for the sole use of the Sioux Nation by way of the Fort Laramie Treaty of 1868, and thus, you have no jurisdiction over me, nor any of my guests, as you are an illegal occupant and officer upon our Treaty Land." He soon became visibly frustrated and left the room, huffing and puffing. But, before he left, he asked if he could search my car. "Absolutely not!" I declared. "You have no legal jurisdiction over me, my property, or my guest, Eddie, and I am not giving it to you via verbal consent!"

However, about thirty minutes later, Heinle came back into the room, and announced that I was being placed under arrest. He smugly declared that he broke into my vehicle – without first obtaining a warrant or my permission – and found what "appeared to be stolen items from a recent robbery at Mount Calvary Baptist Church." He informed me coldly that my son would be taken into the custody of CPS, while I was detained. I burst into tears and gripped my son tightly to me. I told him to be strong, and that I loved him very much! I had absolutely no clue that this would be the last time I'd have custody of my son to this very day! It was October 12, 2010, just over ten years ago at the time that I write this. Tears still stream down my face, as I still mourn my baby boy

Cuauhtémoc, who was only eighteen months old at the time of our separation.

I was then booked and placed under the "supervision" of Pennington County Jail (PCJ). At twenty-eight years old, this was my first time being in legal trouble, and my first time being arrested. I saw a Native girl in the "drunk tank" for the first time as well – a specialized holding cell within jails for intoxicated individuals to be held until they sober up. I learned shortly after that it was a common place for many Natives to "visit."

I noticed at once that every PCJ correctional officer was of European descent, and soon came to realize that every representative of the entire judicial system in Rapid City, from the lawyers and the police officers to the judges and even the juries, were also of European descent! It struck me harshly that 99% of the inmate population were of Lakota, Dakota, or Nakota descent! The imbalance was shockingly obvious.

The next morning, I was called before a Judge by video and charged with "Third Degree Burglary" and "Grand Theft by Receiving Stolen Property," two felony charges with a potential twenty-year prison sentence. I pled "not guilty." A $15,000 bail was placed upon me, with the full amount being required to bail out. I was considered a "flight risk" because I had "no immediate connections to the state," even though my family lived on the reservation on the other side of the state! That was conveniently not taken into consideration.

Within the first few days of being locked up, I confronted a correctional officer because she was such an arrogant asshole. "Who in the hell do you think you are?" I asked. Then, I promised her that, "One day, I'll stand where you are, and you'll stand where I am, and where will your false power be then?" She called in back up and threatened to mace and tase me if I refused to go into my cell for lock down. I stared at her for a long time and finally went. I was locked in my cell for the next three days.

I remember trying to reason with the girls in there. Why didn't they fight back? Didn't they see the numbers? A 99% Oceti Sakowin inmate population, compared to a 100% European law enforcement system? Most shrugged it off, saying that there was nothing they could do about it. It was "just the way that it was." But I never gave up imagining my escape! Every night, I dreamt of breaking out of there, however, I was also having terrible nightmares of my children being horribly abused by Izz, or of my stepfather trying to rape me again. Being in a physical jail snapped my psyche back to the prison of my childhood and my first relationship. I relived it every night in my dreams, and awoke in prison every day, for the next twenty-eight days.

Yet, I was given an incredibly beautiful dream one night that provided a much-needed relief from the nightmares that otherwise tortured me. In it, a mystical, tall white horse galloped up to me. He spoke gently to me, "Climb onto my back." I did and we galloped away! He took me in the darkness to a far-away land. I looked up into the sky of this strange land, and there I saw seven rainbows suspended in different locations above us. "Remember this place," he advised, and then my dream ended, giving me the hope I needed to carry on in the trying times that were ahead.

While incarcerated, I was given hour-long weekly visits with my son that were fully supervised by CPS. During our first visit, my internal battle truly began! I was taken into a dreary visitation room in the lower level of PCJ. Temoc was brought in, and instead of running to me to hug me as I envisioned, he threw himself on the ground and refused to allow me to touch him.

He was covered in bruises, scratches, and bite marks! I told him that I loved him, and continuously reached out for him, until he finally allowed me to hold him. What he freely expressed is how we both felt. The confusion and trauma of our separation had extremely adverse effects on the both of us. When he finally relaxed and released his tension into me, I rocked him in my lap and soothed him as best I could for the last half hour of our visit. Then, he was taken from me again.

I asked the CPS caseworker that brought him in about his injuries. It was obvious that it was physical assault, but she claimed that CPS "noted his markings and determined that they were nothing more than age-appropriate marks that were normal for a boy his age to have." I countered, "He never had markings like that when he was with me!" She agreed to disagree, and thus, discounted both his markings and my concern over them. Then, she told me that CPS had full plans to return my son to me after I was released from jail.

Periodically, these CPS caseworkers came in to question my ideas about parenting in private interviews. They told me that I was "one of the best mothers that they ever met," and ensured that my son would be reunited with me soon. My comments on my son's markings and traumatized behavior continued to be "noted," but were otherwise ignored.

I looked forward to every weekly visit with my son, but with each visit his behavior and anger towards me worsened, and his markings became more obvious and serious. He even came in one week with an open cut under his eye, where he was obviously struck, most likely with a closed fist! Every time I saw him, he had bite marks all over him, and one time, his lip was cut, swollen, and badly bruised. Each time I questioned these markings, the caseworkers robotically informed me that the markings were "age-indicative and that I had no reason, nor did CPS have any reason to be concerned." They tried to divert my concern by continuously ensuring that he would be returned to me immediately after I was released.

After twenty-eight days of being held on a continuously high bond of $15,000, I was finally taken in for my second court hearing, and my bond was lowered to $1000. My father quickly bailed me out, and I was released. I immediately contacted CPS to have my child returned, but instead they informed me that he was now in their temporary custody! The morning before, a court hearing was held, that I was neither informed of nor present for, during which a CPS "Abuse and Neglect" Petition was filed against me. Evidence presented against me in this hearing incriminated me, stating that I neglected my son because of my twenty-eight-day detainment, and therefore, CPS requested that my child be retained in their custody, and that my rights to him be "temporarily suspended in the best interests of the child."

Without allowing me to represent myself or my child – in other words, without giving us any due process of law – Judge Davis signed the order and thus, Temoc remained in the custody of Child Protective Services! Once again, I was given only once-a-week, hour-long supervised visits with my baby and additionally, ordered to satisfy the requirements set forth by CPS to have my legal rights as his parent restored. In this hearing, Judge Davis also immediately terminated Tonio's parental rights to our child, simply due to his status as being a citizen of Mexico.

Crushed, I dedicated myself to doing whatever I could to have my son returned to me! The night that I was released from jail and received the news about Temoc, I traveled to Bear Butte, a Sacred Site to the Oceti Sakowin. I chose an isolated hill to sit on for hours and prayed until I finally fell asleep. I awoke just before dusk to the hoots of a white owl that perched right above me. A light snow fell like wildfire ash, and I shivered uncontrollably. It was time to head back down the mountain.

I knew I needed to understand more about my legal rights through federal and state laws. I spent most of every day after that in the Rapid City Public Law Library, researching Indian law, CPS's rules and regulations, state law, and even international treaties that regulated the rights of Indigenous peoples, mothers, and children. I discovered that a myriad of laws were violated in our case, and that right from the beginning, the detective entered my vehicle without my permission or my consent – under the "color of law" – and thus, illegally detained myself, my son, and Eddie! Furthermore, all evidence gathered against us, which was used to place a high bond, seal the indictment, place two felony charges, and to eventually file an abuse and neglect case against me to remove my son, were also illegally attained. I learned that we had certain supposedly "unalienable rights" to a fair and speedy trial, and to due process of law, and that my son and I were deprived of those rights throughout the entire duration of our case!

After speaking to my lawyer, Bruce Ellison, about these violations, I realized that he was unwilling to fight on my behalf. Instead, he encouraged me to plead guilty to the Grand Theft charges, so I decided to fire him and stand on my own. I compiled lists of all the violations that were committed in our case and presented them to Judge Davis via proper court procedures, and in correct "pro per" status. I intended to take the case to trial. However, all the documents I filed while in "pro per" status were blatantly disregarded and ignored, teaching me that if you didn't pay for – or more correctly, weren't able to afford – a high profile lawyer, then you didn't win! Point blank. In other words, the amount of justice you received was related to the amount of dollars you paid, and the amount you "played their game." I didn't meet their standards in those categories.

I also provided CPS with copies of the violations of their own rules and regulations they committed through the removal of my son. They were also ignored. I soon realized that no matter what evidence I found against the State's actions towards us, that the State would do whatever the fuck it pleased, because truth was, we had no rights in their eyes. It was all an illusion right from the get-go, and I learned it the hard way.

Thus, I publicized my case, using social media as a platform to share what my son and I were going through. This led me to Gwen, a fierce advocate against the removal of Native children via Child Protective Services. She opened my eyes to numerous cases where Native children were removed from their biological parents, with little cause or sound legal justification, and placed within Euro-American foster care placements. She labeled it as "cultural genocide," and she was right! Gwen advocated on our behalf, and we submitted every legal document, in any form possible, to have Temoc returned, and both cases dismissed. She also encouraged me to stay with her throughout this entire process, thus becoming a major support system, and a good friend.

A potent dream came to me, after weeks of pouring myself into researching, preparing, and filing legal paperwork on Temoc's behalf. In it, Shawn, my older brother who passed, stood over my shoulder, and observed my calculations. He was considered a mathematical genius during his lifetime, so I trusted him when he told me that I "was doing it all wrong!" He grabbed my calculations and reworked them for me. When he finished, he set them proudly down before me and exclaimed, "There, it's all fixed now!" I looked down and saw that the corrected calculations had transformed into a perfect tile of a white buffalo calf! My brother smiled smugly at me, then, I woke up.

I had another dream soon after that reminded me of my original home, which I forgot existed. In it, I walked into a restaurant. I didn't recognize anyone on the lower level, so I walked upstairs. There, I saw spiritual leaders and mystics from all cultures. They stared at me intensely as I walked by them, then each of them smiled and enthusiastically welcomed me home! An Indian warrior, who felt remarkably familiar to me, and who was intensely handsome, tall, and solidly strong, walked up to me and embraced me with a big bear hug. He wore a single eagle feather in his hair and a painted buffalo robe around his shoulders. He grabbed my hand and took me outside. Then, he pointed up into the star-filled sky, and shared Star Nation stories with me. He held me close to him as we huddled together as one underneath his beautiful buffalo robe. The stars sparkled in his eyes, and I knew he was the one that I loved. I was awoken eventually from that dream too. However, it strengthened my heart enough to carry on through the hell my son and I were in.

In the meantime, I followed every "reasonable request" CPS made of me to grant Temoc's return. I obtained more than suitable housing, attended every visitation, and received counseling in the form of horse therapy. However, when CPS overstepped its legal boundaries and demanded, out of the blue, that I begin taking random drug tests, I refused, not because I was using drugs, but because I refused to be their bitch! I already knew through my legal research that they had no legal standing to ask me to take a drug test in the first place. No drug or alcohol use was connected to either the criminal or abuse and neglect case, and according to state statutes, the use of either was the only condition which allowed for drug testing.

I finally knew for sure that they were fishing for absolutely any information to hold against me! So, I calmly refused in writing, stating that they overstepped their legal boundaries, and cited the statute that told me so. However, I got tested anyway just to prove to them that they had nothing on me and passed without a trace of substance use! Nevertheless, CPS held my child from me, and the weeks painfully grew into months, as he continued to come into our weekly visits laden with the signs of physical and emotional trauma – which CPS continued to disregard no matter how much I complained! My will and soul were tested and drained beyond their limits. I began to falter.

One chilly day, I sat alone in the gorgeous Black Hills cabin that I rented specifically to appease CPS. That day, the entirety of the stress, trauma, and realization that my son wasn't going to be released to me, no matter what I did, finally hit me! I broke down as my body contorted with sobs, and I gasped for breath. I couldn't handle the pain of losing my kids anymore! It was too much to bear. I wanted to die and contemplated it thoroughly.

In the end, the only thing that pulled me out of that despondency was the thought of my children as they filled my mind. I imagined the pain contorting their expressions as they found out I killed myself. "No way!" I decided. I pulled myself up off the bed, wiped my tears, grabbed my C'anupa, and prayed in the sunlight. I asked for guidance, the strength to continue despite my pain, and clarity to help me understand the purpose of this suffering.

The next day, I met my neighbor who lived up the hill. Also Lakota, he confessed that he too was having an extremely difficult time. He was trying to cope with the loss of his wife to cancer. She was the love of his life. On the same day as me, he pulled out his C'anupa *and* prayed for strength and guidance. Our prayers showed us that we had friends close by. He introduced me to the beautiful art he created, which channeled his pain and transformed it, reinforcing the idea that our creative energy is a powerful, healing force.

Soon after, I was contacted by Chaska Denny, the founder of the "Sovereign Nation of the Dahcotah Sioux Nation of Indians," whose establishment was based upon the Fort Laramie Treaty of 1868. He saw some of my posts about my case with Temoc and stood up to offer the support of his Nation, of our Nation. Thus, I began working with the Dahcotah Sioux Nation of Indians, which advocated on our behalf to enforce our sovereignty and to demand Temoc's return.

However, all our efforts to declare our sovereignty were ignored by the State once again, so we prepared to take the case before the World Court, the International Court of Justice that is the principal judicial organ of the United Nations. Unfortunately, Chaska suddenly passed, and thus, all efforts involved with the Dahcotah Sioux Nations of Indians ceased. Chaska did all that he could to protect Temoc and I from cultural genocide during our time of need and taught me that the struggle to assert sovereignty is an uphill battle that seems to rarely succeed.

As our case progressed, it became clear that the State was not going to return my child, no matter what approach I took to get him back. So, I asked a friend of mine to follow the CPS caseworker while she transported Temoc back to his foster home after our visit. As soon as he gave me their address, I drove straight over and knocked on their door. A European couple answered timidly. I announced who I was and demanded that they return my son to me at once!

They refused, saying that he was now "in a Godly place," and that he was not safe with me. "How dare you judge me!" I scolded. "You know nothing of me. My son being placed with you is the epitome of cultural genocide! Furthermore, my son carries evidence of abuse and physical assault on his body, and in his behavior, and as his mother, I demand that he be returned to me for safekeeping!" Lightning struck almost immediately in front of the house as I said this!

This couple, however, took it as a sign from God that they were "doing the right thing" by keeping my son from me. I laughed at them and reminded them of their disconnection. "Do you know the power of the Wakinyan, the Thunderbeing? Do you even know what a Wakinyan is? How could you? For you are a stranger to this land, a stranger who's earned your place here upon the blood, bones, and theft of the land of our people upon whom your people have benefited for generations! You do not understand natural law, otherwise you wouldn't violate it by keeping my son from me. Why in the world would the Wakinyan," I questioned them, "who is not bound by human law, side with you?" They had nothing to say after this, and only threatened to call the police to report me for trespassing. I told them I was giving them a chance to stand on the right side of history, but they made their choice. Then, I left, not wanting to make my case worse with yet another arrest!

After this, I had just one more weekly visit with Temoc. When I walked out to leave, I saw two beautiful bald eagles that circled in the sky overhead! I thought it was a sign that my constant prayers were answered, and that I would soon have Temoc returned to me. However, this was the last time I would see Temoc to this day. Their message was an entirely different one: a reminder that our prayers would be heard despite nothing seeming to go in our favor, and to hold on to our strength until they were answered, even if it took decades, or a lifetime, to see it through.

Finally, the day of my trial arrived! I walked into the court room with my head held high and my back tall and straight. All my documents were meticulously prepared, and my statements ready to go. Yet, I saw no one present except for the notorious, red-faced Judge Davis. He smugly announced that my trial was cancelled, pending my now "court-ordered psychiatric evaluation!" My mental health, and therefore, ability to represent myself, were now in question due to my unexpected arrival at Temoc's foster location, and my later demand for his return. It was incredibly ironic that my sanity was now being questioned because I was willing to do anything to have my child returned to me, especially knowing that he was being abused while CPS did nothing to protect him!

I left the courtroom in utter frustration. After processing the delay of my trial, and discussing this new information with my support team, I decided to announce to the State via the proper paperwork, that I would no longer willfully comply with their requests to attend court hearings. Why should I follow their laws, rules, and regulations when they clearly didn't follow their own? I chose to step fully into my sovereignty, and to take the matter before the World Court.

I soon met Duane Martin, a Lakota Warrior Society leader, who began to advocate on our behalf. Also known as Canupa Gluha Mani, he and his Warrior Society supported my efforts to enforce our sovereignty. However, what I thought was solely a professional relationship between us, took a nasty turn as he picked me up one night, carried me into his bedroom, and tried to rape me. He "explained" his behavior with his grandmother's teaching, "When he sees beauty, he must take it for himself." I did not agree! I pled with him to stop, but he ignored me.

A few days before, he grabbed one of my hairs without my permission and wrapped it around his eagle feather – which I later realized was the beginning of some sort of spiritual curse, or "hold" against me. Even though he touched me without my permission or my desire to be touched, I felt oddly drawn to be with him anyways. It took me many months to realize that he preyed on me spiritually and used his sacred instruments and the power that came with them to do so!

This man soon revealed his true colors as an insidious liar who tried to rule over women. At events, he refused to listen to a woman if she did not "wear a skirt," as if her choice of dress determined the worth of her voice! Men were never held to the same standards or expectations. He screamed in vile language during every speech, and years later was accused of the molestation of his own daughter. He was also hopelessly obese. He was extremely controlling, and I became sickened by his compulsive lies, vile outbursts, and hypocritical manner of attacking everyone else, without first correcting his own flaws.

Eventually, I jumped out of a moving vehicle to get away from him. My sacred items were in that car, and my original birth certificate with my biological father on it. He refused to give them back, threatening that I'd have to "talk to his Elders" to get my belongings. I didn't have the energy for that, to go up against his Elders who were fed all his lies! I just lost my son. Those things mattered little to me now, especially because I knew it was a trap. So, I let go once again of sacred items – the eagle feathers I found on my reservation, some of my dance regalia, and my original birth certificate that was the only proof I had at the time of my "American Indian – Sioux" heritage.

During the time I struggled to escape Duane's insanity, my parental rights to Temoc were terminated. It happened during a final hearing that I did not attend for several reasons. To start with, I already notified the courts via affidavits that I declined their requests of me to attend any further hearings due to their inability to follow their own law, and due to my right to enforce my own sovereignty. Secondly, if I entered the courtroom for the termination hearing, I'd be arrested.

When I chose to assert my sovereignty and refused to further take part in their system and play their game – because it obviously did not serve us – a warrant was issued for my arrest. Therefore, I knew that I was "damned," whether I went to the court hearing or not! If I went, I'd be arrested, and it would be held against me as it already was in the removal of my child in the first place. I knew they would not restore my parental rights no matter what I did. They made their intentions painfully clear throughout the entire process, and my son paid the highest cost!

What I find most absurd is that the court hearing to terminate my parental rights was held *before* I was convicted of, or pled guilty to, the criminal charges upon which the abuse and neglect case were based. How is this even possible? Where was our supposedly "unalienable right" to "due process of law" as is written in the United States Constitution? Why were my parental rights to my child terminated before I was convicted of a crime? This proves that some of us are actually "guilty until proven innocent," rather than "innocent until proven guilty."

Held in a chokehold, I fought to uphold my sovereignty and legal rights, while they extorted me with my own child. I was damned either way. If I showed, my parental rights might not have been terminated, yet I'd be detained due to the warrant, giving them the fuel they needed to go ahead and terminate my parental rights. If I didn't show, my parental rights would be terminated, but I'd remain in the free world until they caught up to me. I accepted the risk and planned to spend every free moment I had left fighting for my boy, and hopefully to have our case overturned via an international lawsuit.

After evading Duane's insanity and side-stepping the court system, I began traveling to the Pine Ridge Reservation with friends I made while in PCJ, so that I could hide out and continue processing my plan. Meanwhile, my face was plastered all over the "Most Wanted" signs in Rapid City, so I wasn't safe there anymore. In Pine Ridge, I was introduced to Merle, a talented Lakota ledger artist, and through him, I met my soon to be hunka, or adopted family. The women especially took me in with open arms. They taught me how to make gabubu bread, a Lakota-style skillet bread, and how to bead. Most importantly, they gave me much needed shelter and safety. I traveled everywhere with Merle, helping him to sell his masterpieces. He gave me a percentage of his sales for transporting him. In the meantime, I stayed on the lookout for support, funds, and options to get Temoc out of the hands of the State, along with a safe place to hide him.

I met with a woman on the rez who heard my story and wanted to start a Women's Warrior Society using the story behind the tattoo etched on my left hand. The Mayan symbol for "nineteen," it stood for my dedication to the path asked of me during my C'anupa Pipe dream. This woman, who called herself "Pte San Win," – which loosely translates to White Buffalo Calf Woman – later turned against me, smearing my name for years to come because, she claimed, I was "a white woman posing as a Native woman for gain." The gain that she thought I received by "pretending" to be Native always perplexed me. I mean, what benefit did I ever gain from being Native? All I can remember is pain, trauma, and suffering beyond suffering! I'll never really understand what she thought I was taking from her, simply by being myself.

The night before our meeting, I dreamt of a dangerous woman. I watched as she dug out a deep pit and filled it with black water. She then sent children into that hole, leading them down the wrong road. I confronted her in the dream, calling her out for misleading the children and for playing both sides. After meeting "Pte San Win," I realized that she was the woman in the dream from the night before. I saw her as she hustled drugs on the rez to the youth, while simultaneously leading those same children into Ceremony and resistance movements. She revealed during our Women's Warrior Society meeting, that she was waiting to have *the* "White Buffalo Calf Woman dream," where she expected to be given a Pipe and a responsibility. She was the first of many female false prophets I witnessed, both Lakota and not, who purported themselves to be the reincarnation of White Buffalo Woman herself.

One beautiful morning, as I visited with Merle, Iktomi walked in the door. He was a tall, young, and handsome Dakota warrior. We connected instantly and talked for hours. I learned that his parents were spiritual leaders in the community, and that their family started the Dakota 38 + 2 Memorial ride, an annual winter horse ride that began on the Lower Brule Indian Reservation, and ended in Mankato, Minnesota. It honored and brought attention to our thirty-eight Dakota ancestors that were executed in a mass hanging by Abraham Lincoln on December 26, 1865. The "+2" honored the additional Dakota warriors hung on November 11, 1865.

Iktomi and I started seeing each other, and soon I moved in with him and his family on Pine Ridge. I used to pray with them in their Inipi lodge and create beautiful Traditional Dakota art with his family. One evening after lodge, he told me that his dad saw the spirit of a young boy, Jonathan Quick Bear, who committed suicide a year earlier, enter the Inipi and sit down next to me. That haunted me for years. Why did that boy send that message to all of us? Why was he following me?

Eventually I understood that Jonathan's spirit still roamed the Earth. He was only eleven when he took his life, and the tragedy it brought to his community and family is still felt to this day. His grandmother told me that she found him and had to cut him down. Through tears, she yelled in her pain about the day before, when he told her that his white teacher yelled at him in front of all his classmates and embarrassed him. Next thing she knew, he was gone, and she found him! She was never okay again after that. She painfully, yet fondly recalled that he was an otherwise happy kid, and the relationship he had with his horses was unlike any other. "Boy, he could make those horses dance," she exclaimed, "and they loved him!" They were also never the same after he passed.

I think I was connected to that boy because when I came to Pine Ridge, I took care of his horses. Even if it was freezing cold and snowing outside, I was still out there every morning making sure those horses had fresh water. I also used to ride Stranger, the tall Appaloosa that was Johnny's favorite, that also quickly became my favorite. He was so beautiful with his gray, black, and white coloration, and those mystical black spots that dotted his otherwise white rump! I used to ride him with Johnny's sisters and cousins. We rode for miles a day, bareback, doubled, and even tripled up, laughing, racing, and joking!

I also taught those young girls how to Fancy Shawl dance. We spent a lot of time together. I wanted my own kids around, but couldn't have them, and they wanted parents, who just weren't around. So, it worked for all of us. I used to hang out with those horses and girls whenever I felt alone. They became my best friends on the rez. The days we spent chasing and catching those half-wild horses, then riding everywhere on them, became our temporary escapes from the chaos that otherwise surrounded us.

Iktomi had a beautiful, incredibly well-trained horse of his own. We saddled up every other day, and rode thru the hills doubled up, with Iktomi in the saddle, and me riding bareback as I held onto him from behind, somehow staying on as we ducked and dived, galloping through those hilly plains. Iktomi was always on the lookout for a deer, so he rode up front with his shotgun in case he got the opportunity to bring home some good meat. We really did have a *lot* of fun. I suppose that's what I needed after months of practically dying inside during my incarceration and the loss of my little boy.

However, I still panicked, constantly brainstorming ways that I could get Temoc out of the foster care system in Rapid City. I asked Iktomi to help me liberate Temoc so I could hide him on the rez. He could not support it though, and although I didn't understand that at the time, I can see now how much I was really asking of him. I don't blame him anymore for not being able to be there for me in that way. It would never have worked out anyway. Regardless, at this point, I realized that his love for me wasn't as deep as I wanted it to be, so I let him go, and we drifted our separate ways.

In the meantime, December 26 drew near, and after learning about my own connection as a descendant of the Dakota who were displaced after the hanging, I committed to joining the Dakota 38 + 2 Ride. I carried a fellow rider with me as I traveled across the rez to meet up with the other riders. Merle found out I was passing through and called. He wanted to know if I could pick him up, then drop him on the other side of the rez. When I arrived, the cloud of turmoil from the fight he was having with his lady still clung to the air. My presence angered her even more. Merle told me she was threatened by me. This jealousy pushed her to call the cops right after I picked Merle up to report that I was transporting drugs across the reservation.

Fifteen minutes later, two BIA cops pulled us over. They asked if they could search the vehicle. A few months before, I put my vehicle in Merle's name to keep my name from being traced through the system, and to prevent my warrant from being pulled up. Thus, Merle had the authority to give consent to search the car and allowed them to! The cops found the pound of weed he had in his bags, which I didn't know about, and then arrested both of us because I was driving! The woman who rode with me, Mel Jean McGregor, saw all of this, and advocated on my behalf via social media.

I was charged with "Drug Possession with Intent to Sell," and imprisoned again on felony charges, this time in the Pine Ridge Adult Offenders Facility, and this time for something I truly didn't do. Merle, my supposed hunka uncle, was soon bailed out, and told the prosecuting attorneys that the pound was mine, allowing me to take the fall for his actions. I was majorly derailed, and instead of riding with the Dakota 38 riders, was forced to celebrate the 2012 New Year behind bars on the Pine Ridge Reservation. Once again, I was held on a high bond that was difficult to pay.

After about six weeks of my incarceration passed by, I rashly confronted a correctional officer, calling her out for treating her own people like trash. I accused her of acting like the colonizer, and scolded her, telling her she should be ashamed of herself. Apparently, my outburst required my subsequent solitary confinement. As two officers came to transport me to my place of quarantine, one aggressively grabbed my wrist, and I reacted without a second thought, punching her and twisting her arm behind her back before she even knew what happened! I spent my last week of that nearly two-month lock up in solitary, my only break being a visit from my lawyer, Jo-Anne Spotted Bear. She came to make me an offer that showed she was obviously working with Merle and the prosecutors: "Admit that you transported drugs through the Pine Ridge Reservation with intent to sell, sign this document, and you are free to go, as long as you never return to Pine Ridge again." I laughed in disbelief at her! I said, "Hell fucking no! They weren't mine! I'm not taking the fall for this!"

I refused to sign and returned to solitary. I never worked with Spotted Bear again. Even to this day, we just nod as we pass by one another. Another lawyer came in to speak to me at the beginning of the case. He tried to prove to me that I wasn't "Indian" based solely upon my last name, which at the time was still Newburg. I said, "It's an adopted name, you idiot. Haven't you ever heard of adoption, or marriage?"

These Tribal lawyers based most of their information on gossip, rumors, and little thought, insight, or research. Additionally, the Pine Ridge legal system could not lawfully hold me for *any* length of time if I wasn't truly "Indian." The prosecuting attorney knew this and gathered enough information on my Native descent to hold me for the two months that they did. She did more work to research who I truly was than either of my lawyers did, or anyone who has ever claimed that they were entitled to treat me with indifference because they didn't think I was "Indian enough."

Tribes have no authority over anyone who isn't of Indian descent, thus they cannot legally prosecute any non-Indian who comes onto the reservation and commits a crime, which has become a huge problem on the reservations. white men who know this have repeatedly come onto the reservations and committed heinous sexual crimes against Native women and children and are not prosecuted because the Tribe is not legally enabled to do so. Thus, Native women and children are easily kidnapped, and sex trafficked, or raped and murdered, and the Tribe can do nothing about it because they are legally *incapable* of prosecuting non-Indian assailants.

Therefore, the only way I could be held in the Pine Ridge jail for the two months that I was, is because I was "Indian enough" for its legal system to have authority over me, otherwise they would've been forced to let me go immediately, no matter what I did. I've faced this issue my whole life, of being "Indian enough" when it came to being targeted by the justice system, white supremacists, and predators, but not being "Indian enough" for some people when it came to receiving credit for my actions in activism, restoring Traditions, or using my voice to speak on behalf of my people. I've finally concluded that I know who I am and where I come from, and other's opinions and ignorance of that cannot matter to me or hold me back. I do not have to prove who I am to anyone, especially when their opinions are based on assumptions, lies, and gossip.

In the meantime, I fucking hated being locked up in Pine Ridge. Not only did I not do what I was accused of, but I was arrested while on my way to a spiritual horse ride, a Ceremony! Furthermore, the man that I trusted as an uncle set me up to take the fall for him. I felt like I was being punished by Creator. I prayed constantly, and finally received guidance that I was not being held there in spiritual punishment, but instead to be shown the worst side of the disease of separation. I came to understand that part of my mission on Earth was to experience extreme injustice and suffering over the course of most of my life, and that one day, it would serve a great purpose.

While I was in solitary, I was dealt another huge blow. It came in the form of court papers served from the State of Indiana that announced their intentions to have my custody rights to my three oldest children removed, and full custody given to Izz, due to a neglect case that was filed *against him*. The kids broke into a neighbor's house to find food, plus, they weren't enrolled in school, and CPS was now involved, but it was *my* rights to the children, not his, that were now in the motion of being removed due to my current state of incarceration. It was also written in the paperwork that Indiana CPS communicated with South Dakota CPS, and thus, Indiana CPS claimed it knew all it needed to about me based on the previous case with Temoc. I didn't stand a chance!

I almost lost my sanity at that point, but instead used my voice to keep from sinking too low. I sang with all my pride and strength throughout my imprisonments. During my solitary confinement in Pine Ridge, I sang all day with the guy who was locked up next to me. It was the only way we kept our sanity through the long days of having absolutely nothing else to do. Everything was taken from us. We weren't even given soap, or toothpaste and toothbrushes! We had nothing to read and nothing to write with. We had only our cells with their hard beds, and in it, our thoughts to pass the time. So, we sang, like caged birds, to free our spirits and our minds.

I did, however, find some things to enjoy during my incarceration, mainly the weekly serving of warm frybread and wojapi, a delicious pudding, or jam, made from chokecherries, one of our Traditional staple foods. We did eat well, at least compared to how they fed us in Pennington County Jail. That good food introduced me to BJ, one of the inmate workers that helped serve our food trays during mealtime. He took a liking to me and hooked me up with extra food and supplies. He also snuck notes under my food tray that declared my beauty and his confessions of love that were sparked from the first moment he saw me.

In my state, I started having feelings for him too, but even then, I wasn't sure about meeting up with him outside of jail, because there was something off about him. But he kept sending those notes, and my broken heart felt a glimmer of attraction and hope, as he continued to take a risk for me, relentlessly slipping me extra food and commissary during this lonely lock up, especially while I was in solitary.

When my dad found out about my solitary confinement, he pushed as hard as he could to finally bail me out, raising $1,000 on my behalf. However, this was the second $1,000 that was gathered for me. Several of my friends, especially Shell, fundraised on my behalf after Mel, the woman who rode with me, let everyone know about my unjust arrest and promised that she was working hard to raise the money to bail me out. Yet, after my friends sent her the money, she stole it for herself and left me to sit in jail. Once she received the money, after pretending to advocate on my behalf, she laughed and called those who raised the money for me "bitches," while she took off down to Mexico with the money. So, my dad decided to bring in the money his damn self to ensure that I was released.

Just after getting bailed out, I attended a pre-hearing phone interview with an Indiana CPS caseworker. He asked if I knew about the "substantiated" sexual abuse case against Izz with our daughter. "I was the one who initiated that case," I replied angrily, "but I was told it was *un*substantiated, and that CPS was not going to press any charges! Why am I now being told *years later* that it was substantiated?" There wasn't much of a reply to this. The phone interview was soon over, and a few weeks later, the hearing was held. My custody of my three older children was quickly removed, and full custody granted to Izz.

What I found most shocking, was that this decision was made after CPS admitted that it substantiated the sexual abuse case against Israel with our daughter. Full custody was granted to him after CPS had to *force* him to get the kids into school, and after he was investigated for *proven* neglect! After all the proven abuse and neglect Izz committed against our children, he was still considered a "more-fit" parent than me. Furthermore, I was granted only supervised visits with my children, with him as the supervisor. I couldn't believe the insanity of it!

I called CPS one more time after this to report another case of suspected abuse by Izz against my daughter, after seeing her constant suicidal posts on Twitter, and after seeing him rape her in my dreams. I noticed that she showed the same signs I did as a kid around the time I started being molested by my stepfather, when I didn't want to wear girl's clothes. She also shaved half of her head, a drastic change for a ten-year-old girl. Yet, once again the case went nowhere. Izz called me his "enemy," and told the kids I abandoned them, and that I wanted them to go to foster care, therefore, I was their enemy too. Even their grandmother perpetuated this. Any time I visited, she told them they better not go with me because, "I'd abandon them again." I had now lost custody of all my children, and it was clear to me that they were in unhealthy and dangerous placements, and furthermore, CPS and the court systems were the enforcement behind it. I felt powerless to do anything to change it. So, I lost my hope and faith and slipped into a deep depression.

After my release from Pine Ridge Jail, I took the bus to my hunka auntie's home in Evergreen. It just so happened that BJ was released at the same time as me and rode the same bus. Thus, we met for the first time outside of jail, and another seemingly destined romance began in my life. However, after only one week of seeing him, on my thirtieth birthday, he beat me so badly that I couldn't stand up by myself for days! He was so insecure, that me talking to any other male was perceived as a serious threat that sent him into a demonic rage. So, after he heard me talk to my twin brother on the phone, he beat me mercilessly, punching me in the face with a closed fist, hitting me in the ribs like I was another man, and kicking me after I fell.

After only three weeks of dating him, I feared for my life. I almost never left the house, didn't look at or address another man, and was forced to give up all access to my own phone and belongings. He tried to control every aspect of my life! I was terrified that he was going to kill me. I begged him to stop drinking, but he never did, and in the meantime, I took a beating every day because of the control those "spirits" had over him.

Finally, the day came when he left me alone with my phone for a few minutes. I called my hunka auntie, told her what was happening, and asked if she'd come get me. She said she'd be right over! I also called my dad and twin, hurriedly telling them what happened. I gathered my few belongings and threw them under a mattress behind the house. BJ was just coming back up the driveway and didn't notice. Just then, Auntie pulled up and asked for me. "Go see her bitch!" he snarled in a whisper at me. I grabbed my stuff, limped-ran to her car, and jumped in.

She raced off, and I left him in my dust that day as she took me straight to the hospital.

I was evaluated with a broken rib, several severely bruised ribs, a black eye, swollen lips, and deep bruises all over my body. The nurse told me that they "weren't required to report the abuse, and that little could be done about it." The ironic reality is that I quickly forgave BJ, despite receiving the worst physical beatings of my life from him, because I understood *why* he did what he did to me, although I never excused his behavior, nor did I ever return to him!

I realized that he was infected with the ultimate disease of separation, caused by generations of genocide and colonization. Firsthand, I discovered how this sickness claimed our beautiful, strong warriors and transformed them into tools of the colonizer – men who do not protect their women, but who instead threaten their emotional, mental, physical, and spiritual health. I recognized in BJ the final stage of genocide, when the oppressed becomes the oppressor, and I knew that I was lucky to have survived.

Many women on the reservations and in our Indigenous communities, regrettably, aren't as fortunate, and become further victims added to the extensive list of Missing and Murdered Indigenous Women, an epidemic that is grossly ignored and unacknowledged. It is easy to see why, based upon the nurse's reaction. She brushed me out of the hospital without reporting the abuse, turning me loose with no protection, while my assailant was free to continue his behavior without consequence. If it weren't for my hunka auntie, my dad, and my twin, who made it possible for me to leave that day, I don't think I would have survived.

My dad and brother soon arrived. We went to Merle's house to retrieve my car and belongings, but when we got there, he refused to give me my keys. I broke into my car anyway and saw my things were strewn all over the floor. Most disturbing, pictures of my precious kids had fallen to the ground and were stained with the imprints of dirty shoes. Merle took all my dance regalia, feathers, sacred items, and anything of value, and sold them while I was locked up for his bullshit.

I demanded the return of my keys, but he refused. "I'm taking your car, cause you're a fucking white woman, and you deserve it." My hands were tied. My dad and brother forced me to leave Pine Ridge that day, with nothing but bruises, my survival story, and a broken heart. My dad took me under his wing then, with the promise of a new beginning, as he carried me with him to his world in Texas.

Figure 12. My twin teases me, lightening my mood. My face is swollen and bruised, and I can't lift my right arm because of a broken rib.

CHAPTER SEVEN

TEXAS HONEY

It was February of 2012 when I arrived safely in Texas with my dad. I still moved slowly as I recovered from my injuries, but I was beyond excited to be there! My dad promised that I could work with him on the honeybee farm he managed, and I was stoked to finally gather the resources I needed to pursue a case in the World Court against the State of South Dakota! I was determined to assert our sovereignty and to have my children returned. Although I still had a warrant issued for my arrest in South Dakota, I didn't worry about it and focused instead on this new opportunity. I believed that Texas would be good for me.

Shortly after arriving, I contacted Dr. Curtis Doebbler, a renowned international human rights lawyer. I explained the details of my case and asked if he would consider representing me in a human rights violation lawsuit against the State of South Dakota before international courts. I received a reply a few days later. My case "passed all the initial checks," so he was interested in meeting with me! I hadn't started work with the honey company yet, so I borrowed money from my dad and booked a flight to New York City to meet with Dr. Doebbler.

During our meeting, Dr. Doebbler suggested that my case had a "good fighting chance to win," and furthermore, if it did win, had the potential to become "a landmark case that could help all Native American families faced with the same situation." He accepted the case "pro bono," but required that I clear up my warrant before we took any further action. As we parted ways, he looked at me kindly, and with a slight smile and raised eyebrow, shared his opinion. "You are exceptionally intelligent. I see all the paperwork and research you've done. You could one day *be* the judge if you wanted to! You should consider going back to school." His belief in me made an enormous impact, and I left feeling inspired and renewed with hope.

I returned to Texas, excited by the prospect of a future international case, and by the immediate promise of new work with the honeybees. However, the employment my dad's boss promised us still wasn't happening. It turns out his wife was extremely against me working! My dad told me that she was threatened by me and didn't want me around her husband. Her jealousy kept the boss from hiring me, even though he promised my dad I could start working as soon as I arrived, which is the entire reason I was brought to Texas in the first place!

Therefore, I was left alone in my dad's small trailer with his girlfriend Connie for company throughout the days, while I waited for work. I didn't enjoy her energy at all. Her presence thoroughly irritated me, and I shared this feeling with my dad. She had sica, or bad, energy. I even told him about the strange dream I had a few months before, way before I felt her sica vibes. In it, I beat the living daylights out of her! In just a few weeks, what before was a peaceful respite from Pine Ridge and Rapid City, soon became an equally toxic situation, only with different faces, colors, and names.

I soon reached my threshold of being able to tolerate Connie on the day she coldly announced that my dad "didn't really like me but just pretended to." I stood straight up and clocked her square in the face! She struck right back, and we tumbled through the trailer. I unleashed all my stress, tension, and disdain upon her. She screamed out grotesquely sexual things about my father to me, as if we were in that sort of competition. So, I choked her with one hand, while holding both of her wrists behind her back with the other, until I realized I was going to kill her, so let up a bit. Then, I kicked her out of my dad's trailer and told her stay the fuck out of my sight before I finished the job! She left at once.

For weeks leading up to this point, since my arrival, I was forced to see her addiction to pills and substances, which led her to believe that it was acceptable to sit in the trailer all day and do nothing but surf the internet while my dad worked. He took care of her, while she did nothing to take care of him. She wasn't working, lived off his paycheck, and still wouldn't make him food on his lunch breaks.

I hated her and her ugly, lazy energy. I felt like I was cooped up in that trailer with an actual demon! I found out later that I broke her wrist the day we fought and bruised her up badly. My dad was pretty upset with me but admitted that he saw it coming. I warned him many times that I needed to work and begged him to get me away from her because her energy and attitude drove me crazy. He was irritated with her too, but of course felt bad when he saw her all beat up and hurt. I respected his concern for her, but never felt any regrets of my own. In contrast, I felt an enormous relief! To this day, my dad speaks of the demons she carried within her and acknowledges that I played a huge role in chasing that energy away.

One day, I ventured outside to sit by the retention pond that became my space in the chaos where I found peace. As I approached it, I spied an enormous, white wolf dog lying by the waterside! He startled me at first because of his size, but then, I noticed that he looked extremely sick, and quickly my fear was replaced with concern. I called out to him to test his character. He tried to lift his head but could barely even do so. He looked like he was near death! My dad heard me talking to him and came out to see what was going on. He gasped at the dog's size and cautioned me not to go near, but I did anyways, so he grabbed his camera and documented the occasion.

Slowly, I approached the mysterious wolfdog, but he made no reaction as I came closer and closer to him until finally, I sat right next to him. Still, he made no motion at all. Finally, I reached out to touch him and gently stroked his head. I realized that he was not a threat at all, but was extraordinarily ill, so I asked my dad to carry him into the trailer so that we could take care of him.

Figure 13. Getting close to the sick wolfdog.

Earlier that day, I cooked an enormous amount of chicken taquitos. Everyone was already full, so I had plenty to share with the wolf. Slowly, I fed them to him one by one. He took each one with gentle grace and caution. When he ate the last one, I held a bowl of water under his head. He drank his fill, then laid his head down and passed out for the rest of the evening.

The next morning, he looked like he felt better. Although he could still hardly move, he was obviously getting his energy back, and with effort could sit up. I asked my dad to carry him outside, so he could relieve himself. Afterwards, Dad carried him back in, and he rested for most of the day. Over the next few days, we nursed him in this way, until he was finally healed enough to walk around and even run a bit!

Figure 14. A much happier and healthy wolf-hybrid looks up at my dad while I observe from my workstation.

Thunderbird Rising

His arrival coincided with me finally getting my own little studio on the property. So, I took him with me to stay in my new place. At first, he followed me everywhere, but then slowly became more independent as the week passed and his health returned. One evening, I was awoken in the middle of the night by his piercing howl! I opened my eyes to see it as his head turned towards the sky, and he howled with everything he had! It was the most beautiful and haunting sound I ever heard. I felt it throughout my entire body! I knew then for sure that he was a wolf. Or at least a wolf-hybrid.

The next day, I visited my dad at his place. The wolf dog followed me there and waited outside. He howled for me, but my dad was engrossed in a deep story that I didn't dare interrupt. He howled once more, and then grew silent. After a few minutes, I wrapped up my conversation with my dad and walked out to see what he wanted. But he was gone! I looked everywhere for him. He was nowhere to be found. I realized then that he was saying, "Doksa ake," the Dakota phrase for "until I see you again." In our culture, we don't say goodbye when we part, because we know that all of life moves in a spiral, and that we will always see our relatives again. I was sad to see that he left, yet happy that I was given the opportunity to help him along his enigmatic journey. I knew that I'd see him again!

Meanwhile, the days ticked by and there was still no work allowed for me at the honey farm, no matter how much my dad asked, and it was all just to keep the boss's jealous wife happy! I did my best to make the most of my time by beading earrings, Pipes, bracelets, and lighters to make any money I could. My dad finally got angry enough and threatened to quit if I wasn't allowed to start work at once. Only then did the bossman finally stand up to his wife. I was invited to start work the next day if I wanted to! I got fitted up in a beekeeper's suit and began early the next day.

I worked closely with the hives, and quickly became fascinated with the honeybees. I didn't think there was anything better at the time than heading out before sunrise to work hard outside all day in Nature with the bees! It was still early in the year, and only a few flower species were in bloom. The bees, therefore, didn't yet have enough of a natural food source to fully sustain their hives. Thus, we had to feed each hive with a corn syrup supplement. I was devastated when I saw that hundreds of honeybees drowned during the early season, as we doused the feeding area of a hive with corn syrup in a mad rush to feed thousands of hives before the day was over.

My dad worked for a multi-million-dollar honey company, which had thousands of hives strategically placed over multiple locations, miles apart, to produce the maximum amount of honey possible. Their methods of taking care of the bees took the welfare of the bee into little consideration, and like any multi-million-dollar corporation, were designed with the highest priority being to maximize profit, and to get the final product onto the shelf. The bees were the slaves of the company and were pushed extremely hard to produce as much honey as possible.

It was 2012, and entire hives were dying from beetle invasions, mystery fungi, and illnesses. My dad worked in the bee industry for a few years afterward and confirmed how much money the beekeepers lost, as entire hives simply died off or disappeared! It is now 2021, and the population of the honeybee, one of the most important pollinators in the world's ecosystem, and of a third of all our food, continues to decline. A world without honeybees would radically change our lives, and that of every other being living on Mother Earth. They deserve our respect, our attention, and our understanding, before it is too late!

In the meantime, I loved observing the mystery of bees. Sometimes I opened a hive and saw dozens of honeybees connecting themselves together from head to rear, in a bee-chain that spanned across the length of the hive. None of the beekeepers could explain why they did this. It was also incredible to open a hive and hear the hum of "air conditioning" – the sound of thousands of tiny bee wings as they tirelessly fanned off the hive to create a natural air current that reduced the temperature in the hive and kept the honey from overheating!

One day, my dad walked up to me, and proudly announced that he was watching me as I worked. He was "running an experiment," so said nothing as I stepped in front of the entrance to a beehive. He was surprised to see that I wasn't instantly attacked and stung as he always was, but instead was left alone. As a result, he was convinced of the "purity of my heart" and made sure I knew about it! He explained that the bees were extremely sensitive and knew people's energy. They reacted differently to diverse energy fields. Thus, some people were always attacked if they came too close to the hive entrance, and more rarely, others were accepted as if they belonged to the hive!

I enjoyed the hard manual labor of moving and stacking hives on top of each other to prepare for the honey production season. I loved that my muscles grew, and that I fell into bed with exhaustion every evening! It felt so good to spend entire days in Nature caretaking these hives. However, I didn't agree with how the bees were taken care of, nor did I understand some of the terminology of the beekeepers. They used to say that the bees "robbed honey," a reference to the bees eating the honey *we* took out of their hives. I mean, weren't *we* the ones who robbed the honey, not the bees who did all the work and made the honey themselves? It came off as a very entitled and backwards way of thinking about the bees. Furthermore, not giving back to the honeybees is why the industry was beginning to fail. Their survival depended on better treatment, along with a revamp of how they were viewed by industrial beekeepers. They are a precious species we should be taking exceptional care of, rather than using as a resource that is exploited for only monetary gain.

Figure 15. Thousands of honeybees tend to their hive while I observe.

I loved extraction season, the time when we finally opened the hives to pull out columns of thick honeycomb, rich with pure golden honey! I munched on bits of honeycomb and honey all day long, their rich, nurturing sweetness satiating both my thirst and hunger at once. However, it sucked getting stung all day long in the extraction room by displaced honeybees that struggled to find their way back to the hive and who were lost without their queen. They didn't attack me but instinctively stung me when they crawled under my arms, or behind my knees, and were unintentionally crushed as I bent my arm or legs to pick up the next box to place into the extraction machine. I felt for every one of those beautiful worker bees who died in that way, as if it were the death of my own sister!

About two weeks after I started working, a handsome Lakota man unexpectedly showed up to work. He was tall and fierce looking, catching my eye at once. Especially because the night before, I dreamt of a new man that was going to enter my life, and I knew this was him when I saw him! I asked my dad about him and found out his name was Daniel. He was sent down by my uncle from our rez to work for the summer. Daniel and I started to hang out, and soon we became inseparable. Our romantic connection became the most satisfying I ever felt in my life. The way he held me thru the night enlivened me, and I could see us being together for a long time, even though he was nine years younger than me.

My budding romance with Daniel awakened the dream I had about twelve years earlier, when my biggest celebrity crush at the time, Damian Marley – who became the epitome of my ideal lover because of his revolutionary ideals, spirituality, talent, and good looks – came to me and told me that I had to choose a lover from my own Tribe, who was my own color. This connection with Daniel felt right. He was my color, was from my Tribe, and we were falling deeply in love. I thought that I found "the one" that I'd spend the rest of my life with!

In the meantime, after hearing me complain about feeling tired from work, my dad pulled me aside to confess his secret cocaine habit. He claimed that it helped him have the energy to get through the long days at work with minimal food intake and additionally, made him feel quite powerful. He invited me to try it. With no kids around to keep me straight, and after having endured all that I had, I didn't see why I shouldn't! Plus, I didn't give a damn about anything anymore. I wanted to numb the pain of losing my kids with substances. Furthermore, the international lawsuit was pending because I wasn't ready to deal with my warrant yet. The last thing I wanted to do was to go back to jail!

Thus, it was easy to say yes to the temptation, and Daniel and I both began snorting cocaine multiple times a day. I found out it was true what my dad said. I didn't have to eat as much. I had more energy, and I felt more powerful. I could, for the first time in my life, talk to people that I hardly knew without hesitancy. I believed my cocaine habit helped me deeply connect with other people and get more work done. I didn't feel as depressed anymore, and had more drive, *but* I had to keep using it to feel this way, and it rapidly became a habit for all of us.

My dad believes that he's been led by, possessed, and taunted by "legions of demons" for most of his life. It was his explanation for decades of crazy behavior and addiction. He was never able to escape them. He also romanticized his heavy use of meth, claiming that it allowed him to "see more deeply into other dimensions." I could agree with that, however, which dimensions? I doubted the places he gained access to, via methamphetamines, were the most enlightened places to go. However, my dad, from the time he was a young boy, was steeped in hellish environments via his forced attendance at a strict missionary school. His soul, like mine, had dissociated from this abusive environment into a dark place, and struggled to find its way out.

I lost contact with my dad for years after our time together in Texas. He began "experimenting" with meth again, and basically fell out of touch with everyone he knew. Just a few months ago, from the time I now write this book, I dreamt of him returning suddenly from a long trip in the jungle. He looked disheveled, with incredibly red and irritated skin. He hardly remembered me but smiled wildly as he realized that he had finally escaped from that dark place that held onto him for most of his life! Sure enough, my dad contacted me after I had that dream, after years of no communication, to tell me he was "set free." So far, it is true, and he is trying his best to practice sobriety, which is quite a change from the dad I knew seven years earlier that introduced me to cocaine. To him, it was once seen as a healthy and suitable way to escape the harsh reality he's always known.

In the meantime, Daniel and I struggled to overcome our own substance abuse, a common problem in "Indian Country." We are all survivors of continued colonization and genocide. Substances like alcohol and drugs offer an easy way to numb the pain that otherwise is too much for most of us to handle. It allows us to exist in a make-believe, seemingly better reality other than the one that is our truth.

One fateful morning, I slept soundly after another intoxicating night spent with Daniel. A loud knock on the door startled me suddenly out of my sleep. "Who the hell is knocking like that?" I wondered. Daniel, who already left for work, shared the studio with me. If it were him, he'd just walk in. If it were my dad, he would've knocked much softer. No one else would even bother me. I stumbled to answer the door, and my heart buried itself into the Texan soil when I saw that a federal marshal stood behind the mystery.

"Good morning, Stephanie! I am here to collect you for a federal warrant issued by the State of South Dakota." I sighed, oddly calmed by his southern manners and drawl, and asked if I could take a shower first. Of course, he said no, and at once required me to place my hands behind my back. He handcuffed me and gently placed me into his truck. I interviewed him about his life as a federal marshal as we pulled away. In an instant, I was given no other choice but to leave the honeybees, my dad, Daniel, and the substance use behind. A beautiful rainbow arched over the honey farm as I was carried away. Little did I know that I wasn't the only one being taken to jail that day!

CHAPTER EIGHT

FLYING DREAMS

I ride in the back of a cop car. I'm handcuffed, but easily break free. I fling open the door and run to the trees! I fly in the usual way, by flapping my arms, which are wings, and my feet effortlessly leave the ground as I depart into the sky! The cop chases me but can't keep up. He shoots bullets at me as I soar above the treetops. I see Temoc and pick him up. The bullets whiz by us, but never touch us. We fly far away now, but suddenly, I'm jolted awake as an alarm sounds, and a prison door eerily creaks.

"Role Call!" the prison guards screech, and I stand up groggily at 4 a.m. as I did every morning at the same time for the last week. It was just a dream. I woke up to the reality that I was back in hell, in a Texas prison! I was so tired, and my back ached. I missed him, Daniel. We never got the chance to say, "Doksa ake," so, I was looking forward to his visit and my dad's. In a full panic for a week, I desperately dreamt of ways to break myself out of jail. I hadn't yet accepted my fate. They had me once again!

Those who haven't been to prison, or in my case, county jail, will never understand the simple luxuries of a hot cup of coffee or tea in the mornings, or of cooking your own meals and peeing without supervision. Privacy, free time, and conversing with your loved ones at will are no longer options. Going outside and breathing fresh air, listening to music, and even wearing your own underwear or making a phone call without strict regulations are impossible. Absolutely everything is monitored, and free will severely restricted. It is a place that I've worked extremely hard to never return to. It was absolute hell for me.

I recently saw someone that had no family, and no responsibilities, express through social media that his jail experience was a "fun relief" – which to a homeless person it might be! I didn't agree, however, with his perspective that anyone could also find relief and joy in their own jail stay. I never found an ounce of relief in being forcefully separated from my family and my free will, nor in my inability to communicate with my loved ones. Once again, I was ripped away from my family, from talking to my kids on phone, from my partner, and from my physical freedom. Only someone who already had nothing going on for themselves would label a concrete cell, locks, chains, constant surveillance, terrible food, poisoned water, and forced isolation as "fun" or as a "relief."

When I was booked into the Texas jail – my temporary holding place until I was transferred to South Dakota – I was given a pregnancy test to determine any health care needs while incarcerated. It was negative. However, after a week, my moontime, or menstrual cycle, was late. I started feeling sick every morning, wanted to do nothing but sleep all day, and my breasts grew larger and sore. I knew my body, and I knew that I was pregnant, despite the results of the first pregnancy test.

After two weeks of being held, and after putting in multiple requests for another pregnancy test, I was finally given another, which came up positive! I was carrying Daniel's child, and a new beginning was upon me. Immediately, the jail approved me to receive supplemental meals for my pregnancy. I was given extra juice, milk, peanut butter and jelly sandwiches, and fruit. I accepted these extra morsels of food with a level of delight akin to winning the lottery!

During my first week there, I willingly joined prayer circles that prayed to Christ, the spiritual figure that I swore off ages before. However, my perception of him slowly shifted into that of a prophet, whose original message was intentionally skewed by modern-day religions. I read the Bible, at first because it was the only piece of spiritual literature available to me, and secondly, because I could decipher the deeper, hidden messages within it.

All the inmates in my cell block were also mothers, and we prayed hard for our children and for our reunification with them. We were all hurt, confused, and scared. In that state, there was no separation between us. However, my behavior soon took a drastic shift. At first, I socialized and prayed with the other women, but by the time a week passed, I withdrew into my own cell. The other girls checked on me often. I didn't hide that I was utterly depressed and now felt terribly sick. I slept all day as I detoxed and prayed with all my heart to Creator and my ancestors to magically get me out of there, to open the doors, send a natural disaster, to just somehow free me again! How I abhorred being there!

Every time we went outside, I fantasized about jumping the fence and running. Whenever I dreamed, I broke free. No matter how many times I was jailed during that two-year stretch, I never stopped planning my escape, not realizing that it was exactly where I needed to be at that time, for the baby's sake, and for my own path of healing! I didn't know that it would take years of focus, and a complete shift in my perception, for me to finally be freed from the internal prison within me that was built by the trauma I experienced. My imprisonment forced me to confront my issues, my pain, and my past.

It was time to find that little girl within who dissociated to a safe place a long time ago. Whether I wanted it or not, it was also time to know what it felt like to lose absolutely everything outside of me, but to find that there was something within me that could never be taken, touched, or tainted no matter what I went through. My faith and my heart were being strengthened!

Finally, my dad came to visit. I was expecting and really hoping to see Daniel too, but instead, my dad proudly announced that he successfully drove Danny away after telling him he wasn't good enough for me. I still expected him to come though, no matter what, to find his way there with or without my dad's approval, but he never did. Thus, his pattern of absence began. I told my dad to let Danny know that I was pregnant, hoping that it would inspire him to show up for me.

During the few weeks that I was incarcerated in Texas, I read Winnie Mandela's book, *Part of My Soul Went with Him*. Winnie Mandela was a South African activist, political leader, and the wife of Nelson Mandela, who was incarcerated as a political prisoner for most of their marriage. Winnie was also arrested multiple times, but never stopped fighting for the rights of her people to their freedom, land, and sovereignty.

Her book inspired me deeply, and I thought constantly about her perspective of the injustice that was the justice system for her people. Her strength was reflected in the raising of her children. She taught them that no matter what they went through, they must not cry in front of their oppressors. They could never let them know that they were being affected. Thus, no matter the circumstances, they had to remain strong. The difficult journey that Winnie, Nelson, and their family endured, assured me that I too could continue to endure my own challenges. I realized that the oppressor would do whatever it could to break my spirit, and that I had to find a way to carry on no matter what.

Finally, the day came when I was called out of my cell early in the morning to switch out of my stripes. I was then handed over to several Rapid City police officers. It was time for my transport back to Pennington County Jail. With handcuffs on my wrists, and chains on my feet, I was led through the airport for our flight back to South Dakota. They were smart to do so because the whole time I sought my opportunity to run. Yet, an inner voice told me to remain calm and to just face this. I remember how grateful I felt when the female police officer bought me one of those hot pretzels with the cheese dip! Food from the "outside" was a thousand times better than anything we ever ate on the "inside." Plus, I was pregnant, and therefore appreciated its delicious taste even more so.

Even though I knew where we were headed, I made sure to enjoy every moment outside of a jail cell, in civilian clothing, in the fresh air, and with sunlight touching my skin, that I could! We enjoyed a delicious meal on the plane, and I nearly cried as I was given the privilege of watching the stunningly beautiful sunset from the airplane window, as we left my honey-filled Texas days behind. While I looked through a magazine with beautiful pictures in it during our flight, I quietly tore out my favorite ones when the cops weren't looking, so that I could decorate my future jail cell with them as beautiful reminders of the outside world. A few hours later, we landed in Rapid City, just as a booming thunderstorm hit!

CHAPTER NINE

ROUND TWO

It was June of 2012, two years after my first arrest and twenty-eight-day incarceration in Rapid City, and almost one year after my parental rights to Cuauhtémoc were terminated. I still hadn't been given a trial or pled guilty to the charges upon which the loss of the rights of my child were based. Once again, I was booked into Pennington County Jail, the notoriously racist and prejudiced correctional facility that obviously targeted Lakota and Dakota people.

I switched out my comfortable black and white dress for the baggy and unpleasant grey and white PCJ stripes, along with the terribly pink t-shirt, panties, and socks that were worn underneath. Then, I slipped my feet into the notoriously ugly, bright-orange crocks that had already been worn by other inmates hundreds of times. This became my daily attire for what slowly turned into the next six months! The only change came when I swapped out my small shirts for larger ones as my belly continued to grow ripe with child.

The only time I'd go outside again during this second round at PCJ was to walk the short distance to the courtroom for several hearings, to walk back and forth to cop cars for my pregnancy check-ups, and finally for the brief transport to my sentencing hearing on November 19, 2012. I used these opportunities to gulp in the fresh air and sunshine on my skin like it was the first time I experienced either of them. In that six-month period, I was outside for no more than a total of fifteen minutes! Lack of sun and fresh air certainly does strange things to a person.

I needed someone, anyone, to help me contact my lawyer, Curtis Doebbler, or anyone else who might be able to help me, but I couldn't get in touch with anyone for months. Furthermore, no matter how much I prayed for Daniel to contact me, visit, or send money to help buy extra commissary to feed the baby, he never did. I kept waiting patiently for him to show up, until finally, after about five months of absolutely nothing, I gave up on him. I accepted that I was alone in my pregnancy and incarceration, and through many prayers, I received the guidance that Daniel would not be involved in the raising of our baby for at least the first ten years of our child's life. I let go of the man that I thought I was going to marry, and it broke my heart in a million pieces to do so, but I was given no other choice.

The only in-person visits I received were from my neighbor from the cabin I had in the Black Hills and my court-appointed Pennington County lawyer. My twin brother was the only member of my biological family to contact me, and he sent monthly letters that helped lift my spirits. I had no extra money for commissary or phone calls, and for a few months, was completely cut off from the world while I was physically, mentally, and spiritually starved.

A few of my social media friends eventually heard that I was incarcerated and sent heartfelt and uplifting letters. These few correspondences, combined with reading, praying, writing, singing, and playing card games, saw me through one of the most isolated and depressing episodes of my life. After I was released, some of the people who tried to contact me told me that their letters were returned from the jail, even though they had my correct address. I realized then that the jail must have purposely restricted my contact with the outside world!

On the morning of October 22, 2012, I woke up at sunrise and saw a beautiful rainbow arching through the sliver of my cell's window. I knew it was a message, a sign of some important news. Later that day, the news reached us. Russell Means, the co-founder of the American Indian Movement (AIM) had passed! Instantly, I traveled back to the day I met him two years earlier. I attended an International Treaty Meeting on the Rosebud Indian Reservation. Russell walked in the door dressed in jeans, a cowboy hat, cowboy boots, and a red button-up shirt. He walked right over to me and stared straight into my eyes for about thirty seconds. I stared back awkwardly, fully aware of who stood before me and boldly stared me down! Then, he simply shook my hand, asked my name, and where I was from. After telling him, he handed me a copy of the Fort Laramie Treaty of 1868, then turned around and strutted back out the door.

I studied that Treaty intensely afterwards and used it later to assert my sovereignty with the cops that unsuccessfully tried to gather information from me; with the detective who arrested me and kidnapped my son; and then, for the ensuing duration of most of my legal battle. Russell Means saw something in me that day as he stared into me. His actions were simple, but powerful, and had a profound effect on me. He empowered me with the gift of information, and with the truth of knowing what rights I inherently held as a descendant of the Lakota and Dakota Nations. He helped me make a stand, or even *asked* me to, not only for myself, but for my children, and all Treaty descendants. I pondered this deeply from that point forward.

After lunch each day, the correctional officers went on their break and changed shifts, so we were locked into our cells. The door that was usually closed between the men's cell block that adjoined ours was opened, enabling one officer to watch over both blocks. We women "lilili'd" as loud as we could, and the men war whooped! The sound echoed through both blocks, and we laughed and hollered even more! This angered the guards, and they shouted at us to stop, threatening lockdown for the rest of the day. We stopped for five minutes, then went right back to it! We enjoyed seeing their frenzy at our ancient expressions.

The girls always asked me to sing. While on lockdown, one of the girls would beat on the wall, making a drumbeat, and I'd chime in with everyone's favorite song, an Indian love song I learned years back. *"When the sun sets over the world, I'll be thinking of you. I know you are far away. Heya heya. No matter where you are, I still love you just the same! Heya heya."* For all of us, it reminded us of our loved ones, and brought them to us, and us to them, even if just for a moment. It was our temporary break from that place, and even an act of resistance, because the guards always yelled at us to stop.

I also sang every time we were in the rec room. One time, the vent window was open in there, and I began to sing. For some reason, the guard on duty quickly raised the window, so no one outside could hear me! I don't know why, but that really affected me. Why were they trying to hide my song, my voice? Were they trying to punish me for singing? The fresh air was one of our very few luxuries, however, not even that getting taken away could convince me to stop.

We also had no privacy, which was very unsettling because we had mostly male correctional officers in our all-female cell block. The toilets were positioned right next to our cell door, so if a guard walked past while we used it, they saw us naked. It felt gross and violating every single time, to be seen and treated like female animals, rather than as the sacred women and Matriarchs we truly were.

Thunderbird Rising

Every afternoon, the diabetics received an afternoon snack, with an orange and a peanut butter sandwich, while we pregnant girls received nothing but an extra milk with each meal, and a daily pre-natal vitamin. Both sickened my stomach, and I quickly realized that I was lactose intolerant. At my request, they switched me to soy milk, which was more digestible, but whose taste made me nauseous. When I asked the jail nurse why we weren't given any extra food to feed our babies, I was told that our "condition" did not qualify us for an extra meal, and that the "vitamins and milk we received provided us with all the extra nourishment our babies needed." I found it ridiculous how differently Texas and South Dakota jails viewed the nourishment needs of pregnant women, but I was not surprised because I already knew what South Dakota was willing to do to our children. However, knowing that did not make the unbearable hunger go away, or the constant cravings my baby caused, which were his way of begging for proper nourishment.

During my incarceration in Texas, I read only the Bible's last chapter, Revelations, but in Rapid City, with no other spiritual options available to me, I read the King James Version of the Bible from front to back. Over the course of six months, I finished it, and as I did, my perception of the teachings of Christ forever changed. My view of religion, however, fell even deeper into the gutter! I realized that he was a prophet, just like White Buffalo Woman, and that his message of upliftment to humanity was skewed by narcissistic religions that abused his image and twisted his message for their own gain.

As I read the book of Ezekiel, my heart filled with the prophecies and visions shared within it. I realized that the name of my coming baby boy was being revealed to me! I was to name him Ezekiel, after the most badass prophet from the Bible because of what he saw:

> [4] As I looked, behold, a storm wind was coming from the north, a great cloud with fire flashing forth continually and a bright light

around it, and in its midst something like glowing metal in the midst of the fire. ⁵ Within it there were figures resembling four living beings. And this was their appearance: they had human form. ⁶ Each of them had four faces and four wings. ⁷ Their legs were straight and their feet were like a calf's hoof, and they gleamed like burnished bronze. ⁸ Under their wings on their four sides were human hands. As for the faces and wings of the four of them, ⁹ their wings touched one another; their faces did not turn when they moved, each went straight forward. ¹⁰ As for the form of their faces, each had the face of a man; all four had the face of a lion on the right and the face of a bull on the left, and all four had the face of an eagle. ¹¹ Such were their faces. Their wings were spread out above; each had two touching another being, and two covering their bodies. ¹² And each went straight forward; wherever the spirit was about to go, they would go, without turning as they went. ¹³ In the midst of the living beings there was something that looked like burning coals of fire, like torches darting back and forth among the living beings. The fire was bright, and lightning was flashing from the fire. ¹⁴ And the living beings ran to and fro like bolts of lightning.

²² Now over the heads of the living beings there was something like an expanse, like the awesome gleam of crystal, spread out over their heads. ²³ Under the expanse their wings were stretched out straight, one toward the other; each one also had two wings covering its body on the one side and on the other. ²⁴ I also heard the sound of their wings like the sound of abundant waters as they went, like the voice of the Almighty, a sound of tumult like the sound of an army camp; whenever they stood still, they dropped their wings. ²⁵ And there came a voice from above the expanse that was over their heads; whenever they stood still, they dropped their wings.

> ²⁶ Now above the expanse that was over their heads there was something resembling a throne, like lapis lazuli in appearance; and on that which resembled a throne, high up, was a figure with the appearance of a man. ²⁷ Then I noticed from the appearance of His loins and upward something like glowing metal that looked like fire all around within it, and from the appearance of His loins and downward I saw something like fire; and there was a radiance around Him. ²⁸ As the appearance of the rainbow in the clouds on a rainy day, so was the appearance of the surrounding radiance. Such was the appearance of the likeness of the glory of the Lord. – (*King James Version*, Ezek 4 – 28)

The prophet Ezekiel was chosen to receive a beautiful vision of "God," and even, the way I see it, of Star Nation beings! Whatever they were, they were most definitely out of this world. He saw cherubim, or angelic winged creatures from above that were the chariot of an angelic, godly, or extremely sacred being, and Ezekiel was carried back up into the sky with them to receive their prophecy.

I could see that Ezekiel received a visitation from the Spirit World in the same way that the Oceti Sakowin received a visit from White Buffalo Woman nineteen generations ago! It felt perfect to honor the child in my womb, who was imprisoned with me, who endured this hardship together with me, and who was undergoing the biggest transformation of my life with me, with the awesome energy this prophet carried. Furthermore, I began to realize that this special baby boy I carried was chosen by Creator to be birthed by me. I was picked up by the federal marshals before I even knew I was pregnant and was kept incarcerated for long enough that I had *no choice* but to carry him. I wouldn't have if it had gone any other way because of everything my children and I already endured. I didn't want another child to go through it as well. However, it was beyond my choice, and Ezekiel became another miracle baby. Because of the way he came to me, I knew he deserved a name of such caliber.

Meanwhile, a transformation unfolded within me that happened only because it was forced to. *Every* night, I relived the traumas I endured as a child and during my relationship with Izz in my dreams. Being confined in the physical hell that PCJ was for me triggered all my buried traumas to rise to the surface as I dreamt. Once again, I dreamt of my stepfather raping me over and over, or of Izz maliciously hurting the kids to take revenge upon me for leaving him. At first, I was just having these dreams, but then I started fighting back! One night, I cut my stepfather in half with a sword after he tried to assault me. The next night, I beat Izz to shreds with a whip and my bare fists after watching him hurt one of the kids. I was imprisoned on the inside and the outside, but I was beginning to break free, at least internally.

Slowly, cautiously, I took responsibility for my actions, acknowledging that I chose to go through everything I endured. I did this to take my power back, to take it away from that which oppressed me. I came to realize that I had the power to release myself from being the victim. When I asked for the forgiveness of Creator, I learned how to forgive myself and others. I forgave myself for any action I took that separated me from my children and myself. I forgave others for inflicting suffering and pain upon me. I thanked them for making me stronger and for showing me the hardships that my people have endured for generations. There is something beautiful to be found within suffering, because this type of stress causes rapid evolution. I was being forged from the fire and forced to rise from my own ashes! I was a diamond *and* Phoenix being created! When I realized that, I broke through my own veil.

Although I still had nightmares, I also had dreams that revealed "behind-the-scenes" information. In one, Judge Davis asked, "Why are you fighting so hard?" He was red-faced and drunk, just like he was every time I saw him in court. I had another dream that told me of an important legal defense for my case: duress – doing something one would not normally do, due to extenuating circumstances. I suggested this to my lawyer, and he agreed, but never presented it as a defense. He always told me that I instead had to learn how to "play their game" in the courtroom. Eventually, for Ezekiel's sake, I took his advice.

One day, my lawyer brought in the footage of me and Cuauhtémoc on the day I was interrogated by the detective who arrested me. I can't even remember why he did because as soon as he played it, I sobbed hysterically! I absolutely could not bear to watch the footage of the last few moments my son and I had together. I struggled to talk through my tears, and he had absolutely no idea how to behave. I couldn't even look at pictures of Temoc up until this point without breaking down, and now, our last moments together were nonchalantly shown to me. But I held on just long enough to see that Eddie did *not* rat me out like the Prosecutor said he did during our first incarceration, and that Detective Heinle had truly taken it upon himself to enter my car, without a warrant, or my permission to search my vehicle!

In the meantime, I had absolutely no idea when I'd be given a trial. Each time I went into court, my trial continued to get delayed by the Judge. At first, it was to await the results of his court-ordered psychiatric evaluation. I waited months until the day came when I was finally transported to the South Dakota Human Services Center, a nice name for the psychiatric ward that was assigned to observe and evaluate my mental health. I was handcuffed and chained by the ankles, and after an extremely uncomfortable, long, cold, and bumpy ride, we finally arrived.

After the first few hours of being there, I prayed that I'd get committed! The food was a thousand times better, along with the treatment of me as a human being, plus I got to sleep in a much more comfortable bed. I was entitled to walk alone to the showers, and to be unsupervised while I dressed. Furthermore, I realized that I could relate to many of the people there. I didn't see insanity as simply an internal or personal condition. Rather, I saw it as a reflection of the effect our environment has on our internal state of well-being. It's not "crazy" to be negatively affected by mass consumerism, abuse which is swept under the rug, the imbalanced and biased justice system, generations of hidden and unacknowledged genocide, living in a country that was built from legalized slavery, and absurd societal norms. Instead, it is often a symptom of being awakened and aware.

My roommate was a beautiful young Lakota girl that was suicidal. She confessed to me that her grandfather back home was molesting and raping her. She "cut," or sliced her wrists, to relieve the pain. I was the first person she opened up to. I supported her as best as I could and tried my hardest to let her know that it was okay to turn him in and to protect herself. She didn't need to shield him, especially when it cost her the sanity and well-being of her spirit.

I also read a book there about narcissists. It helped me realize that both my stepfather and Izz carried every single trait of one! Either of them could have written, "The Autobiography of a Narcissist," and my stepfather could have added in, "The Psychopath," as a subheading. I began to realize why they were so good at being such seductively horrible people. However, I could also see how incredibly miserable they were. They had to devour the light from other souls to feed their own darkness. They were so sick that it was beyond repair! I survived some of the best. In that discovery, I found another reason to hold my head up higher.

The day finally came for me to receive my official psychiatric evaluation. After an hour interview with a psychologist, I was finally diagnosed with Chronic PTSD – Post Traumatic Stress Disorder – stemming from my relationship with Izz and my childhood. The doctor determined that, despite my condition, I could uphold myself in a trial. She recommended that the case move forward immediately! Unfortunately, I wasn't committed, and after only a week of the luxury of being there, I was sent back to PCJ to continue the long wait for a trial.

Upon returning to PCJ, I wrote constantly, feeling a dire need to express myself. I wrote letters to whomever I could, trying my hardest to get into contact with someone from the outside. Eventually, I contacted my friend Stephen, and sent him the following poem, which he posted on social media for me. I wrote it on August 13, 2012, from inside PCJ, which is in the heart of Lakota Sioux territory:

Chained up in the Black Hills, heart of the beast pumps fast still! AIM song resounding thru my mind, I wonder how much longer I will be forced to serve "their" time? Baby growing in the heart of my womb, Daddy's lost in alcohol and cocaine abuse, half of which I shared with him, before the marshals brought me back in. Lost in the chaos of losing my babies, I thought maybe my numbness could save me, from the pain of loss by genocide that plagues all people wrought by oppression and lies. Day before I left, I saw the rainbow! Beautiful and promising like God's halo!

I think back on such a wonderful sight.... Creator must have good things for me in mind. I miss my pa, my sibs, my seeds, especially my twin brother. I gotta accept this separation's got ways of bringing us closer. I miss my love and the long nights we spent. Wrapped up as one after many crimson sunsets. Texas scenes of cowboy boots and honeycombs, switched tragically to lonely nights in ugly prison clothes. Oh, how I miss those days gone by! And all my friends with whom I flew so High. But I smile still to think of coming lullabies.... In the law of dreams, I am set free, there I spy my destiny: Illusion broken, the dreams shift, to burdens serving higher purpose!

AIM song reenters my wandering mind, heartbeats pump along with mine. We are all connected in the web – judge, lawyer, CO, inmate – no different. So, what continues to hold me here? What is it about me that brings them so much fear? Non-violent but armed with warrior tongue, they say that I rant and rave about what they left undone – we had an agreement – your ancestors and mine! Fort Laramie Treaty on which both sides signed! I need you to know that you can't go on forever, pretending that my people you can always sever, from the truth that this land has always been ours.

This jail you hold us in has its power only in bars, only in lies, deception, and theft, did you gain what little we had left! I am Lakota and winyan at that! I know that I am not a taker-of-fat! I do not buy into hypocrisy and lies but am weak and want to plea to slide by, hoping for release, for this place is killing me! But Tunkasila says no! Here you gotta stay, until the role I've given you is prophetically displayed! So, since I can't go my warrior mind brews, with thoughts of exposing genocide and truth, to the world which has no clue, what we're struggling thru....

Warrior song blasts out my throat! As my warrior brother leads in resounding notes! As we travel together on this Red Road, bound in unity as one in a chain gang load, being delivered to Judge Davis' monotonous court, whom since 1979 has been presiding over lies, of enabling this invisible genocide. I'm so done with this game he plays with our lives! But I think deeper and realize it's time for things to be made right. What one sows one shall reap! So, be careful of sowing your holes too deep! Vengeance isn't ours but belongs to the Spirits. Our preparation is perfected with patient endurance.

Realization is acknowledging that their debts, aren't protected by indoctrination and theft, and concealing that true law isn't with them, but is with the One that created the people with perfect vision. We each have a purpose uniquely intended, and were given a homeland for all seasons, yet change is the constant I'm constantly reminded, and I must face that the past can't be rewinded. So, I seek out all allies and friends, of all colors, backgrounds, and blends, to stand as One Blood, One Love, Oyate Wanji, to fulfill what prophecy has spoken we must be! One heart, one spirit, united in vision, of love over hate, unity over division!

The shift that's coming is only the end, of our own paradigms which entrap us like lead. Freeing our minds from the illusion of the System, means the liberty to be what Wakan Tanka intended. So, here I center my focus.... As I wait in chains and hope this... Chaos and confusion will soon come to an end... Meanwhile, the AIM Song resounds thru my head!

Day after day, and week after week passed, while my belly continued to grow. I realized that I had to make my decision. I could await my trial, which my stubbornness ached to do, and risk losing another child, or I could accept their plea deal. In South Dakota, if you give birth to a child while incarcerated, the child is immediately taken into the custody of Child Protective Services, and you lose your child. My other choice was to plead guilty to the felony charge of "Grand Theft by Receiving Stolen Property." This "grand theft" charge, by the way, was for items which were worth barely one-thousand dollars! If I took the plea, I'd get released before Ezekiel was born and go under the supervision of Florida's probation system. I incessantly collect-called my mother until she finally accepted my calls, and after I begged her, and promised that I'd "be nice," she agreed that I could come live with her in Florida, have the baby, and start my life over as I worked to get my other kids back.

So, I made my choice. I was not willing to risk the loss of another child, plus I was at my wit's end! I told my lawyer that I was ready to accept the plea deal. Promptly, I was brought to court for sentencing, and given a four-year suspended prison sentence, thirty days jail time, and transferred probation to the state of Florida. I was granted "time served" for the thirty-day jail sentence, after having already been held in jail for over 230 days without a trial! However, I still wasn't released after sentencing. Judge Davis didn't want me free on the streets of Rapid City. He demanded that I be held pending "proof of transfer to Florida." Thus, I was held for another two weeks until my father finally came to pick me up, and I was flown directly out of Rapid City.

During the sentencing hearing, Judge Davis told me how "smart" he thought I was, and that he hoped I'd "be a good mother to *this* baby." I simply said, "Thank you." Yet, in my heart, yes, I agreed that it was my "smarts" that caused me to see through their biased justice system from the beginning. My intelligence allowed me to see the truth, that they legally kidnapped my son, and used him to break both our spirits as punishment for my apparent insanity in standing out against the system. My "smarts" even caused me to realize that I must give in for now, to prevent another child from getting caught in their grip through the foster care system, because I knew they would've held me without a trial until I gave birth to him.

I knew I'd be back, but in the meantime, I was deeply humbled, and ready to accept responsibility for whatever I needed to do to get my life in order, so that I would never be put in that position again if there was anything I could possibly do to prevent it! I was ready to accept my need for help and healing, although still questioning my readiness to bring another child into the world.

It was December of 2012, and even the correctional officer was excited for me that day, as I gathered the stacks of my journal writings, the letters from my bro and my friends, and thus, finally waddled out of that cell block hopefully for the rest of my life! The next day, I flew away on an airplane, forcefully transferred out of South Dakota for many years to come. I was headed to Florida, where I'd continue the long walk towards the greatest transformation of my life.

CHAPTER TEN

MOONLIGHT BAY

I arrived at my mother's house on Moonlight Bay Drive filled with delightful anticipation and giddy excitement. I could finally enjoy "free" life again! I swelled with happiness and with child as I matured into my eighth month of pregnancy. My mother lived in a beautiful home in Panama City Beach that was built right next to the bay waters! I was thankful that my mother finally said yes to my arrival, and that her husband also agreed to it. I hadn't met him yet, but soon found out that he was filled with boisterous energy and always added to every conversation. He was the type that would tell a corny joke, and then laugh loudly at it afterwards, while someone like me would just lift a corner of my mouth in an obligatory response. I wish I could say this was a fresh start to me having a healthy relationship with one of my mother's husbands, but it simply wasn't.

For a moment though, we did enjoy each other's company. It meant so much to me to finally be free, and to have the support of my family. My mom helped me stock up on baby supplies, and even had a room prepared for me and the coming baby. She was the Chief of Staff at the hospital on the Air Force base she worked at, as well as their practicing OBGYN doctor, thus she worked *a lot*, and so, I was alone with Patrick plenty. At first, I liked how he cooked for my mom and spent much of his free time playing the conga drums that she got for him. But quickly it started bothering me deep down that he didn't work, that he drove a BMW that my mom bought for him, and that he called my mother's money "his." In fact, he was quite boastful about it: "Oh yes, *I* can buy you that! It's nothing!" He used "his" money to ship in cases of premium quality beer for himself and high-priced wine for my mom. "His" money made sure they stayed well supplied when it came to "spirits."

When my mother came home from work, she went straight into her office with a glass of wine and played games online for hours. Everyone knew better than to interrupt her. This was her "let down" period, the time to herself when she detoxed from work. She hated her job as much as she hated the military. Afterwards, she came out to eat and watch her usual television shows with Patrick. Sometimes, I joined them just so I could spend time with her.

I enjoyed being back around my mom for a short while. I really believed that I could mend our relationship and begin a healthy, harmonious, and transformed mother and daughter experience. However, every time I mentioned my pain about Temoc, and my desire to get all my kids back, she went silent. Eventually, she told me that she thought Temoc was better off with my little brother than with me. I cried, but her eyes remained dry, so I learned to be quiet to her about the injustice I felt regarding Temoc.

For many years, most people, especially my mom, disregarded me and thought I was crazy when I said that the state of South Dakota continued its cultural genocide against our people by kidnapping our children through abuse and neglect cases, with little to no due process of law. Things thankfully changed as the years passed, and more people were awakened to the truth. In December of 2016, an article written by Lacey Louwagie for the Courthouse News Service reported that, "In the spring of 2015, U.S. District Judge Jeffrey Viken blasted Pennington

County Circuit Court Judge Jeff Davis, presiding judge of South Dakota's Seventh Circuit, for his 'five-minute' hearings that removed Native American children from their homes without giving parents the chance to cross-examine witnesses, view the accusations against them or consult with an attorney – all rights guaranteed under due process and the Indian Child Welfare Act."

Currently, anyone can see for themselves how the U.S. government blatantly mishandles migrant Indigenous children – by separating them from their parents and detaining them in cages on the border. Thousands of reports of physical and sexual abuse have since arisen, along with several deaths, and gross neglect. I use my experience with Cuauhtémoc to inform those in this situation that they cannot trust certain U.S. government officials, and that they must do whatever they can to keep their children free from their hands.

In the meantime, as soon as I arrived at my mother's house, I contacted my little brother Joe, whom South Dakota CPS permanently placed Cuauhtémoc with, and who later adopted him. I tried to open the channels of communication once again between my son and I, who was now known as "Chuck" because Joe couldn't say "Cuauhtémoc." However, he coldly replied with a lengthy list of demands that must be met before he would "even consider allowing me to have contact with 'Chuck' again." These demands included that I shut down every social media site I created, especially ones linked to activism; and that I denounce my Indian heritage, and any activity related to it.

Obviously, I still have not met these demands to this day, and therefore, my own little brother and mother have colluded over nearly a decade to sever any possible contact between my son and I, including going so far as to have secret family gatherings with him that I was not invited to, and keeping his location a secret from me to this day. My little sister, who was once my best friend, took part in these gatherings. The betrayal of my mother and little brother was deplorable to me, and my sister's inability to stand up for my right to see my son soon became equally inexcusable. I couldn't believe how these members of my own family turned against me and encouraged, even orchestrated, the continued separation between my son and me!

In the meantime, I seriously doubted my ability to raise the new baby that was coming. I even considered giving him up for adoption. I was in so much pain and depression from losing my other children that I thought I couldn't bear having another. I also felt incredibly guilty. How could I bring in a new child, who would certainly take all my time, energy, and attention, when I already had four that I was still fighting for? I contacted several adoption agencies, and nearly agreed to give up baby Ezekiel for adoption, but after praying and trusting my intuition, I decided to keep him.

Ezekiel's due date came and went, leaving me surprised and physically frustrated! I felt like I was going to pop! I carried him longer than any of my other babies. Another two weeks passed, and I finally had enough. I was rendered into an uncomfortable waddling watermelon. So, on a stormy, full moon evening, I ventured out on a ten mile walk in the pouring rain, demanding his wombly departure and earthly arrival. I returned home, and several hours later, my contractions began! At 3 a.m., I woke my mom and told her it was time!

She rushed me to the hospital, and at 5:54 a.m., I gave birth to my beautiful Ezekiel. My biggest baby yet, the pain of pushing him out was so unbearable that I almost couldn't handle it. My mom was there for me in that moment of crazy pain. Her OBGYN training came out and took control, navigating me through the pain, and together we birthed him without me losing my mind! In that moment, she showed me what a mother is for. No one could help me better than her. Even though my mom hasn't been there for me often in life, she certainly was in that moment, and thus, was given the blessing of bringing Ezekiel into this world with me.

I gave him the middle name Wicapi, Dakota for "Star," to honor the "Ring of Fire" annual eclipse that occurred at the time of his conception. It also honored our endurance together while awaiting trial in Rapid City, the full moon under which he was born, and his Lakota and Dakota heritage. Ezekiel became a star in my life, awakening my heart again to the joy of motherhood, and repairing parts of my broken heart. I poured my love into Ezekiel, and learned to smile, laugh, and feel hope again!

When the baby was a few months old, I began communicating with Te Ngako, a Māori spiritual and cultural leader from Aotearoa, or New Zealand. Adorned with the Traditional Tattoo markings of his people's culture, called Tā Moko, over his entire body, he became the first Haka Dancer in New Zealand to take on the full body Tā Moko. He bravely committed himself to revitalizing a part of his culture that was nearly decimated through colonization, thus becoming a Pathfinder amongst his people. At the time, he also pursued his PhD in Māori Traditional culture. He spoke with a high level of eloquence, deep respect, and intelligence that captivated me.

We were familiar with one another through our social media connection that already existed for years. I thought of a post he wrote back in 2010. At the time I read it, I sat outside Pennington County Jail, praying for Eddie's release while Temoc and I slept in the car. It was just after I found out we were stranded in Rapid City. Te Ngako's post encouraged me to keep on going despite the struggles we endured, thus, I always had mad respect for him. So, during our first phone conversation, when he admitted that he was interested in me, and asked if I'd consider dating him, I said of course! We talked for hours and shared some of our deepest secrets and visions with one another.

I told him that I was just released from jail, had a new baby, and was entirely committed to making the most of my purpose on Earth. He supported me fully and shared some of his own trials and tribulations. He also shared that he was training for a marathon, and that because of it, his body was "amazing." I believed him, and deeply admired his intellect, spirituality, and dedication, which far surpassed that of any man I communicated with before. I never knew a man to express such deep admiration and respect for me despite the hardships I endured. He became my doting, long-distance partner for the next three years.

I was given a beautiful vision of his spirit in a dream one night. In it, he stood in what I later found out was a marae, a Traditional Māori gathering place of the people. As he stood before me, and joyfully made me laugh, I suddenly saw an iridescent rainbow light emerge from the spaces in between his Tā Moko. Creator spoke to me and said that He was pleased with his markings, and I knew then that Te Ngako's spirit was intensely beautiful and authentic.

He lived in Aotearoa, the land of the "Long White Cloud" of the Māori people, known to most as New Zealand. I was comfortable with the idea of a long-distance relationship with him, which forced me to take the long road to getting to know him, and which gave me plenty of time to work on my own healing until the time aligned when we would finally meet in person. We fell so in love with each other's spirits, that after a year of talking on the phone, without even having met, we agreed to marry. I believed that he was the one for me, and he felt the same about me. I glowed with the love he showered over me, and he became my support system in my mother's environment, which quickly faded from picture-perfect to poisoned.

Four weeks after having the baby, I jumped back into training. I just got some money from a tax return, so after sending most of it to my other kids, and after spending a huge part of it on my restitution and probation fee, I invested in a jogging stroller. From that point on, I loaded baby Zeke up at 5:30 a.m. every morning, and headed out for a morning jog, which quickly became my daily meditation. I figured that since I hated running long distances, I'd start doing exactly that until I came to enjoy it. At first, I could only handle three-quarters of a mile. Then, it increased to a mile and a half, until finally, I ran up to eleven miles a day! I went for as long as Zeke allowed before he woke and needed a feeding, which was usually around two hours.

I loved the serenity I felt during those runs! Not seeing another human besides Zeke, while running through Nature, brought a sense of peace and empowerment that I hadn't felt often in my life. It took me back to those days in my youth, when things were briefly normal, back to when I'd take off with my dog for the day and get lost, or get found I should say, in the deep enchantment and mystery of the woods, creeks, and rivers.

The times I spent in jail, all alone, with no support from Zeke's dad, and nothing but the Bible for support, taught me how to reach deep within and follow my inner guidance. It also showed me that sacred items and tools that took a physical form outside of me were not needed for me to connect directly with Creator and to pray! Thus, I learned that I could communicate directly with Wakan Tanka. Creator assured me that I deserved love, to be forgiven, and to live a good life. I believed it, and my belief shifted. I accepted the "Christ Consciousness," *not* Christian indoctrination, as a teacher of the manifestation of our needs and desires with effortless asking and then belief. "Ask and you shall receive" became my daily meditation.

I researched the psyche, and discovered teachers like Dr. Bruce Lipton, who taught the "Biology of Belief," or the theory that the way we think, whether positively or negatively, shapes our world, and that we thus have the power to transform our experience, simply by changing our perception. I began a yoga practice, and after a few months, repaired the injuries in my back and thus, drastically straightened my posture. I also meditated underneath the clouds as they shifted into beautiful pastel pinks, purples, and oranges during the rising and setting of the sun, while I sat upon the deck that led out over the water of the bay from my mother's back yard. I never saw anyone out there besides Zeke. It was a safe place for me to reconnect with Mother Earth, and through her, myself.

From that deck, I had many incredible natural experiences, like watching as pods of dolphins jumped and played in the bay waters or seeing a giant manta ray as he swam through the water directly beneath my feet! He was bigger than me, and the sight of him sent my heart racing! Once, I looked over the clear, still waters, and suddenly a flock of water birds came flying *out* of the water! These interactions with Nature always coincided with my prayers. Nature aligned herself with me, the more I aligned myself with her!

In the meantime, the relationship between Zeke and I became the most incredible mother and baby bonding experience I ever had! He was the sweetest baby and was extremely attached to me. He refused to take a bottle, wanting only to breast-feed. So, I co-slept with him, and he quickly learned to feed himself by latching on without my help. This way, I got the rest I needed, while he learned more self-sufficiency early on. He became "the joy of my world," like Lauren Hill described in her song "Zion."

However, the relationship between my mother and I quickly digressed to its normal "strained" place. When the baby was about six weeks old, I sat with my mom on the deck, enjoying the sunset while he slept inside. After a little while, she went back in. I wanted just a few more moments to cherish the sunshine. I soon followed her in, suddenly feeling the need to check on the baby. Sure enough, I heard his cries. I reached him just in time to watch my mother pick him up, and scream in his face, "Shut the fuck up!" His cries exploded then! I ran in and grabbed him from her without saying a word.

I locked myself in my room, and cried as silently as I could, while feeding my hungry baby. "He is only six weeks old!" I thought, disturbed at her overly-aggressive, verbal assault on an infant. Suddenly, I was thrown back to the days when I was an infant, and I wondered if I was seeing how my mother dealt with me. My heart told me that I most definitely was, and I became even more saddened to realize that I was negatively affected as an infant by my mother's inability to love and nurture me when I expressed my needs in the only way that a baby could, by crying. Furthermore, I realized that I saw my son's first traumatic experience, inflicted by my own mother at only six weeks old! I learned to create space between us from that moment forward and kept the baby's cries as far away from her as I could.

Unfortunately, my mother has struggled with substance abuse for as long as I've known, but not obviously, unlike my father. A "high-functioning alcoholic," she also used a plethora of pharmaceuticals to mask her inability to deal with her childhood trauma. Effectively, she buried her pain in work, in the pursuit of materialistic success, in co-dependent relationships, and in substances, for my entire life.

Thus, I was not given a good example of what it means to be a good parent, which forced me to learn how to parent on my own. Observing my mother so closely as an adult, now with five children of my own, allowed me to realize that I repeated my mother's cycle, by joining into dysfunctional and abusive relationships with men that negatively affected my children. With Zeke, I was given the opportunity to break this cycle, which is also known as "intergenerational trauma."

It was around this time that I noticed something very unusual about Zeke. He had a white hair! At first, I thought it was one of the dog's hairs, or even a broken piece of one of the hairs from the white streak in my own hair, but when I pulled on it, his scalp lifted with it, and I realized with a jolt that it was his own! I saw it as a mark of his destiny to become a Healer and leader in his days to come. I was lucky to notice it, because two weeks later, it fell out and his hair has been evenly dark ever since.

In the meantime, Daniel found out that I was out of jail and tried to come back into our lives. I gave him the opportunity, but he was extremely inconsistent, and I realized that the premonition I had about him while in jail – that he would not be involved in the raising of our baby for at least the first ten years – was true. I decided that I would always let Zeke know who his dad was, and where he was from, but let go of having any expectations towards Daniel's ability to be there for us.

Spring break approached for my other kids, and I was incredibly excited to see them! Their dad and I agreed that if I sent him most of my tax return, he'd send them down to be with me for their break. Part of that money was to pay for their trip, but after he received the money, he didn't fulfill his part of the bargain. When I confronted him, he acted like it was no big deal, and that it was even my fault. I realized he was using the kids to get back at me because I rejected his recent attempts to get back together.

When he offered his partnership a few days before, I calmly told him, "My feelings for you are gone, but I'd love to work together to responsibly share and raise the kids. We are capable of this." However, he only wanted things to be "his way." Thus, he did what he could to make it exceedingly difficult for me to see the kids, using the court case, the court-ordered supervised visits, and my probationary status to his advantage.

Shortly after, however, I had an incredible dream that gave me the strength and wisdom to stop pushing so hard, and to allow time and destiny to work for me. I dreamt that I tried to plan with Izz so that I could visit our children, but he blatantly mocked and ignored me, and instead focused his attention on another woman. I felt something rise from deep within me, and looked up into the sky as a white cloud descended all around me. I looked at my hands, arms, and legs as they morphed into the appendages of an animal. My whole being shapeshifted into another form, and as I looked at myself from above, I realized that I turned into an all-white panther! A voice guided me and informed me that the white panther was amongst the rarest of spiritual forms, and now it stood with me. Izz saw me shift, and immediately changed into his other form as a black panther. I growled at him, "It's the white panther versus the black panther now!" As soon as I spoke my own personal prophecy, I awoke.

This dream helped me to accept that it would take time to get my children back, and in fact, there was nothing but time that would help me, along with the acceptance of the path the dream showed me to take. I was transforming into a being that would one day move "the mountains" that stood in between me and my children, but I had to keep my faith, and fully accept the new road to my personal transformation.

In the meantime, I looked for ways to make income from home, so that I could stay with baby Ezekiel full time. A friend turned me on to the idea of selling an anti-aging beauty product that sold for $80 a bottle. I gave it a go, but of course my sales didn't go too well. Selling anti-aging products for a multi-million-dollar corporation wasn't part of my destiny, but I went for it in my determination, so that I wouldn't have to put Zeke in daycare. I also started beading again. For hours a day, I basked in the sun as I created peyote-stitched art. Once I finished a piece, however, I didn't want to sell it, and didn't even have the audience to sell it to for the price I needed to match the time put into it. So, my twin hooked me up with a few jobs building websites for other entrepreneurs. I built his website, and that of several others who were just beginning their own businesses at the time, and who later became extremely successful. Building these sites for them helped me to eventually build my own website, business, and success.

Meanwhile, the relationship between Te Ngako and I deepened. We still hadn't met in person, but he became the person I relied upon for emotional and spiritual support. We enjoyed long conversations every night. We often just left the line on without talking, a form of spending time with one another without the need for conversation. At night, we video chatted and sometimes even fell asleep while doing so. By the morning, the video feed was always turned off.

One night, however, we both fell asleep this way, and in the morning, I looked at the chat. The video was still on. As Te Ngako slept, the light of day illuminated the feed. Thus, his body was exposed to me for the first time, and I saw that he was not in the "incredible shape" that he claimed to be, but instead was extremely overweight, even obese! He stood up to go to the bathroom, and for the first time, I viewed the reality of his vessel, realizing in an instant that he blatantly lied to me by hiding his true shape for months!

I switched off the camera and instantly sank into a deep depression. This man that I shared some of my deepest hopes and dreams with, including the need to have an honest man in my life as a partner, had deceived me the entire time! I refused his calls for a few days, until I settled on the best action to take. After deep contemplation, I finally told him what I saw, and that I was open to hearing his side of the story. Even though I at first felt like cutting him off and never talking to him again, my heart told me to forgive him, despite feeling so betrayed.

Thunderbird Rising

After a long talk, we came to an understanding, and I expressed my forgiveness. I told him that my trust would take a long time to return, but underneath it all, I understood why he lied. He was scared that if he told the truth in the beginning, he'd never have a chance with me, and truth is, he probably wouldn't have. The trio of spiritual, emotional, and physical fitness were incredibly important to me, so I could not see myself falling for an obese person because I believed an imbalance in one state implied an imbalance in the others. But truth is, I already fell in love with his spirit, and my heart guided me to give it another chance.

Despite his earlier deception, Te Ngako continued on as my support system, helping me survive an extremely challenging time. So too did Nature. One day, I was incessantly attacked by biting flies, and nearly driven inside, but noticed that a lizard watched my dilemma as it clung to the wall behind me. I got an idea and put it to the test! I let the flies bite me, then offered them to the lizard. To my amazement, he ate them right off me! He wasn't frightened at all. So, we did this, over and over, until the flies disappeared. The lizard got an easy meal, and I was no longer tortured. We formed a remarkable symbiotic relationship that lasted for weeks!

Another day, as I sat on the front porch, a mockingbird suddenly dive-bombed me! At least I thought he did, until I realized that a huge black snake slithered just inches away from my feet. The mockingbird dived at it until it was chased away! Later, while I was reading in the garage, the biggest dragonfly I ever saw flew in. He landed only a few feet away, so I couldn't resist placing my fingers gently underneath him. He willingly stepped onto my fingers! He held onto me for several hours before he suddenly flew away.

Every morning, while I practiced yoga, a pair of bald eagles flew right over, encouraging me! I was going through a tough time at my mom's, but the animals, insects, and Nature herself became my best friends. I submerged Ezekiel and myself in her surroundings, from sunrise to sunset, until I absolutely had to go back inside once the biting gnats came out. I am convinced that the natural environment I steeped myself in while there is how I endured that time without utterly losing my mind!

I held Ceremony with the elements in my own way as well. One day, I stood beneath a beautiful storm and offered some of my freshly baked bread. Two eagles circled overhead, as a rainbow that was not arched as usual over the earth, but which circled instead around itself within the clouds, preceded before the storm. Lightning struck directly overhead, as I stood with my arms outstretched to the sky, and my feet submerged in the water. The thunder growled immediately, and blessed electricity kissed the air, the water, and my spirit! I could see the wind approach across the water as the intensity of the storm arrived. The waves picked up with the current of the air, and churned, chanted, and crashed to heights that were rare.

I bowed, facing my temple towards the earth, and my crown towards the storm in respect of its power, while the wind roared and twisted around me. I could feel the anti-gravitational effect as the wind sucked up the energy of the earth and thrashed around in all directions at once! I could see the water as it lifted into the sky. I felt myself being raised as well, as my hair and my dress whipped about excitedly. I didn't know what to do at this point. Should I be afraid? The Spirits said: "Do not fear death, it is only an illusion." So, I stood my ground, as the wind purred around me, and the waves continued to swell, while the wind transformed constantly! I held my arms out to the Earth, breathing deeply, and slowly the storm passed over.

My dreams also helped me through this period. One night, I dreamt of a huge, crane-like bird that swallowed up the night sky. It spread its huge wings across the entire span of the heavens, and then stretched its neck and beak to their limits. In this way, it surged up an incredible amount of electric energy, until suddenly, it shot it out as the thickest bolt of lightning I'd ever seen! It struck the White House below it, splitting it in half!

I then dreamt that I stood in a room on the rez filled with other Natives. Wanbli, Bald Eagle, flew into the room. He circled in a figure eight formation. I waited for the others to notice but they never did. Then, he offered himself as a sacrifice for spiritual purposes and died. The girls noticed him then and fought over his body parts! I asked for the plumes, so that I could honor him with dance, but they didn't want to share with me. I questioned what they did with the parts, and they told me that they sold them to wasicu – takers of fat – for money or kept them for their own regalia so they could win dance contests. This angered me, and I reminded them that they were instructed by the ancestors not to sell our sacred items, but they didn't care, and continued to fight over the parts of the eagle to attempt to keep them all for themselves.

Soon, they took off, and I was shown a little boy that cried. I asked him why, and he said his big sister just beat him up with a group of her friends. I embraced him while he sobbed, and she admitted what she did as if it were something to be proud of! I looked across the street, and saw a drunken middle-aged man sexually abuse a little boy. I cried out for him to stop, but he continued, teaching another man to do the same. I saw the eagle again. He was carelessly discarded. So, I took to working on him, separating the wings from the body to prepare them for Ceremony. Then, I awoke. This dream showed me that many people are lost, disconnected from their ancestors and the Spirit World; that chaos reigns, and abuse is the norm. Yet, the winged ones, ancestors, and Spirits still reach out, fighting for us to remember who we are. It is not too late, even though atrocities abound, for us to make the change!

In another dream, I watched the most intense lightning storm I've ever seen approach from afar. Lightning struck with such intensity that it destroyed entire technological grids. Satellites went down, electrical networks were demolished, and walls of fire rose from the lands behind it. Hundreds of dogs gathered before it, howling at the sky! This became a recurring dream.

In yet another dream, I watched four tornadoes swirl around one another. It was awe-inspiring! Then, they crisscrossed each other, swirled again, and disappeared in an instant. Suddenly, they reappeared as one massive tornado! Then, I woke up. When I went outside, I realized that my favorite tree to sit with was all twisted up. Its branches, which stood strong and upright the day before, were now splayed over the earth. It was split right down the middle, through its core, into four separate directions!

In another dream, I sang on stage with Bob Marley. He coached me to sing "from my throat," and then, kissed me on the cheek like I was a member of his family. Izz sat in the crowd, watching with the kids. He became extremely jealous. I soared through a beautiful sky temple in another dream. When I looked down at my form, I noticed it was that of a dragon! I chased an invading dragon through the temple. As I flew over the temple's sacred altar, I paused and hovered over it, honoring it, yet still caught up with the invader dragon and chased him out of our sacred home! Finally, I dreamt that I flew with a spotted golden eagle. He taught me how to dive, by tucking my wings in at my side, and then just allowing my body to fall quickly to the earth. I practiced over and over with him until I got it right.

My dreams became my internal sanctuary, while the garage and the world just outside my mother's home became my physical sanctuary. Even though I was there all day with Patrick, I created a way for us both to have space from one another, by staying and working outside most of the time. I made a little play area in the garage for Zeke, and for myself to work, dance, and train in when it rained.

Despite doing my best to avoid Patrick, he came out to my space in the garage one day to trip out on me. Accusing me of disrespecting my mother by daring to have the audacity to "move things around without asking," he screamed that I should "put everything back exactly the way it was!" This was *after* I already asked my mom's permission to set up an office in the garage for myself! I suppose he was mad that I didn't see the need to get his approval too. I asked him to clarify exactly what I moved, and where it needed to return to. Furthermore, to explain why it was a problem to begin with. He never specified what I moved, but just kept claiming that I "knew what it was," and I "needed to put it back." I asked again, and still, he didn't specify. So, I asked again, and again, and still no clarification was given, but only a grown man's bitching!

So, finally I flipped on him, "I don't owe you a goddamn thing! I mean, who the hell are you to tell me shit? You aren't my dad, or my stepdad! You are only her husband, and of no real concern to me, especially since I can clearly see how you live off her, use all her money, drive a car she bought you, take her down a deeper spiral of alcoholism by encouraging her to drink every night, and pretend to own things that were never yours to start with, like for one, the right to tell me to do anything!" He left in a huff and called my mom to "tell" on me.

My mom rushed home. She was terribly upset with me and sat down in a huff while he leered over her. She drilled me, "So, Steph, how many kids do you have now?" I calmly answered, "Five, just like you." "And what are you doing with your life?" she continued. "Well, I train every morning by running at least five miles. I'm raising my baby on my own. I'm building my own business through my arts and crafts. I'm practicing yoga, developing my spirituality, and trying my absolute best to change my life. I'm also earning enough money on my own every month to pay all my bills without your help."

She said nothing about those achievements, but instead changed the subject with another question. "Why are you being disrespectful to my husband?" I sighed and replied, "Mom, he came at me. I was in the garage, doing my best to distance myself from him, and he came out to me to create an issue. I can't see how I'm being disrespectful to him. I'm only telling him the truth. Don't you see that he's leeching off you, and passing it all off as if it's his own? How did he get anything he has right now other than by marrying you?"

My mom went off in a rage, "Our situation isn't working anymore. You need to move the fuck out as soon as possible." I agreed! I realized that all the months I spent trying to once again spearhead the healing of the relationship between my mom and I was for naught, as once again my mother chose to stand by her husband, who acted inappropriately towards me, over me. On a deeper level, I also saw that she simply didn't want to accept the truth. I can see now that she was tired, and like any of us, just wanted love, even if she kept a blindfold on to make believe that she was getting it. I stood in the way of that, so I had to go.

This is how I realized that I needed to get a job with a steady paycheck. I talked to my mom about it, and she suggested Patrick as a babysitter, and he said "hell yeah" he'd do it. He was back in school at this point – Mom used her GI Bill on him, paying for his entire college education – and said that he could watch the baby during the times he wasn't in class. I wanted a professional sitter, but didn't have the money for it, so in desperation, I settled for Patrick. It seemed like a good all-around temporary situation, so I could earn the money I needed to pay off my restitution and get the hell out of dodge.

Thunderbird Rising

So, I served tables at Mellow Mushroom, an organic pizza joint with the best pizza I've ever had! It was fun, and the food was incredible, but for the work I did, I didn't make enough money to suit my dreams. I was considered amongst the best, and fastest servers in the place, so I was given the toughest sections during the crazy spring break season of Panama City Beach. I ran my ass off for pennies, as most of my tables were filled with high school and college students on spring break, who were more interested in their next shot than in leaving good tips. However, I did love that my nickname became "Big Eagle." Every time one of my orders was ready, the kitchen staff shouted, "Big Eagle up!" and I proudly retrieved my food.

One day, I served a table of professors at the local college just down the street. Their conversations inspired me, convincing me that it was time to continue my own education. I dropped out of high school thirteen years before, to escape my stepdad and the life I lived at home. Finally, I made the decision to wrap up those loose ends and get my GED. I studied for a few weeks, paid the examination fee, got Patrick to babysit for a few hours, took the test, and passed with an honors score, finally wrapping up my high school education thirteen years later!

As the days passed by while I worked at Mellow Mushroom, I resented that I spent my days away from the baby. I also pumped my milk for him, but he refused to take the bottles. My absence did not work out for either of us. The day finally came when I was pushed to quit my job and leave my mom's house forever. I sat in my car in the garage, getting ready to leave. The baby never liked it when I left, but that day cried especially hard. I told Patrick I was heading out, gave little Zeke a big hug, and left him in the room with Patrick. But as I left, he crawled behind me. I heard his cries as he pounded on the garage door, desperately trying to come after me. It broke my heart to hear it, and usually I pulled off anyway, because he did this every day, but something told me to just keep listening that day – a mother's instinct that guides stronger than any other.

So, I waited, and I listened to Zeke cry, and cry, and cry! After thirty minutes of waiting for Patrick to do something about it, to grab Zeke and to comfort him, to do anything, I realized that it wasn't going to happen. This must've been his method of "babysitting" the entire time – literally just sitting there, while the baby crawled around and cried for me in my absence! I called into work and told them I wasn't coming in that day, and that I wouldn't ever come back. I realized that my baby wasn't being properly cared for, and he came first, so I had to give up my job with them.

I hung up, opened the door, and grabbed my screaming baby. Patrick heard me, and came towards us then, nervously exclaiming, "Oh! I thought you were going to work!" I glared at him but held my tongue. "No. I was going, but I've changed my mind." I didn't confront him and didn't even bother telling my mom about it. What was the use? I learned she would never believe me anyway. I knew who he truly was now, and that was enough for me. I never left the baby alone with him or her again and made plans to leave their house forever.

A few days after finding out about Patrick's negligence towards Zeke, my auntie on my mom's side came to visit. I remember feeling very left out, as they all went out to dinner, and left Zeke and I behind. My heart tried not to hurt, but truth is, I felt isolated and lonely. It was really getting to me how much my mother didn't like me, and in contrast, how much she idolized this dusty, dope of a man. Furthermore, when my auntie came out, the baby and I were automatically left out. I really did like my auntie at first though. I loved her laugh and high energy. She was fun to be around!

The last morning before I finally left, I dressed in my room while Zeke crawled around, playing and exploring in another area of the house. I walked out just in time to see Jake, my mom's golden retriever, snarl, bark, and snap at the baby's face! Patrick sat right next to Jake, but just watched it happen without doing a thing. If Jake were my dog, I would have instantly grabbed him by the neck and slammed him on his back before the baby, teaching him he better be submissive, or else! That is how you let dogs know that they do not come before little children, but Patrick did nothing.

I had reason to be concerned, because years earlier, Jake bit my niece's face, when she was just two years old! He sliced her face open with his fucking teeth. She was rushed to the hospital, stitched up, and still carries the scar of his attack to this day! However, my mother decided to keep Jake, "forgiving" him, and blaming my niece for the violence. My twin still talks about that event to this day, the time when our mother blatantly chose her child-biting dog over her own grandchild. I wasn't about to allow my baby to be bitten by that dog too! I had to run a quick errand that I couldn't take the baby to. So, I took him out to my auntie as she sat by the pool and asked if she'd look after him because the dog just snapped at his face. I needed to make sure he was safe.

Zeke and I moved out the next day. I believed that I left on humane terms with all of them. I told my mom I loved her, and shook Patrick's hand, thanking them both for allowing me to stay there. I felt good about moving on in a good way. However, a day later, after arriving in Sacramento with my brother, my mom texted to complain. My auntie told her that I brought the baby to her to watch because of Jake. My mom *and* my auntie thought it was extremely disrespectful of me to do so. My mom claimed that "Jake didn't mean it. He's a good dog that would never hurt the baby. Asking your aunt to watch the baby because of Jake, is just another disrespectful act towards Patrick, who was perfectly capable of watching him."

That became the last conversation I had with my mother, my auntie, and Patrick. I realized that my mother proved countless times that she'd allow her partners to inflict abuse, pain, and dysfunction into my life, and my children's. I could no longer give her the okay to continue to bring toxicity and trauma into our lives. I chose instead to protect myself and Zeke, and thus, cut the ties between us. I recognized that she had an illness and an addiction that was not my responsibility to fix. Furthermore, Patrick fed off and deepened her addictions, but there was nothing that I could do to help or stop it. I was always the one "doing wrong" in her eyes, and so the best thing I could do was to fully move on and stop looking to my mom to give the affection, support, and understanding of a mother that she was just not capable of giving.

I finally accepted that the state of our relationship wasn't my fault. I did my best, and it was time to move on with my life without expecting her to be a person that I could depend on. It was extremely healing and liberating for me to let her go! My mother taught me that I do not have to have a relationship with someone just because they are biological relatives. If the relationship with them introduced me or my children to toxicity of any form, I learned that it was okay, and sometimes even necessary, to sever ties. I cannot allow anyone into my life that is a threat to my inner peace and sanctity, no matter who they are or what status they hold.

In this way, I moved out of my mother's house, even though I was still on probation. I took a huge risk and flew out to California to stay with my twin. I had to escape the toxic environment in my mom's house, and I also knew that being in California would offer more solid financial opportunities. Once again, I did what I had to do!

In just under a year of being on probation, I paid off my court-ordered restitution fee of $7,500! A year before, this was an insurmountable amount of money for me to come up with so quickly. Thus, I realized that I could manifest the abundance I needed with the right mindset, and this became the turning point in my life from financial lack to more financial abundance!

My probation officer was proud of me and couldn't believe that I had such a high restitution fee in the first place. She said that my crime didn't equal the punishment that Judge Davis placed on me. The felony conviction was far too severe, and probation grossly unnecessary, for what otherwise was a non-violent, victimless offense by a first-time offender that in her eyes, should've been a misdemeanor. Once I paid all my restitution and probation fees, she happily signed off on the papers, releasing me from her supervision three and a half years earlier than Judge Davis planned. I was finally free to move forward without any legal restrictions!

Figure 17. We finally leave Florida!

CHAPTER ELEVEN

THE STANDING ROCK TATTOO

I left my mother's house without looking back and welcomed my next chapter in Sacramento. I enrolled in school at Sacramento City College at once and funded it through a program that aided single parents pursuing their education, through scholarships, and the occasional school loan. A few months before school started, I joined a local Aztec dance group, Kalpulli Ketzalcoatl Ocelotl. I didn't know at the time that I carried Aztec heritage on my father's side that was passed down from my great-grandfather. I understand now that I was instinctively drawn to join the dance group to learn more about myself. I caught on quickly and delved deeply into this powerful, ancient Tradition.

When I immersed myself in danza Azteca, I deeply understood how our dance became our actioned devotion, especially as our group stomped as one, pounding our footsteps passionately into Mother Earth. Our chachayotes – the seed leggings worn around our ankles – moved along with us in unison, rattling in accompaniment with the drum as they embodied the living bones of our ancestors. We became the past, present, and future that moved as one, embodying the circle of life itself, where all things are connected! I dedicated myself to the group and traveled extensively to many Ceremonies and celebrations with them. After our danza on the Buena Vista Me-wuk Indian Reservation, I experienced one of the most terrifying and unsettling moments of my life!

Zeke and I walked alone to our car. Our shelter for the night, it was parked far out in a field by itself. I tucked Zeke in, and he fell fast asleep. I stood outside, gazing up at the stars as I changed out of my regalia. Suddenly, a terribly eerie feeling overcame me. I looked down, and adrenaline shot through my body as I spotted a shadowy figure, about half my height, that intensely stared at me from only ten feet away! Even though it was dark outside, the figure was blacker than the night, and therefore, stood out from it. For a moment, our eyes locked as we pondered one another.

I froze into that moment; in the way one might react after seeing Bigfoot for the first time. My friend "Smurf" approached just in time. He saw the creature, and as soon as it noticed him, it ran away, but not like a human, and not like any animal I'd ever seen before! Smurf yelled after it, and chased it like lightning, but the creature ran faster, so he pursued it until it disappeared past the tree line.

When he returned, he told me it was a Wiwila – the Lakota word for "Little Person!" He explained that the Wiwila, or "Little People," came from another world, outside of our own. The sun died in their world, so they came to ours. "Their" time to come out is when the sun goes down, so we usually never see them. Smurf settled me with this ancestral story. He believed the Wiwila watched me because we just finished Ceremony, so it was attracted to us, but he chased it because sometimes they take us. I had an awfully hard time falling asleep that night. It was my first time witnessing an "other-worldly" being, and it shattered my reality!

The weekend before classes began, Zeke and I attended a Ceremony for the salmon with Chief Caleen Audrey Sisk of the

Winnemem Wintu Tribe. It was held on their Tribal land at the base of Mount Shasta. During the Ceremony, she spoke about the Traditional fire-keeping methods that her people practiced for thousands of years before modern fire regulation. She directly attributed the increasing catastrophic wildfires to the new method, which "overly prevented" forest fires. She also taught us that the forest was adapted to smaller, more frequent fires. Thus, her people traditionally burned the undergrowth of the forest to prevent larger fires.

As we listened to her Teachings, I suddenly heard familiar screams emanating from the group of kids my son played with. With horror, I realized that Zeke was sitting in the center of a giant, wild bee swarm! I rushed over to him. Dozens of bees stung him any place they could, so I swooped in, grabbed him, and sprinted away from the hive as fast as I could! The bees assaulted me too, but I got away so quickly that I was only stung seven times.

I was extremely worried for my son. This was the first time he was ever stung, and he received over fifty stings! I told him that he had to stop crying, so that his blood would calm down and keep the venom from spreading. He did! I carried him swiftly over to the Ceremonial fire and grabbed a fist full of tobacco. I held my son before Mount Shasta, told her what happened, and begged for her to help him! Then, I threw the tobacco into the fire.

It soon became clear that my son was fine! In fact, his stings didn't even swell. It was as if he hadn't been stung at all! I, on the other hand, experienced *extreme* swelling with every sting. It got so bad that most of them also became infected. The power of prayer was made clear to me that day! Before the sacred fire and the sacred mountain, I prayed with all my heart, and my prayers were answered for my son. The swelling of my own stings showed me that a miracle occurred through the power of that Ceremonial circle. The combination of heart-felt prayers, Medicinal offerings, and Traditional Ceremony can and do create supernatural results!

We returned home safely, and classes began. I chose biology, the study of life, as my major, with a focus on environmental biology. I intended to take my education to the PhD level, and eventually use my education to protect and restore endangered species and their native habitats. Te Ngako was a huge support as he helped guide my educational pursuits while he worked diligently on his own. I enrolled Zeke in a Montessori school program that was fully paid for by the state to support my return to school. It was the first time we spent so much time apart from each other, and we both grew immensely from it.

When I first moved to Sacramento, I stayed with my twin for a while. He drank heavily at the time, so understandably we didn't get along because of it. So, after a particularly huge fight between us, Zeke and I left, and moved into a hotel for the first few months of school. I worked extremely hard to manifest the abundance needed to put a roof over our heads due to our $2,600 monthly hotel bill! I preferred an apartment, but the dozens I applied to automatically denied me because of the felony on my record. I ran out of energy and time as the first day of school quickly approached. So, I said, "Fuck it!" and moved into the hotel, paying the high price it cost to do so.

I quickly realized how difficult it was to get approved for anything while having a felony on my record! I didn't stand a chance, even though I turned my life around, didn't get in trouble again, and went to school. So, I wrote several letters to Judge Davis, requesting a "suspended imposition" to remove the felony from my public record so that I could reasonably put a roof over my child's head. I never heard back from him.

Finally, one of my friends introduced me to Nacho, an apartment owner who rented without running background checks. He offered me a small one-bedroom apartment, for an affordable $700 a month, *but* it was next to a registered sex offender. At the time, I had to take what I could get, because living in that hotel threw my money away. I followed my intuition, which told me I'd be uncomfortable there, but safe! Thus, it became our sanctuary for the next two years. It was all we needed. I only left to go to school and back, and otherwise stayed inside to study and take care of Zeke.

During my first semester, I took an astrobiology course that studied the possibility of life on other planets, which I discovered was scientifically "very likely." This course fascinated me, and vastly reshaped my perspective on my own scientific capabilities. I was one of a few students over the *years* to earn a perfect "A" in that class, because of the professor's unique testing style. With no multiple-choice questions on any exam, and with each test consisting of only eleven to twelve essay style questions, students were graded on their ability to "think for themselves," based on their thorough knowledge of the topics covered. This required intense study, a deep interest in the subject matter, and the ability to literally "think outside the box."

Most students failed every question and dropped the class. It was empowering for me, being technically a high school dropout that flunked out of most of my science classes in high school, to now be amongst the few students that excelled in this extremely difficult course! I did so well that I was recruited to tutor it and did so for the rest of my time at the college.

Finally, I found my determination, and now that I was in control of my own life and time, there was nothing that could stop me from rising to the top of the students in every class. I did nothing but study, attend class, take care of Zeke, and train with my twin, who at the time had his own personal training studio. I was also still in a long-distance relationship with Te Ngako, so I never sought to date while in school. I was undistracted and successful for the first time in my life, and it felt incredible! Zeke did well in school too. He was enrolled in the toddler section at Sacramento Montessori, and I felt comfortable knowing that an Indigenous woman was his main teacher.

I worked diligently to achieve my goal of traveling internationally to restore native habitats and protect endangered species. I earned many scholarships with this proposal, and I had full intentions to see it through. I also tried to get my other kids back now that I had my own place and some stability. I hired a lawyer in Indianapolis and took Izz back to court to fight for at least joint custody. My goal was to eventually have the kids come to live with me in Sacramento.

Izz and I had to take part in a parent interview with the courts before our custody hearing. My lawyer told me that a resulting recommendation would be given to the court about the placement of the children that would be "heavily considered" and "almost always followed by the courts." I traveled out to Indianapolis and completed my interview. I thought that I appeared to be an excellent parent. I turned absolutely everything around on paper, had my own place, a steady income, and was now a 4.0 GPA college student! However, when the interview results were given to my lawyer, I found out that the caseworkers strongly recommended to the courts that the kids "remain with Izz." Once again, I accepted that I had to move on. Trying to get my kids back through the system, or by working with Izz alone, never went in my favor. As an activist with a record, I'd never be a good placement for the children in their eyes. So, I let go once again.

One of my favorite experiences during my college studies was the hands-on Mojave Desert Field Study Course, which studied California's Natural History in the Mojave Desert. My relative traveled out from South Dakota to stay at my place for seven days with Zeke so that I could go on this epic adventure. It was the first time I had been separated from Zeke for that long, but it was worth it, because I had one of the best experiences of my life!

For seven days, the biology professors leading the course, and us student biologists-in-training, explored the Mojave Desert. I am the first to admit that I'm a bit of a nerd when it comes to Nature. I'm fascinated by every living creature, plant, stone, and environment out there, except for cockroaches. During this trip, I wasn't the only one "geeking" out on Nature. Each of the thirty people that attended were also on the same vibe! We fed off each other's energy, and soon we realized that we all had it "BAD," an acronym we invented to describe "Biologist Attention Deficiency," the condition of being extremely distracted by every creature, plant, or new feature we meet in Nature.

Our first mornings and evenings there started with netting and cataloging the various bird and bat species in the area, which taught us how to track population trends in local species. We raised nets that harmlessly caught them, and then we carefully removed them, identified their species and gender, measured their wing and beak length, recorded the information, and finally released them. It was an incredible feeling to hold so many beautiful species of birds, and to inspect them so closely! I learned that although the desert appears to be devoid of life, it is host to hundreds of species of specially adapted birds, and dozens of hardy bat types.

An entire day of our trip was devoted to an extremely challenging hike up Kelso Dunes, which stood some 650 feet above the desert floor! When we made it to the top, an awesome reward and adventure awaited us: the "booming dunes," the pounding sound created by our footsteps hitting the sand as we raced down the steepest slope of the dunes back to the desert floor! We laughed like little children as we cascaded in pairs down the dune's cliff.

One of the biologists who came along with us specialized in working with reptiles and poisonous insects. An expert at catching them, he proved it every time we looked at him as he proudly held a poisonous snake, or a lizard that no one else could catch. He also caught scorpions at night and held them in his hands while they lit up like a neon sign under a black light flashlight. He challenged me to catch one of the fastest lizards in the Mojave Desert, the elusive Whiptail Lizard, which to his surprise, I easily did!

Our leading professor during the trip, Dave, was hilarious, and often shared hysterical stories from past group adventures. We fell to the floor with laughter when he told us about his colleagues that allowed themselves to be stung by a tarantula hawk to "study" the intensity of its sting, which is said to be the second most painful in the world. A tarantula hawk is a huge, ominous-looking wasp that inhabits the southwestern desert region, whose sting is powerful enough to permanently paralyze a tarantula, thus enabling it to lay its eggs inside the tarantula's body, transforming it first into the egg's incubator, then, into the living food source of its hatching larvae! Dave giggled uncontrollably as he recounted how these grown men with bulging muscles were reduced to screaming, drooling infants for exactly five minutes after being stung by a tarantula hawk. They successfully proved that the sting *was* amongst the most painful in the world, truly did last for only five minutes, and that screaming was in fact, the only source of comfort they could find during the most excruciating five minutes of their lives!

On the last day of our trip, as we headed out of the Mojave Desert, our caravan of two vans and one truck suddenly lurched to the side of the road! Onlookers saw approximately thirty people of many sizes, colors, and ages rapidly spilling forth from the trinity of vehicles, not even bothering to close their doors. The lot stampeded in the same direction – towards a lone desert tortoise that leisurely crossed the road. Yeah, we certainly had it BAD as we expertly created nerdy scenes, but it was worth it, because after all, the desert tortoise is an endangered species. Therefore, we had to make sure it crossed the road safely, and that we got selfies while doing so!

In the summer of 2016, the opportunity finally came for me and Te Ngako to meet in person! For months, he encouraged me to take on my own "facial soul blueprints," or tattoos. I always said no unless I found evidence of its practice in my lineage. I didn't want to take on markings that did not belong to me genetically. I researched intensely, scouring for any evidence of a Traditional Tattoo culture from my Dakota or Lakota ancestors. Finally, I came across a few sources that confirmed that some Dakota women did have simple forehead, temple, and chin markings just a few generations ago! It was all I needed to go for it in my own way. I had always, even before meeting Te Ngako, been fascinated by the Traditional Tattoos of Indigenous peoples, and wanted to take on those from my own Tribe if I found evidence of them!

Te Ngako arranged for one of the world's most renowned Māori Tā Moko artists, Turumakina Duley, to do the honors of placing the marks. After sharing multiple visions, dreams, and some history of my people with Tu, along with what I could find about the placements of our Traditional markings, he drew the designs that were channeled to him from our ancestors, as is the Traditional Māori Tā Moko method, and then tattooed the outline of the markings on my forehead and chin. A little hesitant at the time to bolden in the lines, I opted out of the fill-in, and thus, my facial tattoos were lightly placed, forever transforming me!

A few weeks went by, and my confidence in the markings grew. I was ready for the lines to be filled! Because Tu had already returned to Australia, his cousin, Stu McDonald, another prominent Māori Tā Moko artist, filled in my facial markings after receiving Tu's blessing to do so. Turumakina, Stu, and Te Ngako, who all carried their Traditional markings on their faces, honored me with intensive koreros, or talks, to prepare me for what would certainly be a long road ahead. They said that I would need the strength of their encouraging words, and to never forget that I was loved and supported in Aotearoa!

Overall, I had a beautiful and incredibly transformative adventure with Te Ngako there. I was enchanted by the natural beauty of the land combined with the power, honor, and presence of the Māori culture. I made plans with Te Ngako to obtain a visa that would allow Zeke and I to stay in New Zealand for much longer. However, I realized that I needed a clean criminal record to obtain a longer visa. So, I contacted the Pennington County Courts to see what I needed to do to begin the process of getting the felony stricken from my record.

When they searched for my record, however, they found nothing! I thought they were joking and asked them to look again. Still nothing! My case was retrieved, and I found out that the suspended imposition was granted, and the felony was removed from my record. In an instant, I realized that my prayers to be set "miraculously free," which began in that lonely Texas jail cell, and endured throughout my entire incarceration, were answered, but in a completely unexpected form! I could now pursue a longer-stay visa without worry, and furthermore, it would never appear on my background checks ever again. I was free!

When I got back home, however, I had many fitful dreams about Te Ngako cheating. I remembered a password he gave me, and with it, I logged into his Facebook account and scoured through his messages.

I discovered that my dreams were true! He did communicate with many other women, seeking their companionship, so I had to let him go!

Thus, the challenge to complete my final semester of college ensued. Recovering from a broken heart, while receiving the stereotypical colonized reactions to my facial tattoos created a whole new reality for me that I had to learn how to handle with grace. It was clear that I could no longer blend in, no matter where I went. Either I was met with stares that were filled with horror and judgement, or stares filled with admiration and wonder. There was no longer any in-between. I quickly learned how to glaze over my vision in crowds, seeing only my destination, rather than allowing anyone's view of me to be of my concern. Although it was an exceedingly difficult transition period, I never regretted the choice that I made.

A few weeks after returning from Aotearoa, in the summer of 2016, I published a story about the meaning behind my facial markings, and why I chose to accept them. To my surprise, it received a massive amount of positive attention and support, and suddenly, my social media following rapidly expanded, bringing new opportunities and connections. Here is that story:

I've had a bit of time to reflect on the changes I've been through over the last few months and would like to share a little bit of my story - my Kirituhi (my Traditional Tattoo for a non-Māori placed by a Māori Tā Moko artist) journey, as they say in Aotearoa, or my sacred soul blueprint/tattoo journey elsewhere. I traveled to Aotearoa, New Zealand, to experience a world that has changed my life forever. A land of beauty, of its people, culture, scenery, and spirit, now haunts me in my dreams and in my waking hours – a profound effect that will never be forgotten. Aotearoa is a sacred place that I will always be driven to revisit. A place I will always be connected to in a special way....

Thunderbird Rising

As many of you have noticed, while I was in Aotearoa, I chose to adorn my face with Traditional Tattoos, placed by Tohunga Tā Moko, Māori Traditional Tattooists, on both my forehead and chin. Te Ngako, my partner, inspired me to do so, but ultimately, it was my ancestors – particularly from the Dakota side – who encouraged me most strongly. Through dreams, I received visions of the markings they asked me to take, as well as guidance in terms of the mana, or power that comes with taking the markings on.

I am not going to deny that I was extremely apprehensive about accepting the responsibility. It has been many generations since women in my Tribe – Dakota/Lakota – have worn markings on the face, and the markings I have taken on are much more elaborate than what they once wore; from the limited information I could find, a few straight lines on the chin, and dots on the forehead, temples, and cheeks were all that used to be worn, and only by select women. But I followed their guidance anyway, and with the synergy created between the Tā Moko artists, Turumakina Duley and Stu McDonald, and Te Ngako, and our ancestors, the designs were chosen and placed, and made tapu, wakan, or sacred. Kia ora! Wopida! Thank you!

Now that the markings are nearly healed, and I've got a bit of experience under my belt in terms of living with them, I've had a few profound insights I'd like to share. I asked my ancestors why they asked me to take these markings on. After all, in "America," these markings place me in a position of huge risk. I will be misunderstood by most, labeled incorrectly, judged, and hugely crossed out of most job opportunities before I've even begun!

Beyond that, there was little physical guidance from my ancestor's tattoos left intact to base my designs on. I could not take on Māori markings but would have to be completely original and have my own designs uniquely created from what little was given to me. I knew that doing so would put me in a position of having to face the criticism and judgement of my own people, and other Indigenous Nations. Yet, the visions of my ancestors were with me, and became more powerful than any risk, so I agreed to take it on regardless.

Thus, I've begun to understand that every time I look in the mirror, or see myself in a picture, or in the reflection of another's glance or stare, that I remember who I am, and where I come from — a long line of Chiefs, of star grandmothers and grandfathers who stand by my side and are proud of who I've become. Secondly, others will look at me and know where I come from. Some will be forced to acknowledge that I come from some people, and some place, they wish could be forgotten and left in the dark. I am a proud Indigenous woman, and I say Indigenous because it means I am of the land. I am also Indigenous in terms of carrying Dakota/Lakota Sioux, and other Indigenous bloodlines, and I'm proud to represent my heritage. The markings have become my voice. I no longer need to shout to the world that we are still here, that you did not wipe us out! Look at my face and know that we made it! That we are the seeds that you tried to bury. Look at us now as we flourish with life!

The markings are a message to my children, and their children to come, and to all our relatives, that it is okay to be who you are. It's okay to defy what the system wants and expects you to be. It's okay to express your true self. It's okay to revitalize our ancestor's ways, and to do so in a modern expression. I've begun to realize that the markings also reflect a change that is occurring in Indigenous peoples all over Mother Earth! We are rising and are no longer afraid to make our presence known! We are beginning not to worry about what the system will make of us taking back what little has been left to us throughout the history of colonization. We are realizing that this is the time when the system buckles under our pressure, because we look up into the night sky, and recognize the never-ending spiral of ancestors that extends beyond each of us!

How will we fail, how will we fall, when we realize, when we see and take hold of our own potential? So, my brothers and sisters, keep on learning to listen to and remember the voices of our ancestors, and follow the path that has been set aside for you, for we are the ones we have been waiting for, and now is the time to reveal our true selves. Remember, and be proud of who you are, and where you come from!

For me, the markings set my path in stone, and for you, well, we are all waiting to see.... Mitakuye Oyasin! Ti hei mauri ora!

Figure 18. *My white buckskin dress and Te Ngako's taonga honor and celebrate my newly placed markings.*

After sharing my story, I was contacted by Elle, a Traditional and modern tattoo artist from Los Angeles, California. A Native Filipino who was actively reviving his own people's Traditional Tattoo practice, he told me that he was looking for someone from my Tribe to pass on the Traditional technique of Handpoke Tattoo, so that we too could revive our own Traditional Tattoo customs. I gladly accepted the offer, although I had doubts about my future success. I never imagined myself as a tattoo artist before this. It never even crossed my mind!

Soon, I entered the final and most difficult semester of my college experience. It was August of 2016. I signed up for a full-time course load, tackling the last requirements needed to earn my associate degree. I took an accelerated chemistry course, cell and molecular biology, and an anatomy and physiology course; some of the most rigorous, time consuming, and challenging courses, all at the same time! Around the same time my classes started, so did the Standing Rock Movement, in which thousands of warriors, or water protectors, stood up against the construction of the Dakota Access Pipeline (DAPL) under Lake Oahe on the Standing Rock Sioux Indian Reservation. On September 3, 2016, water protectors were sprayed with pepper gas and violently assaulted by DAPL private security and trained attack dogs because the water protectors tried to stop DAPL workers from bulldozing a sacred Dakota burial site to make way for the oil pipeline.

When the news reached me, I was instantly torn between continuing school and quitting everything so that I could join the stand against DAPL's installation through our Treaty Lands. I suddenly didn't care as much about my grades and realized that school wasn't as important as I was led to believe it was. I spent my breaks at school watching the live feeds from Standing Rock and sometimes even skipped class to do so. I cried often, triggered by our collective past, and now present, in which history blatantly repeated itself!

Instead of quitting school, I submitted a proposal to present a lecture, for credit in one of my classes, and as a representative of my university, about the Standing Rock Movement. I got approval to ditch all my classes for one week to travel to Standing Rock, so that I could conduct my field research. Thus, I eagerly let all my professors know why I wouldn't be making any classes or labs that week. I was going to Standing Rock, and they cheered for me!

Zeke and I headed out, arriving for the first time at Standing Rock on September 19, 2016! For one week, we were given the beautiful experience of the Standing Rock Movement, when the Oceti Sakowin Camp was just getting started. We felt what it must have been like generations ago, to live as one Tribal community, where we each had our role and place, and when we all looked out for one another.

Figure 19. Ezekiel and I join the Oceti Sakowin Camp on the Standing Rock Sioux Reservation, September 19, 2016.

No major actions occurred while we were there, so our entire experience was steeped in the positive atmosphere of the Oceti Sakowin

Camp life. When I didn't have my hands full with Zeke, who was then just three years old, I washed dishes or served food in the main camp kitchen, attended camp meetings, helped distribute firewood, or visited with the river we were all there to protect, the sacred Mni Wiconi, or life-giving waters.

After returning, I presented an extremely detailed and informative lecture to a large campus audience about the Standing Rock Movement, Native American Treaty Rights, the ongoing struggle to gain the right to govern ourselves, and the need to protect our homelands without governmental interference. I respectfully implored them for their support and understanding of the growing Standing Rock Movement and Indigenous sovereignty. Afterwards, I spent the rest of the semester trying to catch up in the courses that I missed in the week I was gone, but it was worth it in the end, because that week altered the course of my entire life like a life-giving lightning strike!

Elle invited me to create a tattoo design for the supporters and warriors of the Standing Rock Movement, which would be used to spearhead a tattoo fundraiser to support on-ground water protectors. I accepted the offer, and in one night, on November 6, 2016, I created my first tattoo design, the "Standing Rock Tattoo." The week we spent at Standing Rock, combined with my connection to the land and the people, enabled me to pour my whole heart into the creation of the design and its meaning – a Thunderbird with the river of life flowing beneath it. The Thunderbird itself was not a unique design or concept, as it was based on an ancient design, a petroglyph found in our Traditional Dakota homelands in Minnesota. It was the meaning behind it, and the combination of the water, Mni Wiconi, running beneath it, which soon propelled it into becoming a symbol of the Standing Rock Movement.

We launched the official campaign the next day, along with my description of the meaning behind the design: *The Thunderbird represents Great Spirit, who watches over and guides all the protectors and warriors at Standing Rock. The Thunderbird is sacred to the Oceti Sakowin, the Great Sioux Nation, because its arrival in the spring brings with it the gift of life: Mni Wiconi, or the life-giving waters. In the center of the heart of the Thunderbird is a circle which represents all the Nations that have come together as one to stand with Standing Rock. The tail of the Thunderbird is a tipi, which represents the women, the gathering place of Tribal leaders, and the birthing place of future generations. Beneath the tail is the river of life, carrying within it the seven bands of the Oceti Sakowin, whose ancestors foretold of a time when all Nations would heal and unite as one, after many generations of suffering. Together, the Thunderbird, the tipi, and the river of life embody the new path the NoDAPL Movement has created, one of unity, peace, and transformation!*

We set an initial goal for the campaign to raise ten thousand dollars in donations that would be used specifically to support active front-liners. We soon far surpassed our goal, as the campaign quickly grew in popularity, far quicker than any of us were prepared for! Over the course of the next few months, hundreds of tattoo artists joined the campaign, and together tattooed thousands of Standing Rock Tattoos on water protectors and supporters of the movement. The Thunderbird quickly became a symbol of our collective dedication to the protection of Mother Earth and her resources, Indigenous rights, and to the liberation we all deserved.

I was so busy in school that I had little time to manage the Standing Rock Tattoo project, or even to donate any of the money. It also became difficult to decide where to send the money, because of the amount of corruption that poured out of the Standing Rock Movement. It became difficult to know who to trust, and who appropriately managed resources. Thus, I used my intuition along with information from those on the front lines, to donate to specific front-line organizations, groups, and individuals that seemed to not only be doing their best to protect the water and to stop the DAPL installation, but who were *also* in the most need of support.

Our first donation, therefore, was to "We are Diné," a group of Indigenous front line water protectors that were present at most of the major actions. They were also in desperate need of winter gear. We then donated to the Crow Creek Spirit Riders, the group of riders and their horses who were constantly present during front-line actions, and whose horses were injured in attacks by the police and DAPL mercenaries. Next, we supported the twelve Oglala Lakota Youth Runners who ran from Arizona to Standing Rock to raise awareness for the Movement. Then, we supported the Standing Rock Medic & Healer Council, who were present at every front-line action to provide on-site medical attention.

Afterwards, I took some time away from the Standing Rock Tattoo campaign to study for finals. I was justifiably distracted throughout my final semester of college, causing my grades to dip below average. Thus, I needed to ace my finals to pass my courses and earn my degree. So, I poured myself into my studies and successfully aced my final exams, earning the passing grades I needed to graduate from Sacramento City College with an Associate of Science degree in biology! As soon as I finished, I prepared to finally join the Standing Rock Movement full-time!

In the meantime, Elle pressured me to donate to some Standing Rock Sioux Tribal Council members, which I adamantly opposed, due to my personal knowledge of the extreme corruption and embezzlement that occurs within most Native American Tribal Councils. No matter how much I told him that I didn't want to, because I couldn't trust that they would give the money to the people, he kept pressuring me. Therefore, because we were partners, I donated $20,000 of the Standing Rock Tattoo campaign money to a particular member of the Standing Rock Sioux Tribal Council, who promised us that he was going to use it to "purchase gas cards and propane for the people at camp." However, this never happened. All of it was embezzled, just as I suspected!

Before this, I chose only to support people or groups that I knew were on the frontlines doing work. Thus, why I sent the largest donation of all, $45,000, to Winona LaDuke's organization, Honor the Earth. She personally promised me that she would use the money to build a permanent eco-camp at Standing Rock. The eco-camp was never built, however, due to forced evictions, but I found out about a year later that Winona used the donated money to buy land to set up even more warrior resistance camps in Minnesota, which stood against the Enbridge Line 3 Pipeline directed straight through the heart of modern-day Ojibwe and ancestral Dakota territory. Although she seemed to appropriately use the funds to continue resistance efforts, I've questioned even that over the years.

The truth is, my experience at Standing Rock caused me to question everyone! Not one of us escaped without the negative effects that being in a war zone day after day causes. Infiltration and obviously being targeted by federal agents, military soldiers, local law enforcement, and even local and national citizens, did have its effects – distrust, paranoia, doubt, PTSD, extreme exhaustion, and even depression.

Before I physically returned to Standing Rock, we already donated $91,919 of the Standing Rock Tattoo campaign funds to front-line water protectors and related movement organizations, and publicly posted receipts for every single donation. I believe with all my heart that the project was overall a major success because of the thousands of water protectors, supporters, and artists who came together to make it happen. It successfully proved the full power of our synergy! Furthermore, the prayer etched into the design – that we overcome the oppression and abuse that we and our Mother Earth have endured for generations – continues to be carried to Creator through the energy of those tattooed with it.

Elle and I, however, had a falling out over our disagreements, along with his over-bearing communication with me about it, so I ended up terminating my partnership with him on the project. I could not handle being rudely pressured to donate to sources that I knew would *not* use the money appropriately – to sources that have notoriously embezzled from the people since they came into existence! I couldn't work with a partner who didn't heed my valid concerns, and who, furthermore, rudely pushed to have his way. So, I took a big risk and cut all ties with him, taking on the project alone. This would later affect me negatively, when he smear-campaigned me, spreading nasty rumors about what I did with the money to our fellow tattooists at the 2017 Traditional Tattoo & World Culture Festival we both attended in Mallorca, Spain.

As a reputed artist for decades in the tattoo world, most believed him and turned their backs on me, believing that I kept all the money to myself and used it on the "lavish vacations" he accused me of; even though I publicly posted copies of the receipts detailing the donations that were made, and despite the nearly two months I spent on grounds at Standing Rock as an actual water protector! I couldn't believe how easily people trusted outright lies, as I watched them spread like wildfire all around me. I really had to stand strong and hold my head up high anyways because I knew the truth.

Thunderbird Rising

Even with our falling out, and his treatment of me at the tattoo festival, I visited Elle a year later to thank him for passing on the practice of Handpoke Tattooing to me. I was about to step onto a whole new venture in my life – the beginning of my career as an independent Handpoke Tattoo Artist – and I wanted to acknowledge that it was happening because he reached out to me in the beginning. I wanted to thank him for that, to show humility, and to leave our experience forever in the past, at least as far as my energy was concerned.

As soon as I finished my final exams, I closed out my higher education chapter and pulled Zeke out of school. I packed up our essentials and our camp gear, packed up my car, and headed out to Standing Rock with my team. It was time to put in the work!

CHAPTER TWELVE

WE ARE STILL HERE

We arrived in the heart of North Dakota's treacherously cold winter, at the end of January 2017. The eviction of the Oceti Oyate Camp was underway, so I rented a room at the Prairie Knights Casino, and we stayed there until they kicked us out two and a half weeks later because of our water protector status. Our room, while we had it, was open for the use of any water protector who needed to warm up, shower, charge their devices, or crash for the night. We spent every day at camp, and every night at the hotel room tattooing water protectors, conducting interviews, charging our equipment, and releasing the latest news.

A dynamic day and night contrast existed between my first moments at Standing Rock in September, and that of my return in January. Camp had transformed from the empowered, hopeful, and communal feeling of "a return home," into a war zone filled with distrust, the obvious effects of PTSD, infiltrators, and a sense of hopelessness, but nonetheless there was always still plenty of laughter and comradery to be found.

During our stay at the Prairie Knights Casino, it was obvious that the staff considered any water protector a major nuisance. We even overheard the front desk clerk say to a white couple who checked in, and who expressed their concern about the protests, that she wished none of us were there. She claimed that we were "running business away from them and ruining their reputation." It was an interesting belief, because we kept their hotel rooms fully booked during the entire Standing Rock Movement! Eventually, they refused to rent rooms to known water protectors.

The staff retaliated against our presence by purposely leaving their water tanks empty because water protectors filled their water bottles with them. They also worked hand in hand with the BIA and federal agents to coordinate room raids if they suspected any sort of drug use. It was during these "drug raids" that vital video and media footage that were collected by water protectors and journalists "mysteriously" disappeared.

One day, we observed as a long trail of federal agents checked in. They were greeted warmly by the staff as they brought in caseloads of guns, ammunition, rubber bullets, bullet proof vests, and technological gear that would later be used against water protectors. In the meantime, we were treated like pests. Was our money not the same? It was clear whose side the Prairie Knights Casino stood on. Huge BIA satellite vans were stationed in the parking lot of the casino, which were used to disrupt and monitor our cell phones. They also used experimental "Sting-Ray" technology at the casino and at the camps, which caused the power to drain from our cell phone batteries at an accelerated rate.

At camp, the only semi-reliable place to send out updates on our status via social media was from "Facebook Hill," the highest point in Oceti Sakowin Camp, or what later became Oceti Oyate Camp. Facebook Hill became the gathering site for journalists, camp leaders, and water protectors alike. Thousands of smiles, laughs, and frustrations were exchanged atop Facebook Hill, while phone calls, social media posts, and updates were sent out to the public.

We invested in much needed supplies for camp with the money that still flowed in through the Standing Rock Tattoo campaign. We bought a drone that was used to document major actions, and stocked up on memory cards, extra drone batteries, and battery packs for it. Frequently, we bought pizza for the entire camp from a local Native-owned restaurant. We also sponsored several water protectors with winter gear, purchased propane tanks and gas for numerous camps, and paid for countless hotel rooms. The money helped many of us survive the bitter cold as we documented our historical stand for the entire world to see.

Each day at camp was always an unpredictable adventure. Roadblocks, patrolled by the BIA and Bismarck police officers, were strategically set to monitor every person who came in or out. Helicopters flew closely overhead the camps many times throughout the day, watching our every move. Bright spotlights pointed directly at Oceti Oyate Camp, flooding it with bright light through the night, ensuring that we could not use the darkness of night to our advantage. Infiltrators cycled through Camp at such a high rate that everyone was suspect. It's an ugly feeling – not being able to trust anyone while in a war zone. Random camp raids, and attacks by the police, federal agents, and DAPL mercenaries were commonplace. Everyone was on the absolute *edge* with tensions reaching their boiling point!

Many different factions and groups existed within the camp itself. Take for instance, the "Headsmen and Headswomen" of the Horn, who held Traditional Ceremonies, and made decisions for the entire Camp based upon the messages received during these Ceremonies. The decision to extinguish the fire that was lit at the beginning of the Standing Rock Movement, the Oceti Sakowin fire, which established the official Oceti Sakowin Camp, was made this way. They announced that they were directed by Spirit to evacuate the camp and to extinguish the fire. So, they did, and asked all the other water protectors to leave as well before the snow and ice started to melt. This was, however, exactly what the DAPL mercenaries, the BIA, the Army Corps of Engineers, and the Bismarck Police tried to force the people to do all along.

Therefore, most refused to go with them, leaving their structures intact. Instead, they lit another sacred fire and renamed the camp "Oceti Oyate Camp." Leaving, to most, felt like an act of defeat in the face of the oppressor. Standing our ground became an act of defiance that made more sense to everyone else, especially since the majority were not invited to participate in the Ceremonies from which these decisions were made. I'm not saying that the messages they received during Ceremony weren't true, it's just that none of us knew what was happening, who to trust, who to follow, and who infiltrated us by this time! People turned on one another, so staying on the original mission, and holding one's ground, became the most sensible thing for most of us to do.

The "7th Generation Kitchen," a group of young, Native water protectors, transformed a large military tent into a communal kitchen and provided a gathering place for the people. There, they fed hundreds of water protectors with home cooked meals. Every night, the people gathered there to eat delicious food, always with fresh fry bread, while they listened to live hip-hop performances and hand drum singers.

On the other side of the river, on the reservation side of Standing Rock, Sacred Stone Camp, the first camp established, was built high up above the flood plains on land partially owned by Ladonna Allard, a Standing Rock Tribal member and Elder. This camp consisted of mostly veterans and non-Native allies, with a huge online media presence. LaDonna became one of the leading Elders of the Movement and used her platform to support the youth group who were the first to stand up against the installation of the Dakota Access Pipeline.

We helped establish the Cheyenne River Camp, situated in between Oceti Oyate Camp and Sacred Stone. It was a small camp organized and led by Harold Frazier, the chairman of the Cheyenne River Sioux Tribe. Harold was well known amongst water protectors for his willingness to stand on the frontlines with all the others, at every action he could. He was therefore respected, trusted, and loved, as his actions spoke louder than his words. All the camps and groups, despite their differences, were united under the same cause: to stand in the way of the construction of the Dakota Access Pipeline underneath Lake Oahu.

One day, little Zeke and I went out to join the frontlines to document Bismarck police officers, the National Guard, and DAPL mercenaries as they once again tried to forcefully push back the barrier they constructed, which blocked Highway 1806 – the main northern route into and out of the Standing Rock Reservation, and into camp. The barrier was erected just beyond the borders of the Oceti Oyate Camp, and they pushed it closer to camp, preventing water protectors from accessing the pipeline, thus giving themselves a more strategic position for the upcoming eviction they had threatened us with for months.

As soon as we joined the frontlines, Zeke walked right up to the barrier and crawled over, standing on the same side as the police officers and mercenaries before I could do anything to stop him! We all laughed as they awkwardly shuffled about, trying to ignore that a little boy defiantly ignored their barrier. They stepped back as I reached over to grab him, respectfully giving me space as a mother, even though they were fully armed with riot gear, mace, tasers, and rubber bullets! We made a stand that day, and tried to stop them, but there was little we could do as unarmed and peaceful water protectors against their fully armed force besides singing, dancing, and praying.

Over the course of the Standing Rock Movement, hundreds of peaceful water protectors were arrested, repeatedly shot with rubber bullets, sprayed with tear gas, pepper spray, and pepper balls, attacked with sound cannons, or brutally attacked by the police and National Guard during actions involving the conflict over this barrier. It was clearly a strategic part of the police line – consisting of tall concrete blocks, excessive amounts of razor wire, and backed by military vehicles, police cars, and floodlights – all of which served to guard and protect the pipeline route.

My health suddenly took a serious hit, three weeks after being continuously at Standing Rock. I went from feeling fine, to having a high fever, shaking, and vomiting over the course of a day! My friend drove me to a hospital in Colorado to receive treatment, which was how far away we had to travel to receive reliable medical services! I was diagnosed with a severe kidney infection, a potentially life-threatening condition, and immediately given treatment. I never felt so sick in my life!

I found out months later, that many other water protectors also suffered from accelerated cases of kidney infections, and other symptoms such as the "DAPL cough," rapid hair loss, and heart issues. An investigation was later conducted into the possibility of Rozol contamination, a chemical used to poison prairie dogs that made its way into our camp food supply, and which slowly poisoned water protectors. After a week of treatment, I made a full recovery, and we returned to camp.

February 22nd neared, the day the National Guard, the Bismarck Police Force, and DAPL mercenaries promised to forcefully evict any remaining water protectors from Oceti Oyate Camp. I prepared by traveling down to Nebraska to drop Zeke off with my little sister Storm. She gladly took him in and gave him a safe place to stay, far away from the war zone that Standing Rock had become, so that I could do what I needed to without fear of being forcefully separated from my son, or of him being hurt in any crossfire we might encounter. I returned to camp with peace of mind, as far as my son's safety was concerned.

    The day before the scheduled eviction, I stood on the north end of camp, looking up at the cops who gathered beyond the Highway 1806 barricade. Suddenly, a group of about fifteen of them ran down towards us, lifted the fence, and tried to raid our camp, a day earlier than they agreed upon! But just as suddenly as they stormed in on us, lightning struck the earth directly behind them, and streaked overhead in the clouds above them! The thunder boomed and shook the earth! I documented the ensuing moments on a live feed, and repeatedly captured the thunder beings as they struck all around the police cars and Humvees the officers retreated into.

    The Thunderbeings showed us that day that they were on our side, and delivered a message of hope, just as they were invoked to do with the creation of the Standing Rock Tattoo! We won with their help that day, and the war whoops and trills of hundreds of water protectors resounded all through the camp as we realized our victory!

    February 23, 2017, arrived before we knew it – eviction day. The Army Corps of Engineers officially announced the deadline for the water protectors to clear out of Oceti Oyate Camp as February 22, but the day came and went without law enforcement entering camp. The night before the actual eviction, the chaos of enduring months of trauma got the best of many water protectors, who had lived in that war zone for months, and some made the decision to ignite their camp structures.

Many were sacredly built with prayers, and they were not willing to allow their sacred items, intentions, and structures to fall into the hands of law enforcement, who had a history of defiling – by defecating and urinating upon – numerous amounts of sacred items and structures during previous raids. It was a final act of defiance, which created an ominous cloud of smoke and billowing towers of fire, which previewed what was to come the next day.

We slept in my car at Oceti Oyate Camp on the evening of February 22 and were awoken the next morning by one of the veteran water protectors. He saluted us, and declared, "I'm out of here!" Then, he sprinted away, chaotically but comically abandoning what'd been his post for the last six months as an Oceti Oyate security guard. We parked the car at Sacred Stone Camp, which didn't face eviction that day, and traveled into the back of Oceti Oyate on foot, accompanied by the group of veterans who were going to hold the front line. My dad came out to join us that day too, as a Marine veteran, and my personal bodyguard.

It was an extremely cold, windy, and blustery day with side-ways blowing snow and frigid air that stung our lungs. Even though we dressed in thick layers of arctic gear, we still shivered and struggled for warmth. We crossed over the frozen Cannonball River that separated the Sacred Stone and Oceti Oyate Camps. Puddles of melted snow from the occasional warm days stood amongst ice and extremely tall blocks of snow, showing evidence of the approaching seasonal shift. Some days, it was warm enough to melt a little bit of the snow, but most days were still defined as nothing less than "arctic blasts."

As we approached the tipi in front of us, a huge explosion jolted the still air. The canvas of the tipi flew off, and the entire structure was instantaneously consumed in roaring flames! The veterans reacted immediately and ran towards it. A woman and her child stood inside the flaming shell of the tipi. The woman's entire body was covered in fire!

The first vet to reach them grabbed her and dunked her into the pool of freezing water, dousing out the flames. Her hair was singed to the roots, and her skin severely burned. The medics were immediately summoned. I rushed over to the boy while they cared for her. He was around ten years old. I asked if he was hurt or burned, but he just stared blankly ahead, in complete shock. His eyebrows and eyelashes were also scorched, but he was lucky to have no serious burns. The medics arrived, and we continued. Now, we fully realized that we were in a war zone!

Figure 23. Pausing to capture the chaos. Structures burn behind me in Oceti Oyate Camp on eviction day, February 23, 2017.

Structures burned all around us, creating a toxic atmosphere in the air as everything within them ignited, propane tanks included. We warned people to get out, that it wasn't worth someone getting hurt, especially after what we just saw! Any propane tank in the area could explode and incinerate everything around it. We made our way to the front of camp, helping whoever we could, panicked to get out of there before another explosion occurred. The police and National Guard added to the chaos each time they announced, via loudspeaker, that the deadline approached "by the minute" for people to clear out before they entered camp and arrested anyone who remained.

Their forces mobilized on their side of the Highway 1806 barricade – which included dozens of Humvees, Bearcat and MRAP armored vehicles, sheriff deputies, National Guard soldiers, federal agents, and police with riot gear and live weapons. Around 11 a.m., their combined eviction forces descended into camp, where a good amount of water protectors chose to remain. We stationed ourselves on the high hills beyond Sacred Stone Camp, which overlooked the entire Oceti Oyate Camp below, and took turns flying the drone to live feed whatever we could from the mesa.

We shared space with Unicorn Riot, one of the main grassroots media organizations, whose guerilla news reports documented every major action that took place during the entire Standing Rock Movement. Their gear awed us! The zoom lens on the camera they used to capture the footage from eviction day, which ended up spreading like wildfire, was as big as one of our arms! No wonder they got the best footage! We were stoked to see them. The next day, we saw the videos they compiled. As police officers and soldiers clumsily chased water protectors, some fell flat on their faces and made absolute fools of themselves! Thanks to Unicorn Riot, it was documented and publicized with a hilarious musical soundtrack in the background for all the world to see.

While our hearts raced, and our bones shivered, we watched through the drone camera and with our naked eye as the eviction force steadily moved in. Their tactic was to move forward as one line in a slow, but steady walk. Then, when the lead officer yelled, "Charge!" they sprinted towards the water protectors that held the line in front of them.

They ran too, but with a disadvantage because they moved backwards. In this way, the veterans and water protectors were arrested one by one.

We documented the complete take down and arrest of Journalist Eric Poemoceah, via drone video footage, who was live feeding at the time they violently tackled him and broke his hip. We watched helplessly as our relatives were hunted by officers and soldiers, who pointed assault rifles with live weapons at them, as they took them down for arrest. The tears and anguish fell from our eyes as the eviction line moved forward, with fully armored soldiers, military Humvees with assault rifles, and their helicopters circling overhead, in their battle against unarmed water protectors.

While we documented the eviction, we carefully paid attention to our video feed to watch for signs of our drone being "pulled away" with their technology. Every time we caught it, which meant that we were obviously losing control of the drone, we pushed the button that immediately returned it "home." Otherwise, they would have taken it from us, or crashed it, destroying our equipment, and thus, our footage and video evidence. It already happened to many drone flyers before us. As we filmed, a helicopter circled directly over us, so close that it caused the wind to whip all around us! I never looked up though, because I didn't want to give my identification away for easy arrest later, because it was illegal in their books for us to fly drones. The next day, someone posted a picture of the helicopter that circled above us – it was a Department of Homeland Security Customs and Border Protection surveillance helicopter. A fully masked sniper leaned out of the helicopter and pointed a large assault rifle directly at us!

Eventually, the eviction force reached the back of camp, completing its takeover of Oceti Oyate. Then, they invaded the Rosebud Camp that sat on the opposite side of the Cannonball River. At least forty-five water protectors were arrested by the end of the day, including a Lakota Elder, Regina Brave Bull, an AIM veteran that took part in the occupation of Wounded Knee in 1973. She refused to move from her position until the very end!

It was devastating to watch the Humvees and armed soldiers patrol over the sacred land that became our home and the gathering place of hundreds of Nations. It was also where we made our greatest collective stand. As the Humvees rolled over Facebook Hill, I thought of the bones of our ancestors that were buried underneath. I realized that those soldiers didn't know, or didn't care if they did, that Facebook Hill, and all of Oceti Oyate Camp, was a burial ground of the Cante Tenza Okolakiciye, one of the fiercest Traditional Warrior Societies of the Oceti Sakowin! That was something you just spiritually didn't mess with!

Once again, our Treaty Rights and agreements made with the U.S. government, were blatantly ignored for the interests of the exploitation of the resources of Mother Earth, while we paid the highest cost for it upon our own homelands. The U.S. government has always done whatever it pleased, by force, and with absolutely no respect or honor. For our people, all agreements, and all things, were done with honor. So, it was not because of our weakness that we were overcome, but because of their lack of integrity, along with the combined force of their technology and weapons.

However, the Standing Rock Movement revealed the truth of the genocide of Tribal Nations and the motivation behind it – resource and land grabbing – to an international audience, delivering undeniable proof of the U.S. government's atrocious acts against Native Nations that ensued for generations and continues to this day. Through its own actions, the U.S. government proved that its "freedom" is an illusion and its "greatness" a lie. As water protectors, we were asked and guided to remain peaceful, because we had to give them the opportunity to show the world their true colors.

A few days after the eviction of Oceti Oyate Camp, many of us left Standing Rock with broken hearts and an overwhelming sense of defeat and depression that were challenging to overcome. So, I picked up Zeke from my sister's and headed out to join the "Rise with Standing Rock Native Nations March" in Washington D.C., where hundreds of us used our fierce presence to demand that the Trump administration respect Indigenous rights and help us protect Mother Earth and her resources. It was one of the happiest moments I had during the entire Movement, as I carried Zeke on my back, while still live feeding for parts of the march. The best parts, however, came when I put the video down and digested it all. I finally had the chance to process how much we accomplished as a collective!

Thousands of Nations stood together across the world, united in a stand to protect something common to all of us: the resources of Mother Earth. We held our ground for a considerably long time, despite the constant pressure and infiltration from state law enforcement, military soldiers, and federal agents. We gave every person on Earth permission to also stand for what they believed in. For the first time, the struggle of an Indigenous Nation became first page and internationally renowned news!

A year after the evictions, I met a Bismarck-based active-duty Army Guard recruiter, who "served" during the DAPL protests. We stood next to each other in line at a restaurant. My tattoos intrigued him, so we chatted casually, until I noticed his Army Guard shirt. I asked if he served during the DAPL protests, and he told me he "wasn't on grounds there but did recruit and dispatch soldiers there."

He immediately tried to explain himself, claiming that he was "proud to have sent soldiers to Standing Rock to defend what was right," and that the "pipeline was rerouted legally and appropriately through reservation land." He also said that "none of the Indian people objected to the rerouting of the pipeline." I corrected him and said that almost *none* of our people approved of the pipeline, specifically because it would destroy sacred land, and had the potential to contaminate our only source of pure drinking water!

He explained that his commanders told him that "the land wasn't sacred, and no one objected." "They lied to you!" I said, "They always have, and always will." Then, he mentioned that the contract he signed with the government left him no choice but to do what they told him to. I reminded him that he was a human being. He always had a choice, whether he signed a contract or not, to think for himself, and to make his own decisions. Every one of us must face up to the choices we've made in life and will eventually be held responsible for our actions in the form of karmic consequences.

Our interaction helped me understand that the government lies especially to its own soldiers, to coerce them into standing willfully against what the government labels as "militants or the resistance," or in other words, those who take matters into their own hands, by standing against environmental, political, and social injustice. Secondly, the soldiers feel that they are forced to stand against us, or alternatively, excuse it, due to the contract they signed with the government that enlists them into military service. Therefore, those who are not free in any way, are being used to enforce the "freedom" of major corporations like DAPL to do whatever they wish, regardless of who and what it violates!

Figure 24. The Redman statue placed at Sacred Stone during the NoDAPL Movement. It lets the government know that we aren't afraid to look upon them as they commit their acts of environmental, political, and social terror!

CHAPTER THIRTEEN
ARTISTIC FREEDOM

P hysically, the Standing Rock Movement reached its end, but spiritually, it became everlasting! Each one of us who sacrificed our time, security, safety, money, flesh, and energy to become a part of the stand, took a piece of the fire that was extinguished, and carried it home with us, spreading it like wildfire within our communities. Standing Rock became the training grounds for thousands from all races, Nations, colors, and backgrounds to experience how much we could achieve when we united in peace and used our prayers as our weapons against oppression. It is now 2021, four years after we were forcefully evicted from Standing Rock, and the Dakota Access Pipeline was installed under Lake Oahe, despite a resounding *no* from the people. In those four years, we've seen hundreds of similar movements rise all over the world, in which people are standing up and continuing to say no!

We are awakening to the truth of government corruption and its ties to major corporations that are determined to make a profit at any cost, even if it means polluting and draining the resources of Mother Earth. It has become blatantly clear to many of us that we have been lied to, that our governments are not serving our needs, or the Earth's, and that we must stand up to them or they are going to take everything from us and our future generations. They can no longer hide, and most importantly, no longer can we!

We watch in horror now as the oil pipelines we stood against *are* leaking and contaminating water sources! The Keystone XL Pipeline in North Dakota recently spilled over 380,000 gallons of oil, saturating an estimated half-acre of wetlands! The Dakota Access Pipeline has also leaked hundreds of gallons of oil since 2017, across various locations throughout the Dakotas and Midwestern states, yet DAPL is now trying to gain permits to allow *double* the amount of oil to pump through its pipelines on the Standing Rock Reservation!

Furthermore, it's become clear that the U.S. government is arbitrarily and unfairly separating children from their parents and holds these children as prisoners in deplorable conditions – overcrowded cages in which basic survival needs are hardly met – as punishment to the parents for the "illegal" actions they committed, which were truly no more than seeking a better life for their children, while in a state of duress! Additionally, we see that these are Indigenous children that are targeted, as those who seek asylum at the border of Mexico, are from the Indigenous Nations of Central and South America. *Thousands* of reports have already surfaced from these border detention centers of sexual and physical abuse, and even death.

We are also experiencing the effects of intense climate change, and the resulting weather pattern shifts. The entirety of California is now a risky place to live, as fiery infernos spark into thousand-acre fires overnight. Thousands of people have lost their homes, and hundreds have already died because of these unpredictable and monstrous wildfires! Furthermore, wildfires are sparking up on an international level that have reduced forests to ash and pushed people out of their homes with little to no warning due to how quickly they spread. Last year, it was reported from an Australian reserve, that 350 of the six hundred koalas who once lived within it, were incinerated in an unprecedented wildfire. As a threatened species, it was a devastating blow to their already dwindling population. They are now considered "functionally extinct," due to the massive loss of eucalyptus trees during the fires, which the koalas depend entirely upon for food and shelter.

Record-breaking hurricanes are increasing in frequency, and several have absolutely devastated entire islands, killing thousands of people within the last few years. Scientists are now considering the creation of a new hurricane category of "level six" to better define these record-smashing goliath storms that annihilate everything in their path! Glaciers melt at record rates, and coastal areas are submerged beneath the rising waters. Mass fish and animal die-offs are becoming the new norm, and numerous species are facing extinction, or have entirely gone extinct. On an international level, we are seeing changes on our Mother Earth that humanity as we know it has never seen before!

Indigenous people across the world know that these Earth changes align with the prophecies our ancestors have passed down to us. We knew this era was coming, and we hold steadfast, because we are aware that we are entering into the time of reconciliation, in which Mother Earth restores her balance, and the balance of those who have chosen to stand on her side with no fear. Our resiliency is undeniable. Despite every attempt made to wipe Indigenous people off the face of the Earth, somehow, we continue to hold on to life, just like the buffalo. Yet, like the buffalo, we are still confined within small boundaries and fences that restrict and monitor our every movement. Try to roam too free, and you'll get shot down physically or legally. Just ask the Yellowstone Buffalo, or any Indigenous activist!

I dreamt of Donald Trump the other night. I stood in the streets of a city. He suddenly ran up to me and ordered me to stand on a number that was painted on the concrete beneath me. I remained standing there, only because I was puzzled by his odd demand and unexpected presence before me. So, I simply watched, while he sprinted off and climbed into a tall tower. I scanned the streets before me, and saw that many of us stood there, each upon our own designated number. Trump blasted out an order, and suddenly, water hoses and mace assaulted us with full blast! Everyone just stood there, taking it. Not me! I said, "*Hell* no!" and ran for the hills. High fences surrounded us, so I climbed like a madwoman, with only two or three others having the courage to climb with me. As soon as I reached the top, warriors that I never met before grabbed me to help me over. They shielded me as we broke through the barrier, and then took me to a place that was safe and secure. Then, they broke it all down to me – the government conspiracies, the matrix that is everything, and the great illusion. They spoke of the "Great Revolution" that was beginning and told me that I would now be taken under the protection of their underground organization. The Great Shift had begun!

This dream showed me that many of us are, and will be targeted, and that when that time comes, not to be amongst the many who just stand there and take it, frozen in disbelief and fear! To save myself, I had to run and believe in my ability to escape the chaos and confusion. They showed me that those of us who have the courage to escape, or to say no, will be helped, and will be brought to a new environment, free of the oppressor's chaos and insanity!

Thus, I spend my time and energy in preparation of what is yet to come, by doing my best to heal and lighten my own burden. Writing this book forced the most traumatic experiences I've endured to the surface, moments that I before did my best to forget just to keep my sanity. For some of us, forgetting is our survival technique. If we can't remember what happened to us, then we don't have to feel, or re-experience, the pain anymore. However, forgetting, when there is healing that still needs to be done, only buries the pain deeply within, and thus, it spreads like poison beneath the surface. It is time to remember all that we've endured, to face it entirely, with courage and love, so that light will enter and transform the darkness.

Countless times I have fallen to my knees, believing that I reached the end of my rope, but there was always a spark that somehow reignited within me, giving me the sliver of hope that I needed to endure. Every prayer that I've ever poured into the Universe from my heart has always been answered, even if the answer came years later. I learned that in moments of terrible suffering, we are *never* alone! Thousands of our ancestors always stand with us, encouraging us, helping us with their silent love, guidance, and gratitude for our existence. So too, does our Mother Earth and the Creator of our Souls, Wakan Tanka.

All the experiences of my life forged me into this pillar of strength *because* I never gave up! I acknowledge how much I've survived, and the miracle it is that I am still here. If all I went through was just so that I could be here to help others realize that they aren't alone in their suffering, and that they are miracles of resiliency too, then it was all worth it!

On a collective level, serious issues exist within our communities that need to be addressed before we can move forward. In Indian Country, gossip, rumors, and harsh criticism are often used as weapons against others. A tendency to destroy, because we've been destroyed, exists within our communities, and is acted out on our own people. Paulo Freire, a renowned Brazilian philosopher, and author of *Pedagogy of the Oppressed*, understood that "the oppressed, instead of striving for liberation, tend themselves to become oppressors." The disease of separation that White Buffalo Woman warned our people about nineteen generations ago, is all around us. We must follow her guidance, and cling to our prayers and the C'anupa!

Nelson Mandela took it a step further in his book, *Long Walk to Freedom*, suggesting that both the oppressed and the oppressor need healing. "The oppressor must be liberated just as surely as the oppressed. A man who takes away another man's freedom is a prisoner of hatred; he is locked behind the bars of prejudice and narrow-mindedness. I am not truly free if I am taking away someone else's freedom, just as surely as I am not free when my freedom is taken from me. The oppressed and the oppressor alike are robbed of their humanity."

After the Standing Rock Movement came to its physical end, I was severely attacked on an international level, by hundreds who believed, based on rumors, gossip, lies, and assumptions, that I mismanaged the Standing Rock Tattoo campaign, and stole the donations for my personal use. It was a huge blow that was stacked on top of the PTSD I already endured from being part of the water protector force that was attacked and pushed out of Standing Rock by police officers, federal agents, and fully armed soldiers who were prepared for war.

Thus, I stepped away from anything Standing Rock related, especially the Thunderbird design, which I officially announced as a gift to the people for free, unrestricted use. I then disappeared from the scene for about a year to give myself time to heal. However, I still was given dreams that showed that I would never be disconnected from what was truly meant for me.

One night, I dreamt that Zeke and I were prisoners in a concentration camp. We stood in a long line of people that I didn't recognize. Police officers walked along it, pointing a "mind-control" device at each person. It easily kept them subjugated, but when they reached me, I held my wrists up, where my Standing Rock Tattoos are, and crossed them over my chest like a shield. It blocked all emissions from their machines! Extremely agitated by this, they grabbed Zeke and

I and forced us into a structure that had sound-proof padding all over the walls.

Then, they sealed the doors. They blasted us with powerful sonic waves and frequencies that immediately caused us both to collapse to the ground! I crawled over to Zeke and placed my body over his to shield him. The pain of the sound waves destroying my body was so unbearable that I thought we were going to die. Suddenly, I heard the voices of my ancestors: "Sing!" So, I sang as loud as I could, instantly waking up out of the dream and ending their attack! Somehow, our astral bodies were in that place of torture because neither Zeke nor I felt healthy after waking. We both had a difficult time getting out of bed. All our energy was drained, and we felt extremely nauseous. To this day, I cannot tolerate loud noises since that dream because they inflict pain!

Yet, the dream imparted an important message: our tattoos could be used as shields against lower-level frequency attacks, intuitively confirming my research about Traditional Tattoos – that they were used as forms of protection! Furthermore, our songs could be used to nullify their highest-level frequency attacks! I finally understood why we sing in Ceremonies, during our protests, and why our Traditional Tattoo customs were outcasted. They empowered us and gave us a shield that the oppressor could not permeate!

I was soon given another dream about the Standing Rock Tattoo. I dreamt that I arrived at a camp filled with warriors that carried the Thunderbird tattoo. They waited for me, and I was told by Spirit that even though their tattoos had already been placed, *I* had to "activate" them. I held mine up as I made the power fist, and it lit up like lightning! Then, they held up theirs, and they also illuminated. I am still waiting for the full message of this dream to be imparted, but I sense that it meant that our struggle for our rights, to protect our land, and to realize our power, has only just begun, and that we, as a force of protectors, have much more "action" that we will see.

Shortly after leaving Standing Rock, I returned to Sacramento to move out of my place, saying goodbye once and for all to a run-down neighborhood with its child molester and junkie neighbors. I gave all my belongings away, as I've done in my life over and over, and turned my soil completely over. I traveled around California, working on various farms, and finding healing and peace in Nature. Zeke and I slept in tents, or with friends along the way, and I discovered that I enjoyed being away from people, like far, far away from mostly everybody.

After taking this year to myself, Winona LaDuke reached out to me and asked me to place a custom Thunderbird tattoo on her. She claimed that she didn't want anyone else to do this special tattoo for her. I hadn't been practicing at the time, having backed away from tattooing due to my experience at the Tattoo & World Culture Festival, but after lots of praying and her encouragement, I decided it was time to take it back up! Thus, a new chapter began, in which one of the artistic expressions I thoroughly enjoyed also brought abundance and security into my life, and it was thanks to the influence of a strong woman and leader within our water protector community!

Soon, I was instinctively guided to share the evidence I gathered about our Dakota and Lakota Traditional Tattoo customs, along with my intentions to help revitalize them as an emerging Handpoke Tattoo Artist. I knew that the effects of colonialism nearly destroyed the history of this Traditional practice. Furthermore, by way of cultural genocide, most Dakota and Lakota descendants weren't aware of it. I shared my research via social media, which ended up getting a lot of mixed attention, with most of the negative attention coming from the Lakota Nation. I was intensely ridiculed and threatened by my own people, who mostly claimed that I was a "white woman" and therefore could be totally discredited based on that alone. Most based their assumption that I carried no Native blood, or not enough, on the fact that they "didn't know me." I was called a liar, an infiltrator, and a poser, and the evidence I presented, even though it came from reputable sources, was ignored.

It became clear that there was absolutely nothing I could personally present at that time that would change their minds. Therefore, I put my initial focus – the revitalization of our Traditional Tattoos – on the backburner. However, I realized that it was just as important to stand my ground, and not back down when threatened or assaulted. I did not remove my post as hundreds tried to bully me into doing but kept it up with the understanding that in time, the truth always comes out to transform those who are ready, when they are ready for it.

Several sources clearly document the existence of tattoos among the Dakota and Lakota Tribes. John Fire Lame Deer, a Wicasa Wakan, or Holy Man, of the Lakota Sioux, describes the purpose of our Traditional Tattoos in his book, *Lame Deer, Seeker of Visions*:

> From birth to death, we Indians are enfolded in symbols as in a blanket. An infant's cradle board is covered with designs to ensure a happy, healthy life for the child. The moccasins of the dead have their soles beaded in a certain way to ease the journey to the hereafter. For the same reason most of us have tattoos on our wrists – not like the tattoos of your sailors – daggers, hearts, and nude girls – but just a name, a few letters, or designs. The Owl Woman who guards the road to the Spirit Lodges looks at these tattoos and lets us pass. They are like a passport. Many Indians believe that if you don't have these signs on your body, that Ghost Woman won't let you through but will throw you over a cliff. In that case, you have to roam the earth endlessly as a wanagi – a ghost. All you can do then is frighten people and

whistle. Maybe it's not so bad being a wanagi. It could even be fun. I don't know. But, as you see, I have my arms tattooed.

Lame Deer also describes the fork in the sacred cottonwood tree, what it represents, and its relation to tattoos:

> That sacred cottonwood means so much to me. Its leaves are shaped like a heart. When they are twisted, they look like a tipi, and when they are flat they symbolize a moccasin. The trunk of this tree represents the Milky Way. The fork, where a limb branches off, symbolizes the place where an old woman – Hihan Kara – sits in the Milky Way. When we die we have to pass her on the way to the Spirit Land. If we have a tattoo on our wrists Hihan Kara lets us pass. Our tattoo marks represent a kind of baptism. Without them we could not go to the Spirit Land but would have to walk back to the earth as a ghost.

Finally, Lame Deer describes how he received a tattoo from "old Mrs. Elk Head," the seventeenth-generation Keeper of the White Buffalo Calf Pipe. "My prayers must have helped Mrs. Elk Head, because she recovered and lived for a number of years more…. She…told me: 'The time will come when the Indians will rise again with this Sacred Pipe, when it will be smoked by all….' She really was wakan and had the power to see ahead. She also gave me a tattoo and a secret name that went with it." After Mrs. Elk Head journeyed on to the Spirit World, the Pipe, perhaps along with the old knowledge of Traditional Tattoos, was passed down to Stanley Looking Horse, and then to Arvol Looking Horse, the current Keeper of the Sacred Pipe that was given to our people from White Buffalo Calf Woman nineteen generations ago.

Vine Deloria, Jr., a prominent Dakota author, historian, and activist, shared some incredible historical teachings about our tattoo customs in his book *Singing for a Spirit: A Portrait of the Dakota Sioux*:

All Indian children were tattooed, the girls on the chin or forehead, the boys sometimes on the torso, but more frequently on the wrist or some other part of the arm. This custom was carefully observed because of an old tradition. In the days of the wisest men, the 'Milky Way' was thought to be the high road of the Spirits, which led them either towards the happy hunting grounds to the right, or to the left and the abode of punishment. An old man sat along the way to watch the spirits of the dead as they approached. When he saw the spirits of tattooed children draw near, he directed them to the right; but turned the poor little wanderers without tattoos toward the left-hand road.

Ethnographer Karl Bodmer, who traveled through the Great Plains in the 1800s, sketched several paintings of Dakota men and women with tattoos. These are included in anthropologist Lars Krutak's book, *Tattoo Traditions of Native North America*. These paintings clearly document the existence of tattoos on our ancestors, before the boarding school and reservation era was in full effect after 1868, which aggressively dismantled our Traditional practices. These are important artifacts of our tattoo history because the old-time photography process, called wet plate collodion, used in the late 1800s, didn't capture tattoos. I know this because I had my photograph taken by wet plate photographer Shane Balkowitsch, and my tattoos were not visible in them!

LaDonna Allard, a Standing Rock Sioux Tribal historian and Elder, said that her Dakota grandmother taught her that our tattoos are our identity, and allow our relatives in the Spirit World to find us once we pass. She had me tattoo many symbols on her body so that her loved ones would recognize her once she made her journey across the Milky Way. She also taught me that the practice of tattooing women on the face came to its end during the late 1800s and early 1900s due to the overwhelming judgement and prosecution they incited in Christian colonizers, who turned the tattooed women into targets.

Figure 25. A Dakota Sioux woman with a tattooed chin and forehead. Art by Karl Bodmer. (Krutak, 178).

Figure 26. Close up of a Dakota woman's facial tattoos. She is adorned with tattooed chin stripes and an honor mark on her forehead. Art by 1880s ethnographer Karl Bodmer. (1841 – 1843). (Krutak, 179).

Figure 27. The Yankton Sioux warrior Psihdja-Sahpa with tattooed "hand" honor markings. Art by Karl Bodmer. 1833. (Krutak, 167).

Towards the end of April 2018, I joined the 150-year anniversary horse ride commemorating the signing of the Fort Laramie Treaty. The 400-mile ride called attention to our Treaty Rights and demanded that the U.S. government honor its agreements made with our Nation 150 years before. For two weeks, I rode for an average of thirty miles a day on horses that were graciously lent to me. I rode because I loved the feeling of being out in the countryside on horseback with my people. I rode because I pledged to carry forth the prayers and intentions of my relative Waŋbdí Táŋka, Chief Big Eagle, who signed the Treaty back in 1868. I rode because I loved the daily adventures we had. I rode because I loved riding! I rode so much that I got a saddle burn that bled and scabbed over, eventually forming a permanent scar. I rode until my face peeled and reddened with severe windburn. I rode until I could barely stand at the end of each day. In the freezing cold and in the pouring rain, I rode!

There is nothing that can compare to galloping through the countryside of the Great Plains with a badass group of fellow warriors and activists who all stand for the same cause. We rode through the beautiful lands of our Treaty Territory from Cheyenne River, South Dakota to Fort Laramie, Wyoming. We passed through prairie dog minefields that could possibly break our horse's legs; through small redneck towns in which we had to stick close together because we knew we were targets of the Klu Klux Klan; through buffalo pastures where we had to escape before we were charged by the buffalo bulls; and through the territory of the most beautiful wild stallion!

He was tall and muscular, with a sleek black coat and a white rump with speckled black dots. I fell in love with him as he charged us insidiously! It took the guys at least half an hour to rope him up so that the rest of us could get away, while he tried to claim each of the mares in our group as his own!

We raced, joked, laughed, shared stories, and supported one another as we struggled to make it through to the end of each long day of riding. Most importantly, we loved and honored the beautiful and strong ponies who carried us and our prayers for the two-week long journey. We acknowledged that they worked harder than any of us, and that all they asked was that we take loving care of them.

Figure 28. "Stephanie Big Eagle rides with other Fort Laramie Treaty riders along Bombing Range Road on the Pine Ridge Reservation near Scenic, South Dakota, on April 20, 2018." Photo Credit Stephanie Keith/Reuters.

I rode every day until the last day, when there were no extra horses available because everyone wanted to ride for the "grand finale" – the completion of our Ceremony via the final charge onto Fort Laramie, where the Treaty was signed. Despite my disappointment that I couldn't take part in the final charge, I was incredibly honored to take part in one of the greatest adventures of my life and knew that I did my best to honor my relations by carrying that prayer for as many days as I could. I gave my wopilas – thanks – and respect regardless. The first and only ride of its kind, I was absolutely honored to have been included in its history!

After the ride was over, I was invited to join a Movement camp established on the Standing Rock Reservation. I gladly accepted. On the way there, we visited a veteran AIM leader in Pine Ridge. I had quite a bit of respect for him, but soon learned to keep my distance from him when he told the group of people I traveled with, that "I was punishing myself" because I had tattoos on my face. Everyone laughed at me, but I held my tongue since I was in *his* home, and I respected him as an Elder. It was simply not my place to explain myself to him, or to remind him of our Traditions. He revealed however, that the Spirits called me "Pte Winyan," Buffalo Woman! They also told him I'd run all over the world to find a safe place that I could call my home. He said I was welcome anytime at his, but I never returned, having already been made to feel ironically unsafe in his presence because of his judgement and blatant misunderstanding of my markings.

After leaving his home, we headed up to Standing Rock and joined the resistance camp. I was overjoyed to offer my help in any way. I got straight to doing the dishes, then cooked breakfast for everyone. Later, I watched as a tipi was set up. I waited for a while until the woman who pulled the rope around the top of the poles became overly tired. She sat down to take a break, and I stepped up to offer my services. Everyone accepted except her, who immediately chastised the men for allowing me to help because I was "new." Even though I was "new" to their scene, I was not new to putting up a tipi! We put that tipi up anyway, while she glared at me the whole time. From that point forward, she expressed her disdain for me every single time she saw me. She hated me, and for what? For stepping up to help when she was worn out. How dare I!

She wasn't the only one. All the women at that camp equally despised me. Either they ignored me, or they gave me dirty looks if they did acknowledge me at all. I couldn't understand why. I worked my ass off every day to help build that camp. I helped take care of their horses, build fences, plant gardens, erect structures, feed the people, and clean up after everyone when almost no one else did. Otherwise, I explored the grounds or hung out in my yurt with Zeke. I couldn't understand how I offended them so badly. I was beginning to lose my cool.

One day, I was in the camp's main house looking everywhere for my son's shoes. One of those women came rushing in, obviously stressed out that she had to deal with her toddler's soiled diaper. I happened to be looking around in the bathroom as she came around the corner. She saw me in there and rolled her eyes, huffing and puffing away, not even realizing that I was just leaving. I glared at her, intolerant of her impatience and disrespect towards me, which built over weeks. She looked at me and said, "What!?" I retaliated, "Why are you always acting like a bitch towards me?" She dared me to call her a bitch again. So, I asked her once more, "*Why in the fuck* are you always acting like a bitch towards me!?"

She set her baby down and slapped me as hard as she could across my face! I snapped, and triple-combo'd her, striking her across her face and ribs, then kicked her across her legs. She was down on the floor instantly. I dropped with her, grabbed her, and held her in a jiu-jitsu grip with my legs while choking her out from behind. I wanted to snuff her out, but the others pulled us apart. After that day, we became friends. She even brought me gifts and nicely acknowledged me whenever she saw me. I felt incredible after we finally threw hands! It was a much-needed release after experiencing weeks of tension from being treated like shit by everyone for no valid reason.

That place was, however, nothing more than a cesspool of negative energy. Someone was always fighting with someone! It was like a stagnant muck of sickness and dysfunction that tried to infect anyone who came. I never fit in there, no matter how hard I tried, and neither did little Zeke. All the other kids picked on him and cursed him out. I realized that my kid was the one who got bullied. Even the horses constantly fought. The only reason I stayed for as long as I did was because I feigned that I had some sort of responsibility to prove that I was a servant of my people. When my name was drug through the mud after the Standing Rock Movement ended, I felt like I had to show everyone that they were wrong about me. Contributing to this camp somehow seemed like the best place to start.

I quickly got over that false notion, soon packing up my things to abandon the project. The final push came the night that I dreamt of fully armed soldiers that were dropped into the field across from the camp by airplane. They raided our camp before we realized what was happening, and it quickly became every person for themselves. A female soldier headed straight for me. I could tell by the look in her eyes that she trained long and hard for this moment, and now she finally had the opportunity to face me. She mistakenly thought that she could easily overpower me. But, as she approached, I pushed the tsunami emotion of a thousand warriors of the past through my eyes like a lightning bolt and aimed it straight at her heart! The condescending smirk in her eyes transformed into fear as I awaited her attack. I woke up before our fight ensued.

I left that place shortly after that. It wasn't worth it to me to fight with, and for, people that I already shared no comradery with, and who already made me their enemy because I had the "nerve" to show them what a real woman acted like. Later, I found out that almost everyone at that camp was using meth besides me! No wonder we clashed! Zeke and I left and never looked back.

I heard soon after that everyone from that camp accused me of being an "agent." It was so ironic to me that I – the only woman who came in there and worked tirelessly every day, without blatantly causing any drama – was the one considered a "fed." I laughed it off. It wasn't the first time someone put a mark on my head due to their own insecurity, jealousy, and illness, and certainly wouldn't be the last!

LaDonna Allard – the leader of the Sacred Stone Camp during the Standing Rock Movement and the Tribal historian of the Standing Rock Sioux Tribe – heard that I was a Handpoke Tattoo Artist and invited me to come to Fort Yates to place buffalo tracks on her wrist. I gladly accepted. After I placed her markings, she invited me to join them at Sacred Stone, and thus, I ended up living with them for the next few months. I was given my own studio to work out of, where I tattooed many water protectors and Standing Rock Tribal members, while learning some of our Traditional ways.

LaDonna taught me how to collect and prepare chokecherries, wild plums, and juneberries; how to properly harvest our sweet-scented prairie sage; how to dig up yucca root to make Traditional shampoo; and how to make ribbon skirts and other Traditional clothing. I heard many old stories and learned more of our language. LaDonna also shared her knowledge that, for as far back as she knew, her ancestors *always* had tattoos!

For the first time, I gained the personal account of an Elder who confirmed that we had a Traditional Tattoo culture! She explained that the Dakota had varied tattoos, while the Lakota had tattooing that was small and subtle, the main designs being a dot between the eyebrows, four dots in a line from the eyes to the hair line, and a line from the bottom lip to the chin.

After spending nearly six months living at Standing Rock, I decided to leave due to the lack of opportunity I experienced there, which is common to any reservation. I hadn't been able to pay any of my bills and struggled to even keep my phone on. More crucially however, I left due to the dysfunction that is *normal* on every reservation I've ever been to. This dysfunction caused me to make more enemies than friends while living there. I made enemies not because I acted untoward with anyone, but more because I was simply being myself, my full self. I honor LaDonna for supporting my art and for being so welcoming to me and Zeke. She did her best to exemplify what "being Dakota and Lakota" truly means.

Thus, I announced on my social media sites that I was organizing a Handpoke Tattoo tour, and quickly became fully booked across several states. I placed hundreds of Handpoked Tattoos and built my career as a tattoo artist. The day after I left Standing Rock, I saw my guiding number sequence, 919, at the first house I was hosted in during the tour! Thus, I knew that a magical and mysterious journey had begun. My art quickly became a reliable source of income, and for the first time, I wasn't borrowing money from others, or breaking down to work a corporate job, to support myself and my family! I also realized that my work wasn't meant to be restricted to just my Tribe as I originally thought it may have been. I was *meant* to work with all nations!

During the Colorado Springs portion of my tour, I was told that a buffalo herd lived on a nearby ranch that had five white buffalo! I was intensely guided to visit them, and thus my friend and I organized an impromptu Ceremonial trip to see the buffalo with four other sisters and Zeke. We did not contact the owner of the herd to arrange our visit, but simply loaded into a van and drove there, making our intentions to pay our respects to the white buffalo clear through prayer before we arrived. Incredibly, when we arrived, the buffalo were gathered close to where we could easily see them, and where they could approach us if they so desired. We got out of the van and sat on the earth before them, giving them the lead to decide what would happen next.

The first to approach us was a black buffalo. He came within fifteen feet of us, casually yet intently looking each of us in the eye. He did not graze but seemed to just listen to our silent prayers as he loomed before us. We could hear the grunts and groans of the rest of the herd as this majestic buffalo stood before us and simply shared space. He smelled the air before him, smelling us, and then turned his body so that he stood with his full left side facing us. Ten minutes passed during this exchange, then he finally walked past us and returned to grazing.

Slowly, the rest of the herd came closer to us. The black buffalo stood on the outside, some surrounding us, as three younger looking white buffalo stood on the inside of the herd, grazing before us. They were the closest to us. One by one, the white buffalo approached and acknowledged us and our prayers, either with a gentle look, or a gentle approach. Shivers coursed down my spine! The fourth white buffalo now joined us and made her presence known. She was larger than the other three, and a trinity of black buffaloes made a wall in front of her as she approached. Suddenly, they stepped aside, and we were given a perfect view of her! Some of us laughed in pure joy, and all of us sighed as she also acknowledged our presence and prayers.

I felt a *strong* presence approaching, and as I looked past the herd before us, I spotted the last white buffalo! She walked alone towards us from far out in the hills. The shivers overtook my spine as she came closer, and the intensity of the energy of the herd seemed to increase. Finally, she joined the herd, and the buffalo parted in the center as she also approached us! She was much larger than the other four white buffalo and carried the energy of the Matriarch of the herd. She commanded their presence, and especially ours. Her neck was covered in layers of thick, white, curly hair, and she towered over many of the other buffalo. She was magnificent!

We sighed, laughed, and even cried as we came to realize the miracle that unfolded before us! Not only were the buffalo in the only location of the ranch where we could easily access them, on what otherwise were hundreds of acres of private land, but *all* five of the white buffalo gathered right before us, and each of them acknowledged us! We came with specific intentions to share space, Ceremony, and prayers with them, and they heard us and answered! We did not sing or talk, but simply sat on the earth before them in complete humility and respect, and allowed them to approach us, bless us, and receive our silent prayers as they saw fit!

After the arrival of the fifth buffalo, I felt energy descend from the sky, which quickly overcame my body! I shivered and shook uncontrollably even as my sisters piled blankets, hats, and scarves over me to help keep me warm. Suddenly, I felt the energy of the sky shoot through me as lightning, and I became the earth and sky as one! I was incredibly cold, yet so warm in the same instance, and I knew I received a gift! An energetic gift that can only be described as an "activation."

This energy traveled from my crown down through my spine, channeling from the sky to the earth. When it reached the base of my spine, and thus traveled fully down into the earth, I opened my eyes, and the buffalo immediately stampeded! The sound of their hooves beat into the earth like lightning, and dust kicked up in a cloud around them. I was transported back into the genetic memory of our ancestors as they watched the ancient buffalo herds, when there were no fences, ranches, or ranchers to contain them. Back when we were both free, and I laughed, and kept laughing, as some stumbled and broke down fencing, and the entire herd transported itself in a wild instant into a new, far-off location that instantly became inaccessible to us! And so, it was!

We smiled, laughed, and breathed in deeply! All of us were shocked at what happened. We knew we were blessed beyond our wildest imaginations by this mighty white-and-black Buffalo Nation! As we drove away, my sister Feather and I saw a golden eagle the size of a man standing upon the earth! He faced us, and held his wings slightly raised in a V-formation, forming a triangle directly over Unci Maka. We were the only ones to see him as the van whizzed by the field that held him, giving us one last piece of the puzzle to process about the incredible events that transpired that day.

After processing the momentous experience, I received this message to pass on: *We have survived an age of terrible darkness, and out of this darkness we now arise! Not simply as survivors, but as a new species, like the white buffalo, who has come to restore peace, balance, and beauty upon Mother Earth! The imposed boundaries to capture, harvest, and contain our souls no longer bind us, unless we choose to allow it to do so! Those of us who elect to throw off the chains are now free and blessed with a limitless potential to embody our full multidimensional beings, made of earth, sky, and stardust. They can interfere with us no more! So, step forward, rise, have no fear, and be who you came here to be! You cannot allow them to marginalize you anymore. You must take your rightful place upon the throne of your own sovereignty!*

This is also a message to prepare yourselves! Prepare for the cleansing storms and rising waters! Listen to your heart and your gut instinct to relocate to safe places if need be. Prepare for chaos but know that this is all coming to restore bliss and regenerate our sacred Mother Earth! Follow and listen to our relatives in the Animal, Plant, and Spirit Nations! You can no longer stand or even survive alone. Move as one, like a buffalo herd, in a moment's notice if need be.

Thus, I return to where this book began, in Sedona, Arizona. In the year I spent writing my story while still there, Sedona poured its legendary healing Medicine over me! Although the inescapable amounts of cultural appropriation there continued to stifle me at times, I discovered this undeniable connection that existed in the power of the vortex energies that swirled throughout it. My dreams intensified more than they ever had, to the point that I became certain that I was traveling to other dimensions to "work," and even to be tested while my body slept, making me certain of multidimensionality.

One night, I dreamt that I was out in the woods, being led to a house by a stranger in the middle of nowhere. We reached the house, and the stranger knocked at a secret entrance underneath it. A concrete block rapidly unhinged and opened, and a monkey appeared. He laid down, belly up, on a board with wheels, and motioned for me to lay down on him, so I did. The other person left, and the monkey used his arms to push us along this tiny entrance into the building. Finally, we reached the entrance inside, where he announced me, then left.

I then stood in a darkened room, where on the dimly lit table before me, rested a glass filled with magic stones – an elixir! It fizzed and popped. As I watched, the stones that rested at the bottom, alchemizing, popped up. Excited, I placed my hands together in prayer mode, then guzzled it down! I tried to set the stones back up how they were before, but couldn't remember, so I called a man over to help. He instructed, "Remember? You set it up like the cross facing north," but I couldn't do it and he announced that I "failed the order."

Then, I looked up and realized I was standing before an altar, a masonic altar filled with dark occult objects and divination cards. It was all black with a silver hue. Suddenly, an ugly man pulled me brusquely to him. He was "higher up" than me. He had sharp claws and intensely dark inhuman eyes with a cataract look, red hair, and freckled skin. He looked Irish.

He clawed my face with one claw across my cheek. "I bet that looks cool though," I said coolly, with one hand on my hip and my chin lifted. He also pointed out a huge skull of a pig that was hung up in such a way that it could be opened with the push of a button. He was going to throw something at that button to open it, but I showed my comprehension and terror of what that was, so he left it alone.

My terror turned him on, so he took out his manhood and told me I had to go down on him. I resisted, and he tried to force me! A loud struggle ensued, and no one did anything to stop it. Then, he suddenly passed out with his head resting precariously over the stairs! At first, I was confused and wondered if he faked it, but then he stood up and came after me again. Yet again, we struggled, and he passed out, this time even more precariously, so I planned my escape back down the corridor I entered through, but before I could, the "order" was called to attention, and everyone gathered in the next room.

A person who apparently "failed" at something, was picked up by the back and bagged. He was strapped onto a contraption that was surrounded on both sides by two half human pigs, with pig faces, and the monkey who ushered me in. The low sounds of vicious growling filled the room. They were told that they didn't have to do "this part" if they didn't want to, but they all chose to. I knew they were about to tear him apart!

I woke up, and immediately prayed for guidance. Was I somehow part of a dark occult order? I was assured that I wasn't, but instead was shown that they *had always* tried to recruit me. Incessantly, I fought them, so couldn't be turned over! I realized that the dream revealed the truth of the environment I was raised in, and furthermore, that my stepfather was a member of an order as shown.

This was just one example of the many dreams I had during the time I lived in Sedona, where I was given glimpses into the rituals, ceremonies, and horrific ways of these secret societies, whose members practice pedophilia to feed on the souls of innocent children, and who channel demonic energy to gain their power. I also discovered that Sedona was home to several of these high-level orders!

Another night, I dreamt that I was dressed in beautiful silk attire, and impeccably painted as a geisha. I stood in the center of an ancient temple, where I was taught a highly intricate Chi Gong dance designed to change the fabric of space-time itself! I perfectly mimicked the intricate hand and head movements I was shown, and the fabric of reality began transforming before me! Ever since that dream, I've incorporated the extensive use of intricate finger and hand movements into my dance, along with entire body movements and spins, to reproduce what I was shown.

Soon after, I dreamt I was part of a large group in active combat training. We were placed in a virtual reality, into which a *huge* blue and purple dragon was released. We were ordered to escape its pursuit as best we could! After quite an adventure, one man was ordered to charge it and kill it with his sword. He tried, but the dragon bit his hand along with the sword, and he yipped in pain! Our supervisors shut down the dragon simulation, and I burst out in laughter that I quickly tried to stifle. "What a wimp!" I thought.

The simulation started again, but this time a real dragon chased us. He caught up to me and prepared to blast me with a fiery blaze, but I stood before him and sang "off," or minor, harmonies. He couldn't stand it! His eyes rolled back in pain. I sang another set, and again his whole body contorted. I threatened him, "Do you want me to do it again?" He begged, "No! Please!" I gun saluted him, "Ok then! Be nice then!" and held out a giant piece of cheese. He slinked up to me submissively, gently took the cheese, and thanked me "very kindly." Everyone slumped back in utter surprise. They had never seen that happen before! The supervisors announced, "Well then, a new paradigm has begun. We shall integrate this method into our training!" Then, I awoke.

Yet another night, I flew with a warrior friend. Using etheric symbols and words, we conjured storms, weapons, and energy fields around us – our shields against soldiers that violently attacked us. My friend shot at them with his leg and arm that transformed into two semi-automatic weapons! I used chants to create force fields around us, and to launch fire balls at our attackers.

The night after, I dreamt that I was talking with the Star Nation again. They reminded me of who I was, and called me "Black Prayer Woman," and "Reigning Thunderbird Woman." They also showed me another one of my forms – that of a powerful dragon of a mountain, one whom the people left offerings to out of deep reverence, respect, and even fear. The people came to me at the base of the mountain and whispered their prayers. They needed me! I was called to Mauna Kea, to embody the spirit of the mountain, and to rebirth this Earth through my womb! I was to unleash the fury, to shake "them" off Mother Earth like the fleas and parasites they were. I was inside the mountain, and became the dragon awakening within it, and suddenly I felt the fire and lava erupting within me!

Then, I sat at the top of the mauna, or mountain, as the giant mother-of-all Thunderbirds. I sat atop my nest and shot lightning out of my eyes at those who tried to climb up the peak in a bad way; at those who did not belong. The people called me, and I said, "Feed me then!"

I watched as they left offerings at the base of my nest. Suddenly, I was called to create an opening between the dimensions for the trapped souls of children in boarding schools and detention centers to pass through. I could feel the way they felt after being raped, or the feeling of being imprisoned and tortured, so I encouraged them, "Come now! Rise up! *Let's go!*" I took them all with me.

Then, I was taken back to a place where my hands were covered in the blood of our fallen warriors. My husband lay murdered at my feet, and I was covered in his blood as I mourned for him. The infection of colonization wriggled through his blood and seeped onto my hands. I cried and sobbed for him, then washed my hands clean, and suddenly, I was whisked away to another reality. Here, I held my ocean goddess staff to the sky and called the warriors to their stands. "It is time!" I cried. "We are holding it down! We are pushing them out! We are re-writing our timelines. This belongs to us!" Then, I woke up.

I had yet another dream, where I watched a little princess get thrown off her horse. The horse tried to run but I blocked it. He ran straight to me and allowed me to grab him. I held onto him as the little girl got back on and reminded the horse of its Nation's agreement with ours – to carry us on their backs and in exchange we'd take care of them. I suggested that the better he carried her, the sooner it would be over because the rider would be satisfied and worn out. Then, I told the little girl she had to respect and love her horse! She must always remember to take a feather, offer a prayer before riding, and remember the original agreements!

On September 15, 2019, I dreamt that hundreds of white buffalo, and a few black ones, were delivered to my yard. I became their caretaker. Soon after, on the 30th of September, I dreamt of two giant spaceships in the sky above me that shot at each other. One crashed down as I filmed it. One of my friends suspected it was a simulation. On

October 4, the last thing I heard while waking from my dream was someone shouting, "The spaceships are coming! The spaceships are coming!" On 11/11/19, I dreamt that Cuauhtémoc was taken from me again. Repeatedly, I fought his assailants, breaking him out of the cages they kept him in. Finally, I won, and we escaped to a place where they couldn't find us! I believe my dreams gave me vital messages about events that are soon to come!

While in Sedona, I left only a few times to offer tattoos elsewhere, and to attend Ceremony. During the most recent of those excursions, I had a beautiful experience in Ventura, California that reminded me of the healing Medicine and power of the ocean. There, I surfed again for the first time in years! However, the waves were more powerful than I was used to, and I got taken under and rolled by a huge wave, but I didn't panic at all. I just allowed it to roll me, and to clear my energy field, while I held my breath and waited for it to release me. I was gifted because all the fear melted away as I merged with the powerful force of that wave, and my hair and the water spun in spirals around me as I was pushed forward in that saltwater tornado! I recognized in that moment that salt naturally clears and protects, and when combined with water, there is not a more powerful and clearing, yet energizing force.

Then, I kayaked out with my friend Ryan. While we were out there, a pod of about twenty dolphins suddenly appeared! I immediately sang them an honor song, and Ryan played his flute for them. I saw the dolphins take note of this, as some of them stopped swimming and lifted their heads out of the water to look curiously at us, even the baby dolphin! After giving our respects, we kayaked and "swam" alongside them! They swam in front of us, beside us, and even under us as we quickly learned how to maneuver the kayak in sharp turns and circles to keep up with them. We must've been out there for two hours! We only turned back because the sun was setting, and duty called us back to land.

All my worries and concerns disappeared in those moments. My disdain for the insanity of most of humanity no longer mattered. My muscles ached, but my body and spirit were satisfied in the exhaustion earned from such a generous moment shared with the dolphin pod. There is nothing that can compare to the Medicine and magic of Nature, nothing that can replace the beauty of connecting with other sentient beings! My heart was filled simply through the sound of their breath, and their joyous company. Sharing it with my friend and son made it that much more special and hearing the questions of those who witnessed it from the shore helped us to realize how gifted we truly were. "Were they hurt? Were they asking for your help or something?" They couldn't understand why the dolphins spent so much time with us. The idea that we were playing and enjoying the sharing of the same time and space was alien to them. That is where the healing, the transition that this Earth needs, is going to begin, in realizing and honoring our connection to all our relations, for we are all in this together!

I also went home to South Dakota to Sundance – one of the Seven Sacred Ceremonial Rites ushered in by the White Buffalo Woman. For the first time, I fasted from food and water and danced for four days. It was one of the hardest sacrifices I've ever made, physically and spiritually, and when I was in that sacred circle, I danced as hard as I could! For the first time, I got to see first-hand what great warriors my people really are! When we are in that circle, and dance around the sacred cottonwood tree, which stands at its center, we represent the entire Universe. Our prayers then resound throughout all of existence, and we dance to honor the sacred hoop of all life and our place within it! I dedicated my prayer to restoring the harmony in my direct family by healing our intergenerational trauma, and to eradicate the dysfunction and genocide that has plagued not only my family, but all Indigenous peoples worldwide.

Ten years earlier, my grandmother and I drove out to watch the same Sundance together. However, she refused to get out of the car when we got there. The Christian beliefs she was forced to adopt during her boarding school days overcame her Traditional instincts, convincing her that it was a "heinous" gathering, and that she was "sinning" by attending. Ten years later, I prayed directly for her while I Sundanced.

When I returned to her home after Ceremony, she broke down and wept tears of gratitude. She said that the land we danced on, the White Swan area on the Ihanktonwan Dakota Reservation, was the land she grew up on for half of her childhood. She'd still be there, but her family received mandatory evacuation orders from the government, giving them one day to get whatever they owned and abandon the area! The Army Corps of Engineers then flooded the land and created the Fort Randall Dam. She thanked me for dancing, gave me a hug, and then told me that she loved the tattoos on my face. When she said that, *I* nearly cried, because my grandma, up until that point, harshly questioned my tattoos, and now, after I danced, she was blessing them! I felt the power of prayer that day, the power of Ceremony, and realized that it truly is our prayers, our songs, our dances, and our Traditions that will heal the traumas we have endured!

Fully sharing my story, with all its ups and downs, has been the greatest healing process of my life. As Rumi said, "The cure for pain is in the pain." I delved down into my trauma, re-felt it, and as the tears poured down my face, I breathed deeply, allowing myself to "redo" all those moments in my life where I held my breath, or where my breath was once taken from me. Thus, I am ready now to move forward and pursue justice and healing for the experiences my children and I endured. We've been through enough, and so have many other families like us!

Back in 2012, after two years of ripping my son Cuauhtémoc back and forth thru European-based *abusive* foster care settings, and after not placing him with a Native household – which is required by the Indian Child Welfare Act and the United Nation's International Indigenous Rights Declaration – the State of South Dakota finally decided, despite all my requests to put him with other willing family members first, to place my son with my half-brother Joe, whom I now do not consider a brother in any form! Joe carries only a fraction of Native blood from my mother, which he does not acknowledge, and otherwise is a European descendant. Furthermore, he is the offspring of the man who molested and raped me for ten years, and has not received counseling, much less admitted to, any of the sexual abuse he endured as a child.

I know there are good people out there from every nation, but my son was intentionally, or at least recklessly, placed with people who would separate him from his culture, and abuse him while doing so. As a descendant of the people who have survived the largest unacknowledged genocide in recorded history, he *needs* to know who he is and should be provided with an upbringing that connects him with his culture, rather than one which purposefully separates him from it! I will never forget the dream in which Temoc appeared to me and said, "Mom, you think you had it rough? Wait until you hear about my story!"

Over the eight years my "brother" has had my child, he continues to refuse to allow me to have *any* contact with him, unless I meet his requirements to "stop being Indian, embrace only my European-based heritage, shut down all my Facebook pages, and cease any activist activity." I cannot sell my soul out! I will find a way to take this matter before an international audience now that I am finally healed enough to face this again, and I will never stop being who Creator and my ancestors asked me to be. It became an even deeper betrayal when my brother claimed to be "the voice of my mother," who supports his withholding of my son from me 100%. The disease of separation is all around us, and often, our closest family members are the most infected.

As we can see, there is something much bigger at stake here. My son and I are not the only ones who have experienced the devastating trauma of forced separation, which is justified with insane logic, racist reasoning, and under the "color of law and authority" – the use of one's position of authority to deprive another of their rights and using one's position to further claim that this deprivation is lawful. We deserve a better life! We do not have to live according to the racist and ignorant ideas of how others think we should. Furthermore, the children of migrant Indigenous families locked in cages at the borders deserve the same! I refuse to stand by idly anymore, forgetting what happened, simply because it once used to kill me inside to remember.

I am going to use my story and experience from this day forward to empower myself, my children, and my people, and to stand up to these injustices in any way that I can. I don't hate the members of my biological family who act against me anymore, but I abhor the darkness which holds them. I will stand against that at any cost!

Forgiving is necessary, but so also is removing toxic people and environments from one's life and acknowledging it for what it really is. I see one day the State being exposed for its crimes against the people, and I see myself having all my children returned to me, not just in body, but in spirit. Because that's where they've got their hold on them right now, from the inside out, which is cultural genocide in its most destructive form!

A skewed programming runs "America," and other nations like it, in which the appearance of its righteousness masks the dark truth underneath. Murderers adorned in uniform become the government's heroes. Cops with a badge are free from, and above the justice system they enforce upon others. The Native people are homeless and impoverished upon their own homelands. America is owned and run by Europeans, who pass America off as if it is European in origin and discovery. English is its official language, despite the thousands of languages that originated here. This "land of the free" was built upon the backs of slaves, over the bones of Native graves, and via the morally absurd Doctrine of Discovery.

Borders are closed and militarized on this land, which previously thrived through nomadic migrations, and upon which ancient trade routes spanned from Alaska down to the tip of South America! Native peoples, the only ones with an inherent birthright to "American" land, are forced to prove their blood-quantum – their percentage of Indian blood – to the federal government to receive recognition and Treaty benefits. However, when a person is recognized as "Indian" by the federal government, and given a Tribal Identification Card, it is written in federal law that they are now "no longer capable of managing their own affairs" and thus become a "ward," or *prisoner*, of the United States government! They then have *less rights* than any other civilian! The lies are perverse and run so deep.

The brainwashed often have no idea their minds have been hijacked. It takes copious amounts of patience and light to penetrate those walls, and then many years for healing to even begin. This is why children who have been abused, especially sexually, will protect their abusers. Master manipulators love to victimize the innocent and hijack their love. Their love, being pure, is turned against the victim and becomes the warden that holds the secret of the perpetrator safe within the imprisoned mind of the abused. Shame, guilt, and fear build up those walls with each incident, sometimes to the point where the abused doesn't even realize they are being abused!

Experience gives me these insights to speak, for I was once so severely brainwashed that I had no clue I was a victim. All I knew was that every day I wished to die, or fantasies circled in my mind of my abuser's death, which never came. Only when I turned eighteen did I muster the courage to escape, after years of daily abuse! Even then, I didn't realize until six months later that I was raised and victimized by a pedophile. How many other children out there are just like I was? Believing they are alone, that they are the problem, and then trying to take their own lives to end their pain and self-hatred because their souls are imprisoned. How many adults see what is happening and do nothing to stop it? I've suffered terrible things, and today I use that suffering to share my experience with others, so that hopefully they can realize what may be happening to them, or someone else, and will have the courage to act against it.

For me, the cycle of abuse stops here, by speaking of it. This is how I end it. Truth penetrates lies. Light erases the darkness! I am a survivor of the darkest evils of this world, and I face the darkness that tried to consume my soul with courage. I am not my past, but healing from it sure has taken an extremely large part of my life. I wish that upon no one.

White Buffalo Woman taught us that having compassion for those infected with the disease of separation is necessary, but like the bad-hearted warrior who was turned into ashes, sometimes healing can only come when the physical form is disintegrated and returned to the source of creation. The Earth itself has been hurt the most by the disease of separation, therefore, it is inevitable that a change is rapidly approaching; a much needed environmental, spiritual, and physical transformation. There is absolutely nothing we can do to stop it! We can only prepare.

So, my message is to not be afraid. Help those who need it by planting seeds. Share your experience. If you know someone is being hurt, don't wait until their perpetrator dies to speak out, until the victim commits suicide, or until that victim becomes the abuser themselves! Our responsibility in these times is to expose and stand against abuse and oppression of all forms. Our children, our future, need us now.

Mother Earth is beginning to shake her blanket, just as our ancestors foretold. Therefore, we now face major storms, earthquakes, fires, and even social strife. It is time to let her messengers, the animals, guide us, and to follow them! We must learn how to survive by living in balance with the Earth. We must think about the changes we can make to alter our ways of living that take more from the Earth than is given back. Part of this involves taking the time to make offerings to Mother Earth, and to thank her for the resources she provides to us so lovingly. Those of us who are aware, must stand up and accept our responsibility to Mother Earth, to help her in any way that we can. We must start by looking within ourselves first, to heal the disease of sickness within our own beings. Whatever we transform within, radiates without!

I recently had a dream that dangerous storms filled with tornadoes and floods rapidly approached. As I looked out upon them, I watched as hundreds of little children planted gardens during the breaks in the storms! They smiled and waved at me, assuring me that it was going to be okay. Then, I saw a beautiful Hibiscus flower bush before me that they planted. It was filled with hummingbirds of varieties I didn't know existed.

Throughout all the chaos I experience in my life, beauty has been subtly present, becoming my guide out of the darkness. It exists in my life-long relationship with Nature and in the music that lifts me out of my PTSD lows. It is there when I dance to attune myself, and in the visions that help me to miraculously remember who I truly am. I find it in our Traditional Ceremonies and through the creation of art. I feel it when shaping my mind, body, and spirit through physical fitness. I know it in the love for my children and through the guidance of those who walked the path before us. I create it in the moments when I bravely follow my heart. These moments of beauty are the pieces of the puzzle that encourage me to keep going and to stand strong. I cling to their beauty for the life they continue to give as they help me to defy the disease of separation time and time again!

The beauty in the chaos is my serenity, my resistance, and my resilience! May you too find your own beauty amidst the chaos, so that together we can rise from the ashes, and recreate the way we live with, and upon, our sacred Mother Earth. For, with or without us, she is beginning her divine transformation, and whether we continue with her depends on our own ability to transform and to humbly rejoin the sacred hoop of all life. May peace and beauty be with us, and may we forevermore walk gently upon our beautiful Mother Earth!

CHAPTER FOURTEEN
WE ARE FOREVER

A lifetime has passed in the three years since I first published this story of resilience, reconnection, and empowerment. Now, a foreboding sense of inescapable and world-shattering change hovers over our planet, compelling me to share more profound insights gained through inspirational and challenging experiences that can be used to help others better navigate "The Great Shift" that is finally upon us. I've agreed to help during this prophetic era. I finally understand what that means and what it asks of those of us who are stepping into our natural leadership positions during these chaotic times. Thank you for being a part of this story. You are not alone.

In the quaint backyard of my friend's house, nestled beneath Pueblo Peak in Taos, New Mexico, I think, decompress, and write. Since the COVID lockdowns in 2020, Sacred Sites like Pueblo Peak, found within the ancestral homelands of the Taos Pueblo, have been closed off to outsiders and have only recently reopened. However, threats of more lockdowns loom as reports of COVID infections surge and our governments issue increased warnings of potential shutdowns to "control" the spread of infection. Most of us, however, don't even bat an eye at it anymore. We know better. The infamous 2020 lockdowns caused massive changes to our world as we knew it, and many of us realize that we can never go back to our "normal" pre-2020 world. But do we even want to? More people are standing in their power after realizing how much they've been lied to by their governments. They are researching and discovering the true history that has been hidden from them for centuries. However, there is a huge split in the collective — those who are aware, and those who choose to remain blindfolded and hopelessly plugged into the matrix as its slaves. Together, they create a rift between the light and the dark, like two worlds that are separated by a red and blue pill.

Currently, I travel back and forth between Taos and Santa Fe, New Mexico. Both are art epicenters of the world and are thus wonderful places for me to channel my thoughts once again into this memoir, however, even these places are dealing with massive change and transformation that leave an air of uncertainty and stress that exists no matter where one finds themselves in this world. It's inescapable, although some places are still more peaceful than others. When I began writing this memoir, I lived in Sedona, Arizona. There, I was tragically inspired to write this book due to the loss of my friend by suicide. I wanted to show those who were led to read it that it is possible to overcome our trauma and anger, no matter what we've had to survive, and furthermore, to create a path for ourselves to thrive. At the time, I was still separated from my three oldest children, a source of incredible sadness, guilt, and pain that kept me trapped in negative cycles, trauma, and suffering.

Finalizing the memoir and publishing it — the biggest undertaking of shadow work and healing of my life — unlocked the heavy door that before kept us separated. Right before the first COVID lockdowns, in January 2020, after a short visit with my three oldest in Indianapolis, I decided that I needed to do whatever I could to be with them, even if that meant that I had to move back to the city and neighborhood that were what I considered a literal hell, the Fountain Square neighborhood in southeast Indianapolis, Indiana. It became clear that my kids would never come live with me, no matter how beautiful or serene of a place that I found for us, so I had to sacrifice what I wanted, and instead come to them, especially after I saw the way their father, Izz, treated them during that short visit. The way he talked to my oldest and made even the simplest duties that were his responsibility to fulfill into an unbearable burden, such as taking them to complete their driving test to get a license, sickened me. So, I returned to Sedona, and within three days, found a couple to take over my lease. I gave them almost all my belongings, and once again, left with only what I could fit in my car. Within three weeks after arriving in Indianapolis, and with the help of some very generous friends, I raised enough money to rent a six-bedroom house in Fountain Square only a mile away from where the kids lived with Izz. I made it as easy as possible for them to quietly leave their father's home and to move in with me, and in this way, I gained my three oldest back into my life, right before the historic COVID lockdowns.

Even though I was unsure of my ability to provide for all of us, I devoted myself to doing whatever I needed to do to provide my kids with the safest home that I could. Although Fountain Square had vastly improved over the ten years since I last lived there and is now considered an up-and-coming historical neighborhood, we still heard gunshots and random fights every day and night. For the most part, however, it didn't affect us. I quickly transformed the enclosed front porch space of our home into a beautiful Handpoked Tattoo studio and managed to bring in enough clients and money to cover all our bills.

Soon, the COVID lockdowns hit, and I was forced to temporarily stop tattooing. However, I qualified for unemployment as a self-employed business owner and for the first time in my life, I was given a solid source of weekly income by the State without having to work my ass off. It gave me the freedom to rest, and I realized that I didn't want to tattoo just to make money anymore. Like many others, the lockdowns allowed us to look at what we did and didn't want for ourselves any longer. Some of us could see what was truly important, yet others focused only on the pandemic itself and self-isolation, thereby choosing to live in fear rather than using the forced isolation as a time to reflect on the changes that were occurring in our world.

Many contemplated the reality that the COVID lockdowns were part of a "plandemic," an event that was planned by the government to test to see how people would tolerate losing certain freedoms that were enforced through fear-mongering and authoritarian rule. Others chose to believe whole-heartedly in the pandemic and accepted an experimental vaccination into their bloodstreams. Some even shamed others who didn't get it by accusing them of spreading the disease and causing the deaths of others because they weren't vaccinated. However, it soon became clear that even those who were vaccinated still contracted and spread the disease, and even worse, some of them experienced irreversible negative health effects directly caused by the vaccination. Either choice that a person made, due to fear or duress, eventually caused most people to question the government, and to realize that somewhere along the way, they were lied to and have been for generations.

I did not receive the vaccination and did my best to ensure that none of my kids did either. My oldest did, however, and I respected their decision. They received all the booster shots as well. I worry about them now, because ever since, they've had repeated bouts of sickness like pneumonia and bronchitis and have repeatedly contracted COVID despite doing "everything they were supposed to do." I cannot blame them for the choices they made, because their university *required* all its students to get vaccinated to return to school. In this way, many people were forced into the vaccination to keep their jobs or to return to school, placing them in a state of duress that in the end, is the responsibility of the state and federal governments that created and enforced mandatory vaccinations. Ultimately, it will be these same governments across the world that will be held accountable for what they did to their own people during the COVID-19 pandemic, or what some call the "plandemic."

The lockdowns were a blessing in disguise for me. I finally received the much-needed time and space to recover from tattooing and from being the only one that was financially responsible for my family. I used the time to rest, recover, plant gardens, learn new survival skills, and to reconnect with my family. In September of 2021, I received two huge grants from the federal government that provided emergency aid to businesses that were forced to shut down because of the lockdowns. I used this money, right after the lockdowns were lifted and the unemployment funds from the State ended, to open my first licensed, professional, Traditional Handpoked Tattoo studio and brick-and-mortar retail space. Although I didn't want to tattoo just to make money anymore, I had to once again provide for my family on my own, and I hoped that opening a professional studio and retail space would not only offer the opportunity for myself to expand my artistic freedom, but that of others as well.

Thus, Thunderbird Rising Studios opened its doors, and made history as the first Indigenous-owned and operated tattoo studio and retail space in the Midwest that provided Native-made art, tattoos, and products. Everything offered was made exclusively by reputed Indigenous artists and creators, particularly those Native to Great Turtle Island, or what is now known as America and Canada. From the day the studio opened, business boomed, and I realized that I accomplished one of my biggest life goals – to bring my own dream to life, by escaping the 9 to 5 job cycle, becoming my own boss, and most poignantly, creating a safe space to support other Indigenous artists through it while keeping my children with me.

Unlike my experience in Sedona, when I had a bare minimum of clients and struggled to make ends meet, I now had all the clients I could ask for and more. With a fully booked schedule for a year, and with a waitlist of over two hundred names, I adjusted how I offered tattoos so that it more aligned with Traditional aspects, rather than standards set by modern tattoo artists. Particularly, through my ability to channel the designs that were meant uniquely for each of my clients. I accepted only those that gave me full artistic freedom when creating their designs, or those who were Indigenous and wanted to receive a Traditional design from their ancestors. I no longer allowed my clients to decide what their marking would look like and released those who asked me to go back to the drawing board after I already drew their design. In this way, I did my best to ensure that Thunderbird Rising Studios was respected as a Traditional Handpoke Tattoo studio. I also lectured at local universities and museums about the sacred practice of Traditional Tattooing.

It took me many years of research to discover that most Native American Tribes, including my own, the Lakota and Dakota, once considered the tattooing practice to be a Ceremony that could only be carried out by highly trained tattoo artists who were also Keepers of Tattoo Bundles. Bundles are considered incredibly wakan, or sacred, and are usually kept and cared for by only the one who carries that bundle. Tattoo Bundles contain the tools of Traditional Tattooing and other sacred items with spiritual power that help the tattooist to imbue tattoos with special energies, protections, or healing qualities. Furthermore, not just anyone can become a Traditional Tattoo Artist. They are chosen by Creator and have a gift from Wakan Tanka to channel markings that are meant for the person that came to them for the Tattoo Medicine.

This knowledge, combined with experience, inspired me to trust fully in my ability to create through the gift Wakan Tanka imparted unto me – to channel the designs that were meant for those who trusted me to do so. I felt more fulfilled in my tattoo work than ever before, and business boomed for over a year. It didn't take long, however, for me to feel incredibly overwhelmed from tattooing, even though I changed my approach. I realized that I still wasn't fully protecting myself from the unhealed energy of some of my clients. I discovered that Traditional Tattooing is an ancient Ceremony considered amongst the most sacred, therefore, Purification Ceremonies by both the Tattooist and the tattooed would have been held before and after the Ceremony itself. These Purification Ceremonies, such as the Inipi, or Sweatlodge Ritual, and Fasting, protected the energy of both the Tattooist and those tattooed.

Due to the nature of my studio, I could not offer a completely Traditional Tattoo Ceremony because I could not ask each client that came to me to go to a series of Purification Ceremonies before their session, or to Fast. I could only ask them to absolve from alcohol and heavy recreational drugs for a short time before. I still had to pay the rent. I couldn't afford to be too particular. Thus, I became physically and spiritually overwhelmed with the residual energy that I carried from others. When I wasn't tattooing or drawing designs for clients, I was recovering from it. I became increasingly dissatisfied with the business, and heavily considered shutting it down or selling it to other tattoo artists. I needed a massive change.

To my surprise, I started receiving offers to model for Indigenous designers, and to perform as a singer and Fancy Shawl Dancer in places like Santa Fe, New York, Las Vegas, and even Paris, France. I never thought these types of opportunities would ever be mine again once I received my facial tattoos, particularly runway modeling, but I was wrong. I quickly said yes to these offers, especially since I needed the break from tattooing. So, I left the house in the charge of my oldest children, who were then 19, 18, and 16, and traveled so that I could model, sing, and dance.

As I moved away from tattooing full-time and spent more time on the runway or on stage, I noticed huge shifts in my physical appearance. My face slimmed, my cheekbones popped, my waist tightened, and my wrinkles faded. The more I focused on enriching myself, the more I experienced a "glow up." Strangers on the internet even accused me of not being the "real Stephanie Big Eagle" as they compared pictures of me five years ago to the new ones I was posting. What they didn't realize, and what had come into full focus for me, was that I was surrounded by narcissists, what I consider the closest beings in human form to demons, for most of my life.

After getting trapped in yet another toxic relationship with a narc in late 2020 through early 2021, I dove deeply into the study of the effects of narcissistic abuse, particularly how to recognize it, protect myself from it, and how to completely cut these types of people out of my life. What those strangers saw in my pictures from five years before, was a woman who was disempowered and whose life-force was being fed upon by the vampiric energy of the narcissists in her life, including her stepfather, mother, the father of her first three children, and many other relationships in between. It took an incredible amount of shadow work for me to realize that I was giving away my energy and sacred power to people who could not create that energy for themselves, so they had to take it from others through manipulation, gaslighting, and physical, mental, emotional, and spiritual abuse.

I recited daily affirmations that called my power back to myself in a clean, whole, and empowered state from all others to whom I consciously or unconsciously gave it to. Thus, I intentionally protected myself from these spiritual predators, and finally, it transformed my outward appearance once I fully reclaimed my power. That is the essence of how a "glow-up" happens – one takes their power back and doesn't allow others to feed upon it anymore. Once that happens, they start to glow from the inside out, and appear more attractive, beautiful, and empowered than ever before. I have not since allowed another person to take my power from me. I've learned that putting myself first is the best way to stand in my power, rather than being a people-pleaser as the narcissistic abuse forced me to be for my own survival, and which I subconsciously continued for far longer than necessary.

Despite the gunshots and explosions we heard every night, and the neighbor's fights that inspired me to put noise-drowning box fans in every room, I created a sanctuary inside our home that enabled deep healing in myself and in my relationship with my children. My room became my meditation space, the home of my sacred items, and the creation space for music, art, and dance. The disturbances sometimes overheard from the outside world became reminders that it is always up to us to create our reaction to our reality despite the negativity that may swirl around outside us. However, because we are in a time of chaos and confusion, we cannot control the impacts of that negativity that will no doubt affect every one of us, no matter how much shadow work, healing, or protection we achieve for ourselves and our families.

On March 26, 2023, while I was in Iowa recording a song, a drive-by shooting forever changed the lives of my children, their friends, and myself. It happened at our house while my sons and about ten of their friends gathered. My oldest son watched his friend die instantly in our kitchen, then held his friend's seriously injured face together until an ambulance arrived. Meanwhile, my second oldest lay passed out in my bedroom after watching his best friend take a direct shot to the face. A total of thirty-seven 7.62 caliber rounds, used mostly in full-power military main battle rifles, passed through the entire house, from all sides. Almost every window in the house was destroyed, and every carpet in the house was stained with the blood of innocent young people.

Despite the extreme nature of this brutal attack, no suspect was named, and to this day, there is still no suspect for this attempted mass shooting of young people. In other words, the shooting had no apparent motive because there was no connection made between the gathering to the shooting itself. It was a senseless, violent act of insanity that targeted young BIPOC, as most of my son's friends were Mexican and Black. So many questions continue to race through our minds, as all of us try to heal from an event that still causes nightmares and shock. It remains an unsolved mystery that to law enforcement, is unimportant and simply filed as another statistic of normal Indianapolis gun violence.

Despite this horrific tragedy, the landlord of this property hit me with a $12,000 bill despite an otherwise perfect rental history, to "replace blood-soaked carpets, repair multiple bullet holes, and replace shattered windows." Even though none of it was our fault, the rental property had no compassion. After my research and the advice of others, I realized this was illegal, and despite my own need to heal from this, to help my family, and to deal with moving from our home and being forced to close the studio, I had to fight. I found lawyers that accepted my case pro bono, and after several months of going back and forth with the rental company, we finally signed a legal agreement that released me from those outlandish charges and any possible negative reports that could have prevented me from qualifying for future rentals.

I almost didn't contact those lawyers because of the state of emotional distress my family and others were in, but I did anyway. Thus, there was finally a small sliver of justice served. We may never know who targeted my family and my son's friends, or why they chose to leave this scar on our hearts and Indianapolis forever, but at least we didn't have to pay such an outlandish fee for their insane and sick behavior. We cannot allow the increased amount of gun violence and mass shootings that we are dealing with in America, nor the chaos and confusion that is now our everyday reality, to keep us from fighting for justice.

Chaotic events like these are only going to increase as we are carried forward into "The Great Shift" that is now upon us. Many who have not done the spiritual work will be easily overcome by darker energies and will target those around them with their hatred and fear, using their weapons, violence, and whatever is at their disposal to destroy those whose spiritual light irritates their darkness and negative attachments. We must continue to pay attention and remove as many weak-willed and lower-vibrational energies as possible from our own energy. We must protect ourselves. However, this is a spiritual battle, and that means that no matter how much we try to shield ourselves and our loved ones, we will still be attacked, and sometimes, we will get hit, whether it be by a weapon, natural disaster, or an enemy we once thought was a friend. We must surround ourselves with those we love and the ones we love in return. When we do so, we can continue to carry onward no matter what obstacles we may face, because this is a battle that cannot be won alone. We need others now. We need an entire team, and it better be a solid one.

It is the time of chaos, confusion, and survival now, and there is no turning back. This is what we came here for, and this is why, for many of us warriors, our lives have always been chaotic and challenging. We are now prepared to help others who haven't yet been exposed to this level of chaos to survive this shift. We are ready now to lead the way as balance, harmony, truth, and justice are restored. We are the ones who know how to listen to our guidance systems, to trust our intuition, and to remain calm despite being amid gunfire, terrible storms, or any comparable tragedy. We must step up to the plate now. The pitcher has already launched the ball and intends to strike us out.

It is now mid-2023, and the second-worst wildfire in history just obliterated the historical royal province of Lahaina in Maui, Hawaii. My good friend, who is Kānaka Maoli, or Native Hawaiian, contacted me while parts of his homelands burned. "The shift is beginning. Lahaina burning is part of our people's prophecies. There's no turning back now. It has begun." His words weighed heavy as lead as reports from locals surfaced of the thousands of bodies that floated in the water or whose charred remnants still sat in their cars, unable to escape the flames that overtook Lahaina with no warning other than billowing black smoke and flames. Many asked, "Where is the help? Where is the government?" In those questions, they will have to face the truth, as countless Indigenous Nations have, that our governments are not going to help us in times of crisis, and even more shockingly, that they are most often the cause of the disasters that will from this point forward, until the completion of "The Shift," become so common that we will cease to hear of most of them because all of us will be forced into an era of survival that will require us to focus only on what's right before us. It is the final showdown and us warriors of all kinds have no choice but to hunker down and fight in the battle that's been building for generations.

I think back upon the message that was given to me sixteen years ago on the eve of my twenty-fifth birthday as I slept beneath the stars in Honolulu. A hovering star being spoke to me, while an unending spiral of other shimmering stars extended into the night sky beyond it. It warned, "A time of chaos and confusion is coming. In this time, you must find the ones that love you and that you love in return, and be with them at all costs, for it will be the only way to survive what's coming."

What's coming, is here. This is the time of chaos and confusion, and we cannot stop it, but only prepare for it. As wildfires spread, earthquakes strike, monstrous storms unleash their fury, and diseases of the mind, body, and soul prevail, know that nothing but love can guide us into safe spaces or save us. Only true love can overrule the terror that many of us will have to face that would otherwise cause us to abandon the person next to us in a life-or-death situation. Love is the power that overcomes fear, and fear will be used heavily against us now to weaken and separate us.

This type of love is what made it possible for several Lahaina families to survive days of being forced to wade in choppy, wind-fueled water to escape the flames that burned their homes, cars, and everything they owned. This love will help us all to survive similar situations, the seemingly impossible. It will open doors and portals to worlds that otherwise are inaccessible. I finally understand why they gave me that message sixteen years ago, and why I must share it now with as many people as possible.

Last night, as I meditated and listened to my Spirit helpers, they whispered, "We are here. Do not be afraid and pay attention." This took me aback, because for years they've been assuring, "We are coming. Keep holding on tight." Now, they are finally here, and I feel the excitement, yet anxiety at the same time, wondering what that really means. I know that I can do nothing but let go of everything that I've perceived as reality and must seriously pay attention to the changes that are coming as if they are tidal waves that we can only brace for. I am confident that I have done all I can to prepare, but it really does have me on edge, especially after all that my family, friends, and I have recently endured, and what the world continues to.

On July 26, 2023, the U.S. Congress held a public hearing on UFOs during which several notable U.S. government officials confirmed the existence of various alien spacecraft, some of which contained "non-human biologics" that were recovered from extraterrestrial crash sites.

They also acknowledged the existence of UAPs, or unidentified aerial phenomena that possessed technology far beyond any that currently exists on Earth. It was made clear that this hearing was made public to reduce the stigma around alien disclosure and to encourage more people to come forward with their stories, because as Democratic Representative Robert Garcia of California confessed, "UAPs, whatever they may be, may pose a serious threat to our military and our civilian aircraft, and that must be understood. We should encourage more reporting, not less, on UAPs. The more we understand, the safer we will be."

A week before this disclosure, a video of a distressed woman went viral as millions watched her demand to deboard from her plane because she claimed to see a being that was non-human in the seat next to her. Watching it inspired me to publicly share my story of the Wiwila, or Little Person, that I saw back in 2016. Her reaction to whatever she believed she saw reminded me of how I felt the first time I saw that Wiwila, the Lakota word for these beings that are said to be from another planet that now live on Earth. I was completely unprepared for an interaction with an other-worldly being, and it terrified me for days to come. Many now argue amongst each other about whether what she saw was true or not, but I know regardless of her truth, that other-worldly beings do exist, and shortly after her video and mine went viral, the U.S. government confirmed it as well.

These disclosures remind me of a dream I had about a year ago, when I first truly understood who I am and what my mission on Earth is, along with why my life has been so complicated and difficult. In this dream, I packed for a long trip for both me and my youngest son, Zeke. I needed a break after hours of packing, so I ventured outside, but when I looked up, I saw that the sky contained an ocean, and as I looked down, I saw that the ground was instead the sky. "This is completely backwards!" I thought. The terrain of this place was entirely an ochre red rather than brown and green, and suddenly, the memories came flooding back as I realized that I was on my home planet. My comrade interrupted my thoughts as he opened the door, "Are you ready, sis?" I smiled at him, "Yes, bro!" My son and I, along with a group of about fifteen other warriors, grabbed our bags and boarded our ship. We were welcomed onboard and briefed. All of us were hand-selected to accept this mission to travel to Earth to help her ascend. We were told that none of us would remember our true origin or identity until it was necessary to help us fulfill our purpose there. We took our seats, and our ship departed. Then, the dream ended. It wasn't until the government disclosed the existence of star beings and alien spacecraft that I truly began to believe in my own identity as a "star child" and came to understand why such a revealing dream would have taken so long for me to have.

For most of my life, an identity crisis, and a feeling of not belonging or fitting in anywhere has been one of my biggest sources of trauma and pain. The words "half-breed," "pretendian," "fake," and more have been hurled at me, especially recently, by others who've taken a disliking to me and who seek to destroy my reputation without even knowing me. After all that I've been through, and because of the dreams that have guided me along the way, I now understand that the darkness that has imprisoned this planet knows who the warriors of light, truth, and justice are. We carry an energy signature that is made clear the moment we incarnate onto Earth, and thus become primary targets of the beings that feed upon the souls of others. When we don't know who we are, or where we come from, we are trapped in a disempowered state. That is what these vampiric beings want, because when we don't stand in our own power, then we can't help others, much less ourselves, to escape the darkness they create. Without our power, they are nothing, and the only way that they have access to our power, which feeds and fuels their energy in the way that human blood feeds a vampire, is when we give it to them, either consciously or unconsciously. Our lower-vibrational reactions, our unresolved anger and trauma, our fear, our hatred, and our disempowerment, fuel them.

Those of us with the mission to free this planet and her people have had some of the hardest lives of all. In our own disempowered states, our natural light was fed upon by energy vampires, many of whom were first introduced to us through our own families. We've had to learn the hard way to overcome the darkness and to free ourselves, and by doing so, we gained the power and keys to unlock the door to freedom for others that are willing to walk through it and into the light. In this spiritual battle, we can only help others by first helping ourselves.

We also gained unique powers that could only be unlocked through incredible pain and suffering. Like a diamond, we had to survive, endure, and be transformed like the Phoenix before we could ever lead or help others. For me, it was my lack of identity and those who threw arrows at me because of it, that became my brightest inner-Phoenix fire. No one can ever make me doubt myself or my sacred purpose ever again, and I will help others to discover their identity and purpose by standing in my own amongst them.

The White Buffalo Calf prophecy speaks of the children of the stars that will one day walk upon Earth. It says that during the time that she, White Buffalo Calf Woman, will return and physically walk amongst all of us to seed a new prophecy, the original prophecy she brought to the people will have reached its fulfillment. At that time, a living C'anupa will exist in the hearts of children from the stars living upon the Earth. They will recognize her voice, and become the embodiment of her new prophecies, freeing the Earth of the darkness of past ages. The people who were given this prophecy, the Oceti Sakowin, were told that they would know the end of the coming ages were upon them, and her return was heralded, with the appearance of the white buffalo upon Earth. This time is upon us! As more of us awaken to the reality of who we are, and as more prophesized white buffalo and children from the stars are born unto Earth, it will be only a short time before this powerful woman from the stars returns to walk amongst us and to speak in all her power, drawing a boundary line of protection that our oppressors can no longer cross. I believe we will see it happen in our lifetimes, especially as the reality of star beings is made known to us by lower-vibrational entities who are now bound to disclose this information, in particular, governmental entities.

Although the "alien disclosure" from the U.S. government came as a surprise to those who were otherwise skeptical, Indigenous peoples, at least those who are aware of their Traditions and Oral History, have always known about other-worldly beings and our Star Nation relatives. My father's people, the Lakota and Dakota, say that we originally come from the Pleiades, and that we were seeded into this Earth, emerging from caves in what is now known as Bdote in Minnesota for our Dakota people, and Wind Cave in South Dakota for our Lakota people.

Over the past few years, giant sinkholes have opened up around the world. A particularly massive sinkhole was recently discovered in China that is 630 feet deep, has three cave entrances, and an ancient, preserved forest at its bottom that features old-growth trees, flora, and fauna. This discovery helped me to better understand how our own people could have emerged onto the surface of the Earth from such openings. If a lush, old-growth forest can be contained beneath Earth's surface as these sinkholes prove, then certainly we could have emerged from, and even thrived within, the Earth as many Indigenous creation stories recount. I believe that some of us will soon return to inner Earth, as my dreams foretell, for our own safety.

About six months ago, I had an electrifying dream. I stood in a large field, surrounded by many of my Indigenous relatives. A huge flock of snow geese suddenly blackened the sky above us. The lead goose held a staff in its beak. As it passed above me, it dropped the staff. Knowing immediately what to do, I swooped it up and sprinted over to our sacred fire pit. Holding the staff above my head like an axe, I jumped up as high as I could, slamming it down onto the east side of the pit with every bit of force I could muster. I then turned to the south, the west, and the north, repeatedly striking the staff in the same way in all four directions. When I finished, I looked up to the west and saw the formation of the blackest, most ominous thunderstorm I've ever seen. I cried out to the people, "It's time! Do not be afraid! The Cleansing has begun!" Then, a few others and I guided our relatives into an entrance into the Earth, and we descended into it as the storm quickly overtook the surface.

The evening of August 30, 2023, was the rise of the "Super Blue Moon," an intriguing description for a second full moon that occurs in the same calendar month while the moon is close to Earth, resulting in its more magnified and brightened appearance. An astrologically rare event, it coincided with the arrival of a Category 3 hurricane, Idalia, which made its landfall in the Big Bend coastal area of Florida, the first to do so in recorded history. This was only one week after Hurricane Hilary, a Category 4 hurricane when it made landfall in Mexico, made a significant impact on southern California as the first storm in the area's history to cause a tropical storm warning. Although the storm wasn't unprecedented, its path and strength were unusual and thus a major indication of the increasing power and impact of these storms that coincide with massive earth changes. On September 7, 2023, Hurricane Lee, still brewing far southeast of the Caribbean islands, was forecast to turn into a major Category 5 hurricane by the National Hurricane Center. "Current models are calling for remarkable rates of intensification beyond rates normally seen with model forecasts," the center said. The storm's rapid intensification was predicted as it moved over record-warm water in the Atlantic Ocean. The National Hurricane Center predicted an "above normal" 2023 hurricane season due to these climate effects.

On September 6, 2023, United Nations Secretary-General António Guterres issued this warning, "The dog days of summer are not just barking, they are biting. Our planet has just endured a season of simmering – the hottest summer on record. Climate breakdown has begun…. Our climate is imploding faster than we can cope with." In other words, the storms are here, and we can only prepare!

As these storms hit, and chaos ensues, we will have to watch our relatives in the Animal, Spirit, and Elemental realms closely. They are our helpers, and many have agreed to help us during these times. Even multidimensional beings such as Bigfoot will show themselves to those with good hearts and guide them into safe places while Earth cleanses herself. Whether people believe it or not, other-worldly beings are real, and many Indigenous Nations knew of their existence long before modern-day skepticism.

My people, the Dakota and Lakota, call Bigfoot Chiye-Tanka, or Elder Brother. It's a name that shows how much respect and honor we have for this being that can go in and out of worlds as it so chooses. A protector of Mother Earth and her people, Chiye-Tanka has been known to terrorize those who terrorize the Earth, while protecting those who protect her. The Big Man can walk through the forest without being seen, but can also run through it like an elephant, snapping fully grown trees in half as if they are only twigs. He chooses how he is seen, by whom, and when. Bigfoot is also known for its psychic abilities, so they know when people are looking for them or traveling close by. So, if you see Bigfoot, it's by choice – Bigfoot's choice. There are many Nations that have different stories and teachings about them. I've even heard of

Elders that have traded with Bigfoot. They'll leave treasured items out in a specific area, and Bigfoot takes those things and trades evenly for them.

An Ojibwe Elder shared several Bigfoot stories with me, and this one really stuck with me. About twenty years ago, she was kidnapped by group of men that took her up into the mountains with intentions to rape and murder her. They did this to many Indigenous women before her. Creator was looking out for her that day because she found a way to escape! As she wandered the mountainsides looking for her way home, Bigfoot found her and took her into his lodge to protect her. As she stayed in his home, she could feel the heavy thump of his footsteps all through the night as he patrolled the area outside to make sure that those men didn't find her, and if they did, that they wouldn't be able to get to her again.

That wasn't the only time she had a Bigfoot encounter. The first time she saw him was when she was a little girl, while she was lost in the woods. The sun had set, and her eyes were swollen with tears as she frantically searched for her way out. Suddenly, she came across a tall, hairy being with piercing green eyes. He said to her, "Don't be scared! Just close your eyes like this and you'll be able to see through the dark." So, she closed her eyes, and just like Bigfoot taught her, she found her way back home and out of the forest using only the power of her mind.

I've been told that most sightings of Chiye Tanka are warnings. Bigfoot comes to remind us of the balance that is meant to exist in all places. As a multidimensional being whose purpose is to protect all natural things, seeing him is a warning that asks us to beware of how we treat the Earth. It's also a sign of tremendous changes that are coming and a warning to prepare for them. Instead of wondering if he is real or not, it would serve one better to question their relationship with the

Earth. We are being reminded that living in balance with the Earth, means treating her as our mother, with honor and respect.

In May of 2023, I sat upon the hill for my first Hanbdeceya Ceremony, or Vision Quest, under the leadership of our Sundance Chief, Hehaka. One of the Seven Sacred Rites of the Oceti Sakowin, it is an up to four-day period of fasting from food and water, traditionally done alone, to receive a vision that can help us to better understand ourselves and to clarify what we will dance for during the Sundance Ceremony. Before going up on the hill, we purified in the Inipi for four days. On the final night of purification, right before I went up for my Hanbdeceya, Hehaka looked at me during the third round and asked, "Steph! Did you hear that?" I looked up at him while the sweat poured down my face, and breathed heavily, "No!" "Mitakuye Oyasin!" he cried and called for the door to open.

As the steam poured out of the lodge, and we gathered our breath again after singing strong during that round, Hehaka, the son of late Chief Galen Drappeau Sr., the Keeper of Seven Sacred Alters of the Oceti Sakowin, announced to everyone, "Stephanie's ancestor just came into the lodge and claimed her as his granddaughter, and he is a Wakinyan!" I gasped as he continued, "He was dressed in all black and white, and he says that he is *not* going to give her a vision up on the hill tonight." He laughed, and then explained that the Wakinyan is a Thunderbird, and they work with humans through the Heyoka, or the Sacred Clown, a human chosen by the Wakinyan to embody their energy, power, and Lightning Medicine to bring healing to the people. They do everything backwards, even talking, so, he explained, "Your grandfather talks backward because he is a Wakinyan. So, that means he is going to give you a vision tonight!" Then, he put his head back and laughed in the way we've all come to love him for.

I felt an immense swelling of pride and relief pour over me when he shared what he saw. Hehaka has the power of our great Medicine People who have mostly all gone back home across the Milky Way. They can easily see and communicate with Spirits of all kinds. I've seen his power, so I trusted his vision. It felt amazing, even though I already knew who I was, to have this confirmation from our Chief from my Wakinyan grandfather himself. I was thrilled to climb the hill.

I pulled Hehaka aside after the lodge however, because he also announced to everyone in the lodge that I'd be doing Traditional Piercings at our upcoming Sundance Ceremony, and that was definitely news to me because first of all, I had no idea how to Pierce – the cutting of the skin to open it for the pegs that are then inserted and connected to either the tree, or to ropes that are held by leadership until the one dancing "breaks free." Secondly, I thought that only men were allowed to Pierce. When I asked him for clarification, he said, "Oh no, leave the Piercings to the men!" So, I did, and just believed that he said "Piercings" mistakenly, because I was planning instead to bring Traditional Tattooing back to our people during Ceremony, as he and I had already planned.

Thus, I climbed the hill filled with excitement for the vision my Wakinyan grandfather promised *not* to give me. However, that night, I dreamt instead of a disgusting parasite that was sticking out of my leg. I pulled with all my strength, but I simply could not yank it out of me. My youngest son, Zeke, somehow knew about it, and instead of helping me, he rubbed it in! I pushed him off me and cried out for the Wakinyan to help me, but they never did. I was incredibly puzzled by that dream. Not only was it not the vision I was hoping for, but my son and I had a healthy relationship, or so I thought, so why was it showing me otherwise? I had nothing else to do that day but think, and suddenly I realized that the dream was showing me that I was allowing my son to behave disrespectfully towards me without even realizing it!

The parasite that I couldn't pull out of my leg represents the patriarchal treatment of women that has turned me, and many other women, into victims of abuse by men, and even other women, for generations now. It is so deeply rooted into our society, that many of us don't even realize that it exists, and if we do, we can't pull it out by ourselves because we don't realize what it means to truly be honored and respected as women. Therefore, we continue to allow ourselves to be mistreated and fed upon by the parasite of misogyny. I realized that when I allowed my son to insult me jokingly by calling me "brah," or "gay," that I was telling him that it was okay to disrespect his own mother, which in his future, would set the foundation for how he treated other women. He did it for so long that it became his way to greet me every time he addressed me, and I did nothing about it.

I took that dream seriously, and as soon as I came down from the hill, I took my boy aside and told him that the Spirits said that he was no longer allowed to call me names of any kind ever again, and that I would not be allowing it. Furthermore, if he continued to, I would take him into extra Inipi lodges for purification until it was removed from his system. He took that warning seriously, as he went through every Purification Lodge with me before I went up on the hill, and boy were they tough ones! From that day forward, he has never called me a name, even jokingly, and thus, I corrected the misogyny right out of our relationship by following what that dream showed me. We are learning together what it means to be "Traditional" Dakota and Lakota.

I always find the first day of any Ceremony with Fasting to be the hardest. The first day of Sundance and Hanbdeceya, are the days where we "enter into the Spirit World." Our bodies cry out for water and food, and the yearning for both, especially water, is almost unbearable. That first day on the hill, the sun beat down on me like an oven. All I could do was survive and try to quiet my mind. A small thunderstorm finally formed at dusk, offering a small amount of shade, and I napped, but still had no vision.

That night, I dreamt that I was walking along the waterside. My throat was parched with thirst. I realized that I needed to find a loon, because somehow, I knew that if I could find their fishing spot, that it would be a good place to drink the water. Suddenly, a loon appeared and walked right beside me, then it ran, so I chased it and sure enough, it led me to its fishing spot. I dove into the water right beside the loon and quenched my thirst. As I drank, I spotted a figurine submerged in the water beside me. It was ancient and wooden, and carved into the form of a Matriarchal Queen that wore an elaborate crown. In her hair was a double-sided decorative hairpiece made from chokecherry sticks and porcupine hair. I picked up the figurine and tucked it into my pocket.

Although that dream wasn't the vision that I was crying for, it still imparted several incredibly important lessons. First, it reminded me to always look to the animal world for teachings about how to survive. I was thirsty and deprived of clean water in the dream. Thus, I had to find a clean source of drinking water and could only follow the loon to find it. This is a reality that many of us will have to face soon, as many of our Indigenous Elders have been warning about as we enter this time of survival.

Second, the discovery of the submerged figurine of the Matriarchal Queen that the loon led me to, whom itself is regarded as a symbol of leadership to many Indigenous Nations, is a sign of the rise of empowered women into natural positions of leadership – a return to matriarchy, or a way of living in which anointed women and men hold an equal weight in making decisions, an equal amount of power, and equal wealth. It honors and respects women for their ability to lead in a way that inherently honors the Earth, the environment, and the best interest of all the people, while men are honored for their ability to lead in a way that channels the illuminating energy of the Sun and the Sky World.

My Tribes, the Lakota and Dakota, and many other Indigenous Nations, are originally matriarchal. In this way of life, women are honored for their natural energy that comes from their ability to create and carry life. Because of it, women are expected to make decisions using their natural connection to the Earth and its creative force as their guide. Therefore, their equal leadership is only natural and prevents the imbalance that arises when only men are put into positions of leadership. It is said that we will once again return to this form of equal leadership, not just among Indigenous peoples, but worldwide, where both men and women stand in their divine power to respectfully, honorably, and equally guide their people together.

Currently, women around the world, myself included, are realizing their innate feminine power and sacredness that was purposefully hidden or taken from them over the course of especially the last few hundred years. The patriarchal system that made them the property of men through marriage, and which even denied their right to own their own bank accounts, make decisions for themselves separate of their fathers or husbands, or even to own property or land, is being shunned. Even women in other countries that are still heavily patriarchal are standing together to bravely usurp the power that their men have forced upon them for generations.

We have been abused for so long that many of us are only beginning to open our eyes to our incredible worth and innate power. Even our Chief, Hehaka, has announced that it is time for the women to rise again and to step into their natural positions of leadership. The message from that dream, of finding a Matriarchal Queen submerged in the water – the patriarchy – and then picking her up, drying her off, and placing her in my pocket – stepping into my power – couldn't have been more significant for the rise and return of the divine woman during this time. As the Earth cleanses herself, due to our natural connection, so too will the women of this Earth. Although it seems messy, chaotic, and frightening, it is in the best interest of our planet and humanity.

Day three of my Hanbdeceya came, and as the evening set in, so too did a powerful thunderstorm. We were allowed to take tarps and our sleeping bags up with us on the hill, so in grateful preparation, I wrapped myself up like a burrito inside the tarp. The winds whipped the tarp around, swirling in noisy chaos, but within it, I was dry, comfortable, and safe. Lightning and thunder rumbled the ground around me, bringing a calm excitement and feeling of home. The gentle taps of rain danced on the tarp above me and soon soaked the thirsty ground. I closed my eyes and snuggled in for the night.

Before I drifted off to sleep, I saw a Spirit Man standing before me. He wore a black and white feather Headdress, filled with hundreds of black and white feathers arranged just like a Dog Soldier's – an elite and feared warrior of some Plains Tribes that used to stake himself to the ground during battle. His entire body was covered with white paint, over which black paint was used to make spots and stripes from head to toe. He wore only a warrior's robe that covered his legs that looked like it was made from a buffalo hide. His eyes were dark, but with an intense glow. His mouth was dark too, almost black, and within it, he held a whistle.

This powerful being held his arm out to me and said, "Relative, you can come back home with me. I'll take you right now, just grab my hand! Or, you can choose to stay and help the people, and if you stay, I'll be with you the rest of the way." I cried then, because I genuinely wanted to go, to leave this Earth, and return to the place that I knew was home, which wasn't in this world. There have been so many times I've prayed to be released from here and to go back, because of all the hardships I've had here, which still weigh on my soul, but something within me told me that it still wasn't my time. There are still things I need to do here to completely fulfill my mission. So, I looked back at him, and whispered, "I'll stay." He smiled crookedly, blew his whistle, and faded away while I drifted off to sleep. Then, the rains poured heavily from the sky like a thunderous lullaby.

It wasn't until I woke up the next morning, the fourth morning of my Hanbdeceya, that I realized I had my vision! My "Crying for a Vision" Ceremony was complete, and it was time to come down from the hill and to share my vision with Hehaka. After hearing my vision, Hehaka confirmed that I described my relative in the same way that he saw him. What really let him know that my vision was real, however, was the whistle I described. Hehaka didn't tell me about the whistle when he first told me that my relative came into the Inipi to claim me. When he asked, "Steph, did you hear that?" during the Purification Lodge before I went up on the hill, he was asking if I knew that my grandfather was blowing that whistle with all his might right in my face! Hehaka then shared my grandfather's powerful name with me and confirmed that he was a powerful Heyoka that carried a Black C'anupa, or Pipe.

Due to the nature of my vision, Hehaka invited me to complete the fourth year of my Sundance commitment as leadership. Not truly having any idea what that meant, of course I accepted, and thus I was thrown directly into pouring water for the women during Inipi at Sundance. This required me to know songs, which of course I didn't, so I gave tobacco to the women who did know songs so that they'd sing for us until I learned a few on my own. One song, which has always been my favorite to sing during Sundance, became my song of choice. I was told that it was the "Forgiveness Song," but it wasn't until the third day of me singing it within the lodge that I was corrected and told it was the "Piercing Song" – the song that is usually only sung while the people are getting Pierced for their offerings! I laughed and cried at the same time when I found out, because on the fourth day, Hehaka approached me and told me that Spirit told him that it was time to teach me how to Pierce the women and asked if I would accept that responsibility.

With a racing heart, I did, because you do not say "No" to your trusted Chief, and thus, even though I felt completely unprepared, his announcement that we all thought was a mistake made during the Hanbdeceya Purification Inipi came true. I became one of the first women since the era of colonization to perform the sacred responsibility of piercing the women's arms for their flesh offering to Creator – the offering that creates the way for our prayers to be heard. In this way, I was thrown into leadership for our Sundance Altar, learning everything the hard way, but the only way that I have ever known. Thus, I understood with a roar of laughter why the song that really stuck with me was the "Piercing Song"!

In this way, is how I am called to help the people, by standing beside them to assist them while they send their prayers out to the Universe and Creator; By sharing my story that can help guide them out of the darkness and into the light – like lightning; By doing whatever I can to protect, guide, heal, and empower those around me until my relatives come for me once again and it is finally time to go home.

Each one of us has the potential to step into our full power and purpose in this lifetime. I hope that by sharing my story, my visions, my dreams, and a collective survival story turned into one of resilience, reconnection, and empowerment, that others will realize that they too are capable of miraculous, even supernatural feats! Remember who you are, and the divinity that you carry. I will leave you on a high note, with a spoken word poem that soon will become a song that will be heard around the world as we Thunderbirds, Movers, and Shakers, continue to arrive, arise, and thrive!

Thunderbird Rising

Sitting in the sun, in search of a little light.
Tragedies loop through my darkest insights.
Steadily we cycle thru this rollercoaster life.
My relatives and I, traveling a road predestined to strife.
We hear them say, ancestors voicing.
What's transmuted becomes your blessing.
Cycles are breaking, energy's changing.
Warriors endure. Warriors survive. Keep on. Create light.
We ride on. Fierce! Into the sunlight.
Piercing electric eyes carry 10,000 lightning strikes.
Spreading wings, we're diving. Thunderbirds Rising.
The return of our Nations. All our Relations.
Prophecy bridges destiny & elation, for us, the people that survived:
Generational indoctrination via cultural assimilation.
Legal genocide, & boarding school assassinations.
When it seems nothing's changed but the faces and places. Remember.
We are the endurance of generations upon generations of sufferation.
The Calvary Soldier became the federal agent.
We remember. We are forever.
They define who is and isn't "Indian."
We remember. We are forever.
They continue to steal our children via Child Protective Services.
We remember. We are forever.
History lies while genocide presides under "Red, White, and Blue."
We remember. We are forever.
"Land Back" remains only a chant while survival has been our only option.
We remember. We are forever.
We lililili and war whoop, screaming "Mni Wiconi."
We remember. We are forever.
They terrorize Earth's last natural resources.
We remember. We are forever.
Soon we will see truth revealed and injustice repealed. Prophecy fulfilled.

Because we remember. We are Forever.
Amongst the stars, the energies are stirring.
Because we are still here, Ancestors are re-emerging.
Mothers give birth to new Standing Bulls.
Crazy Horse walks this Earth.
Pte San Win, White Buffalo Maiden, returns.
When she speaks in thunder, lightning strikes! Enacting the Sacred Rites!
Will they dare break the Sacred Code? For another million years, no!
Moved forward in an instant. Spirits empowered by ancestral persistence.
The enforcers are released, and the vampires are pushed back, then collected.
It is time. We are returned. No longer can they interfere.
Prophecy fulfills while they're left cowering in fear.
Demoted to watching. Only watching, watching, watching.
Now they are bound and released are we into prophesized action.
We strike the fire pit with our Wakinyan lightning sticks!
Four sacred directions! Four sacred colors! Four sacred foundations!
Called to arise and cleanse this Chaos and Confusion.
We gather, riding in form. As the sunlight storms.
Transforming the land as 10,000 lightning stars stand.
Spreading wings, we're flying. Coming to Earth, we're arriving.
To lead the prophesized arising. Traveling with sacred horses, we are riding.
Listen to our footsteps. Listen to our Thunder.
Watch our lightning destroy your plagues. Plunder your towers.
Topple fake power. Spark the rebirth of sacred Mother Earth.
You can't stop us. We are arriving.
We are walking. We are riding.
We are running. We are flying.
We are Thunderbirds Rising.

BIBLIOGRAPHY

Ben-Saud, Sarah. "White Buffalo 8." 2019. JPEG file.

Big Eagle, Stephanie. *Thank You to all Our Supporters*. 2016. Honor the Earth Annual Report Pg. 32, Callaway. Honor the Earth.

Bison Skull Pile – restored. 1892. Burton Historical Collection, Detroit Public Library. *Wikipedia the Free Encyclopedia*. Digital photo. Accessed 16 Nov 2019.

Brown, Alleen. "Dakota Access Pipeline Leaks Start to Add Up." *The Takeaway,* Jan. 11, 2018, https://www.wnycstudios.org/podcasts/takeaway/segments/across-country-smaller-pipeline-leaks-start-add. Accessed 19 Nov 2019.

Casas, Bartolomé. *A Short Account of the Destruction of the Indies*. United States: ReadaClassic.com, 2009. Print. Freire, Paulo, Myra B. Ramos, Donaldo P. Macedo, and Ira Shor. Pedagogy of the Oppressed. 2018. Print.

Churchill, Ward. *Kill the Indian, Save the Man: The Genocidal Impact of American Indian Residential Schools*. San Francisco, Calif: City Lights, 2005. Print.

"Cultural appropriation, n.1." OED Online. Oxford University Press, September 2019. Web. 16 Nov 2019.

Deloria, Vine. *Singing for a Spirit: A Portrait of the Dakota Sioux*. Santa Fe, N.M: Clear Light Publishers, 2000. Print.

Forbes, J.D. (1985). *Native American Higher Education: The Struggle for the Creation of D-Q University*, 1960-1971. Davis, CA: D-Q University Press.

Forbes, J.D., Martin, K., & Risling Jr., D. (1972). *The Establishment of D-Q University*. Davis, CA: D-Q University Press.

Fort Laramie Treaty, 1868. *The Avalon Project: Documents in Law, History and Diplomacy,* https://avalon.law.yale.edu/19th_century/nt001.asp.

Freire, Paulo, Myra B. Ramos, Donaldo P. Macedo, and Ira Shor. *Pedagogy of the Oppressed*. 2018. Print.

Horton, Alex. "Australia's fragile koala colonies are being ravaged by bush fires: 'It's a national tragedy.'" *The Washington Post,* 15 Nov 2019, https://www.washingtonpost.com/science/2019/11/15/australia-fire-koala-bear/. Accessed 19 Nov 2019.

Judicial and Statutory Definitions of Words and Phrases. West Publishing Company, West Publishing Co., St. Paul. 1914. p. 763.

Keith, Stephanie. "*Stephanie Big Eagle Rides with other Fort Laramie Treaty riders along Bombing Range Road on the Pine Ridge Reservation near Scenic, South Dakota.*" 2018. Reuters, New Hampshire. *The Atlantic.* JPEG file. Accessed 16 Nov 2019.

Knowles, Hannah. "Keystone Pipeline leaks 383,000 gallons of oil in second big spill in two years.*" The Washington Post,* 1 Nov 2019, https://www.washingtonpost.com/climate-environment/2019/10/31/keystone-pipeline-leaks-gallons-oil-second-big-spill-two-years/. Accessed 19 Nov 2019.

Krutak, Lars. *Tattoo Traditions of Native North America*. Stichting LM Publishers, 2014.

Lame Deer, John (Fire) and Richard Erdoes. *Lame Deer, Seeker of Visions*. Simon & Schuster, 1994.

Law Dictionary Fourth Edition, Steven H. Gifis, p. 86.

Louwagie, Lacey. "S.D. Officials Again Blow Off Indian Child Welfare Act." *Courthouse News Service*, 16 Dec 2016, https://www.courthousenews.com/s-d-officials-again-blow-off-indian-child-welfare-act. Accessed 16 Nov 2019.

Mandela, Nelson. *Long Walk to Freedom: The Autobiography of Nelson Mandela*. Paw Prints, 2014. Print.

Mandela, Winnie, Anne Benjamin, and Mary Benson. *Part of My Soul Went with Him*. Harmondsworth, Middlesex: Penguin Books, 1985. Print.

Nesbit, Jeff. "This is the way world ends: will we soon see category 6 hurricanes?" *The Guardian*, 15 Sept 2018, https://www.theguardian.com/us-news/2018/sep/15/hurricane-category-6-this-is-how-world-ends-book-climate-change. Accessed 20 Nov 2019.

The Holy Bible, King James Version. New York: American Bible Society: 1999; Bartleby.com, 2000. www.bartleby.com/108/.

Sinn, Jason. *Art Apodaca Explains the Founding of DQU*. 2017. Unbroken: Native Americans Today, Sacramento. *Jason Sinn Photography*. JPEG file.

Trudell, John. *Lines from a Mined Mind: The Words of John Trudell*. United States: Fulcrum Publishing, 2016. Print

ACKNOWLEDGEMENTS

To my son Cuauhtémoc, "One Who Descends Like an Eagle," thank you my son, for choosing me as your mother. Thank you for becoming an embodiment of the cultural genocide that is still occurring against all Indigenous peoples everywhere, via our illegal separation by the illegitimate corporate government of South Dakota. Thank you for enduring this struggle with me together. Thank you for your strength, wisdom, and warrior spirit! I know with my cante ista – eye of the heart – that you will return to us again one day! I know that you will be a great leader of the people, especially due to what you must endure, and that you will fulfill the responsibility of "Cuauhtémoc, One Who Descends Like an Eagle."

To my son Ezekiel, thank you for being so incredibly patient with me as I spent countless days pouring my time, focus, and energy into writing this book! Thank you for learning how to be extremely self-sufficient so that I could have the time I needed to tattoo, to write, and to heal. Thank you for opening my heart once again to being a mother and for being so protective of me. Thank you for sticking it out with me, there is so much more to come!

To my oldest, Star, thank you for being the first! Thank you for enduring so much with me. Thank you for being relentlessly yourself no matter what anyone else may think. Thank you for following in my footsteps, as the activist you are starting to become. I see you and I am always here for you on this beautiful journey!

To my oldest son, "One Who is as Brave as a Lion," thank you for your strength, for your intelligent humor, and for your respect and integrity. Thank you for always seeming to understand, and for being so forgiving. Even when you are in deep pain, you always carry on. Thank you for showing me how to keep doing that!

To my son Leone, "The Peace Keeper," thank you for coming into my life in the miraculous way that you did. You are literally a miracle! Thank you for being so strong and for feeling everything. Thank you for your infectious smile, your incredible loyalty, and your magic. I can't wait to see who you choose to become!

To my twin brother, thank you for investing in me when no one else could or would! Thank you for having the courage to share your story along with mine; for having the bravery to face the darkness that nearly destroyed us. Thank you for training me and helping me to get into the best shape of my life over the years. Thanks for opening your home to me and the kids countless times! Thanks for calling the cops, for calling 911, and for forcing me to leave Pine Ridge. Thanks for refusing to accept the behavior of those in our family who continue to separate Temoc and I. Thank you for cleaning up after the shooting. I love you bro, and I'm so proud of all you've become!

To my dad, I want to acknowledge you for investing in me and supporting me as I wrote this book. Thank you for also bailing me out of jail twice!

To Shell, thank you for inspiring me to build my own business as a single mom, by role-modeling how you built your own while keeping your boys with you. Thank you for all the times you aggressively advocated on my behalf while I was incarcerated or publicly drug through the mud over the years. Thank you for gifting me my first shawl and opening the door for me to begin Fancy Shawl dancing. Thank you for the years you have provided me and the kids with an endless supply of the best soap.

To M. LaMere, thank you for supporting my research into our Tribe's Traditional Tattoo culture over the years, by sharing your own findings. Thank you also for sharing so many stories and teachings from our Dakota history. I have a much deeper understanding of who we are because of your influence. Thank you for continuing the Treaty work of your father, and the Dahcotah Sioux Nation of Indians. We will one day regain our sovereignty because of the efforts of people like you.

To Gwen, thank you for bravely advocating on my behalf before the Pennington County Court System, using the years of research you conducted about the arbitrary separation of Indian children and parents by CPS and the legal system in South Dakota. Thank you for taking me into your home when I had nowhere else to go. Thank you for showing me what true activism is, and how to support our sisters who are belittled and targeted by the justice system!

To Redhawk, thank you for encouraging my art and activism by inviting me to perform with you. Thank you for welcoming Zeke and I into your home countless times, for supporting my tattoo work, and for your part in the creation of the "Skindigenous" episode. Thank you for also standing up for me against the countless "you know whos."

To T. Gore, who invested in me every month since beginning this book, and who also is one of my favorite and most loyal tattoo clients, thank you for believing in me! Thank you for telling me that it was reward enough to help me build my dreams for you to invest in me! Thank you for spearheading the need to acknowledge Indigenous peoples amongst your community members and thank you for diving deep within your own inner being to heal.

To all my clients who have supported my art by receiving a Handpoked Tattoo, thank you for supporting my path towards self-sufficiency through my passion to create! Thank you for allowing me to assist in your transformation via your skin, and for your willingness to wear my art for the rest of your life! To all my fellow tattoo artists who have fully supported me over the years, thank you so much! I couldn't have done it without your support and encouragement!

To my ancestors, thank you for guiding me throughout my entire life, and for showing me in the most beautiful and mysterious ways of your constant presence and guidance. Thank you for all that you sacrificed so that my children and I, and my relatives, can be here today. Thank you for surviving and persisting through my own DNA. Thank you for showing me that no matter how much they try to assimilate or eradicate us, that you are powerful enough to awaken your descendants through dreams and visions! Thank you for standing with me through it all. I love and honor you entirely!

To Mother Earth and Father Sky, thank you for being *everything* to humanity. We owe our entire existence to your presence, and you ask nothing of us except to live according to the original instructions of natural law. Thank you for the endless moments of beauty and magic that have shown me there is more to life than pain and suffering. Thank you for forming our bodies from your elements and your spirit. Thank you for being patient with us and for giving us so many chances to reform our relationship with you, and with all creation. We will not let you down Ina Maka and Ate Wi! I love you and honor you, and our place beside you, Mitakuye Oyasin!

ABOUT THE AUTHOR

Stephanie Big Eagle is a descendant of the Oceti Sakowin on her father's side. They are enrolled members of the Ihanktonwan Dakota Oyate. They are also Isanti Dakota, and Kul Wicasa Lakota. On her mother's side, she is of Nordic, Baltic, Celtic, and Indigenous heritage.

She is featured in Season 2: Episode 2 of "Skindigenous," a thirteen-part documentary series exploring Indigenous Tattooing Traditions around the world, airing on PBS and APTN television networks.

She graduated from Sacramento City College with an Associates of Science Degree in Biology in 2016. During the same year, she was educated in the Traditional technique of Handpoke Tattoo, and created her first tattoo design, the Standing Rock Tattoo. The founder of Thunderbird Rising Studios, she is an experienced Traditional Handpoke Tattoo Artist, an Indigenous and environmental activist, a public speaker, a singer-songwriter, a Fancy Shawl Dancer, and a fashion model who tours nationally and internationally to share her art, Traditional Knowledge, and presence.

For more information or bookings visit **www.stephbigeagle.com**.

"About the Author" photograph by Jason Sinn (2017).

www.ingramcontent.com/pod-product-compliance
Lightning Source LLC
Chambersburg PA
CBHW051707160426
43209CB00004B/1054